D0900183

ONE GOOD DAY

ONE
GOOD
DAY

MY JOURNEY TO THE GOOD FRIDAY AGREEMENT

DAVID DONOGHUE

Gill Books

Gill Books

Hume Avenue

Park West

Dublin 12

www.gillbooks.ie

Gill Books is an imprint of M.H. Gill and Co.

978 07171 9557 2

Design and print origination by O'K Graphic Design, Dublin

Edited by Tamsin Shelton

Proofread by Ruairí Ó Brógáin

Printed by CPI Group (UK) Ltd, Croydon, CR0 4YY

This book is typeset in 12/17.5 pt Minion.

The paper used in this book comes from the wood pulp of sustainably managed forests.

A CIP catalogue record for this book is available from the British Library.

5 4 3 2 1

In memory of Denis Donoghue
1928–2021

CONTENTS

INTRODUCTION

I had joined the Department of Foreign Affairs expecting to see the world. I was young, restless, eager to experience shores beyond our own. Ireland had joined the European Economic Community not long before and was still finding its feet in this exciting new context for Irish diplomacy. Paris, Rome and more exotic capitals were on my horizon.

The year was 1975. Little did I know then that my career would take quite a different turn from the one I had been contemplating. Northern Ireland stood on the brink of civil war. The Sunningdale experiment in power-sharing had collapsed the previous year and paramilitary violence was rampant. The British Government of the day was out of its depth in responding to these challenges and a dangerous political vacuum existed. Decades of systematic unionist discrimination against the nationalist minority were taking their toll. The deep disaffection of nationalists, the Provisional IRA's campaign against the security forces, the growth of loyalist paramilitary activity and an unprecedented number of sectarian killings on both sides were combining to push Northern Ireland to the edge. A complete collapse of law and order seemed imminent.

On my first day in the department, I found myself assigned to the Anglo-Irish Section. Created in the early seventies in response to the escalating 'Troubles' (as the crisis was euphemistically called), this was the place where much of the Government's policy on Northern Ireland and Anglo-Irish relations was devised. It was, in those days, a tiny part of the department, numbering about 10 staff in all. But I joined a highly dedicated and motivated team and was thrilled to have been given the opportunity to work there. Within a few days of arriving, I was plunged into intensive contingency planning for a large-scale influx of refugees who were expected to come across the border following the anticipated breakdown of public order in Northern Ireland. I found myself on my knees, poring over an Ordnance Survey map to identify where the most beleaguered communities were likely to be in the North and how they could be assisted. We nicknamed it the 'Doomsday plan'. Other maps in orange and green conjured up potential repartition scenarios.

This was where my journey began. Almost 25 years later, it would lead me to Good Friday 1998 and to the agreement bearing that name which has brought lasting peace to these islands. In a sense, I was not to look up again from that map until we achieved the Good Friday Agreement, all those years later.

I began a long-term, frequently frustrating but ultimately rewarding engagement with Northern Ireland. Like others who worked on this extraordinarily challenging set of issues, I found that it laid claim to me in a personal as well as a professional sense. The commitment required to sustain, night and day, the Irish Government's unrelenting quest for a peaceful political settlement. More usually, the strain of managing protracted political stalemates. The endless frustrations and disappointments. The emotional roller-coaster of reverses, followed by small victories, followed by reverses again. The constant demands of crisis management. The solidarity owed at all times to Northern Ireland's courageous political representatives. The threats to one's own physical security at various times.

All of these considerations meant that working on Northern Ireland over a lengthy period was not for the faint-hearted. It required unusual levels of dedication and resilience. When I completed my own journey in the late afternoon of Good Friday 1998, it was a moment of personal fulfilment as well as of deep professional satisfaction.

This is the story of that journey. I begin it in those early years in the seventies, a time of grim violence and despair. I continue it in the mid-eighties, when the Anglo-Irish Agreement was negotiated and I became one of the department's first 'travellers'. This was a term we used for a small group of officials tasked with developing a network of contacts on the ground in Northern Ireland in support of the Irish Government's new role under that Agreement. After a spell in London from 1988 to 1991, where my job was to seek favourable British media coverage for Irish Government policy on Northern Ireland (at a time of exceptional challenge in Anglo-Irish relations), I returned to Dublin in the early nineties as the deputy head of the Anglo-Irish Division.

From 1991 to 1999, I was closely involved in the Northern Ireland peace process, contributing to the negotiation of key documents and to the multi-party talks which culminated in the Good Friday Agreement of April 1998. From 1995 to 1999, I was the Irish head of the Anglo-Irish Secretariat at Maryfield, just outside Belfast. Known colloquially as the 'Bunker', this was the main channel used for contact between the Irish and British Governments on Northern Ireland issues.

All of these roles were important stations on my journey to Good Friday. It is, however, the last part of that journey, the detailed story of the negotiations which led to the Good Friday

Agreement, to which I give priority. This is the first comprehensive narrative of those negotiations to be written by an insider. My account focuses on the nine-month period from the summer of 1997 until Easter 1998, when a combination of circumstances created a basis for the achievement of a balanced and inclusive settlement.

It was a negotiation process of extraordinary complexity, multi-level and multi-faceted. There were many moving parts and a wide cast of actors. There were moments of high drama but also periods when the talks almost ground to a halt. There were pressures of all kinds on the participants, internal and external.

I have tried to capture the ebb and flow of these negotiations, the hopes and fears attached to them, the crises and their final resolution. I have done so from the perspective of an Irish Government participant who was involved on a day-to-day basis in much of the process but was not present at every meeting, as nobody could be. Inevitably this is a subjective perspective, reflecting the priorities and pressures which guided our delegation. But I have sought to be fair to all other perspectives and to give the reader a clear, balanced and succinct overview of how the Good Friday Agreement was forged.

In the end, this Agreement was the work of many hands. Two Governments and eight political parties found a basis on which to manage, and ultimately to transcend, deep-rooted political disagreements. In so doing, they opened up a future based on shared values, respect for difference and the primacy of constitutional politics for all the people of Ireland, North and South.

The Agreement is, of course, not perfect: few human enterprises can claim that distinction. But it remains one of the very few examples of successful conflict resolution anywhere. It has inspired peace processes all over the world. And, closer to home, it is the indispensable bedrock for an Irish–British relationship that has been sorely tested by Brexit.

Twenty-five years ago, Ireland was changed forever. George Mitchell once said of his time in Northern Ireland that 'we had 700 bad days – and then one good day, which changed the course of history'. This is not an assessment of how the Agreement has fared since then, though the vicissitudes have been many. Rather it is an account, tinged perhaps with nostalgia, of a unique political endeavour and collective achievement that, on a snowy April morning in 1998, brought us all to that one good day.

FIRST ENCOUNTERS

I made my first trip to Belfast in 1959. I was seven years old, accompanying my father on a visit to stay with some friends. I remember it like yesterday, my first trip on a train, the excitement of a new city, grown-up talk and different accents.

My father had grown up in the North of Ireland (as he invariably called it). However, as he made clear to me on that trip, it had never been home for him. His own father was a Kerry Catholic, from the Black Valley near Killarney, who had joined the Royal Irish Constabulary as a young man. As there was a practice of transferring RIC officers as far away as possible from their places of birth, my grandfather found himself assigned to various parts of the North. In 1922, confronted with a choice between joining the new Garda Síochána in the South or staying in the North and transferring to the new Royal Ulster Constabulary (RUC), he opted for the latter. It was a choice he would come to regret; as a Catholic sergeant in a small town with a unionist majority, he was never likely to prosper. He retired 25 years later, still a sergeant.

My father grew up in that town, Warrenpoint, and the treatment of his father, whom he revered, was to be one of the formative experiences of his own life. He left the North when he was 18 and never went back.

I went back, in a manner of speaking. Along with other teenagers and young adults of my generation, I grew up with the emergence of the civil rights movement there in the late sixties, the explosion of sectarian violence and the gradual descent of Northern Ireland into chaos. On a visit to Armagh in 1970, I heard for the first time the menacing drumbeat from a Lambeg drum. From my student years, I remember vividly the Bloody Sunday atrocity in 1972 and our deep sense of injustice at the innocent lives lost. But many more innocent lives would be lost over the years to come. A defining moment for me was to be the infamous Bloody Friday, in July 1972, when the Provisionals carried out a series of bombings in supermarkets and the like in central Belfast which killed nine and left 130 injured. To this day I recall the outrage I felt at the news of those utterly futile and senseless killings. In my own engagement with the conflict and how its underlying issues should be resolved, this was a turning point.

A few years later, having entered the Department of Foreign Affairs as a young diplomat, I began what would become an almost continuous professional involvement, in one way or another, with Northern Ireland and the wider Anglo-Irish relationship. This would last for 24 years.

I remember the spring of 1975 as a period of near-despair following the collapse of the power-sharing Executive not long beforehand. There was an ominous political stalemate. Loyalist violence was escalating alongside the continuing IRA campaign. There were forebodings, indeed, about a complete collapse of law and order, and possibly even civil war, in Northern Ireland.

Northern Ireland consumed much of the political energies of the Irish Government of the day. Garret FitzGerald, as Minister for Foreign Affairs, played a key role and his department had much of the day-to-day responsibility for monitoring developments and proposing policy options. In the Anglo-Irish Section, we benefited from the inspiring leadership of Seán Donlon, then a youthful Assistant Secretary in the department and a leading participant in the negotiations which had produced the Sunningdale Agreement. Seán worked very closely with John Hume and the Social Democratic and Labour Party (SDLP), while others in the Section built up contacts with unionism and loyalism (challenging and dangerous as such work was in those days).

With two fellow juniors, Brendan McMahon and Joana Betson, I had the task of monitoring security-related developments. This was essentially a compilation of daily killings, gleaned from newspaper cuttings. We cheerfully referred to it as the 'stiff list'; it made for a rather lugubrious start to our work each day. I also had to compile as much information as possible on a growing number of loyalist paramilitary groups which were issuing dark threats of one kind or another.

Another responsibility I had was to support the Irish Government delegation in a case that the State was taking against the British Government at the European Commission on Human Rights. This case sought to have the treatment of republican detainees at the Castlereagh interrogation centre in Belfast described as torture. The eventual outcome was one which each Government claimed as de facto vindication of its position: a finding not of torture but of 'degrading and inhuman treatment'.

After an eventful year in the Anglo-Irish Section, I was given my first overseas posting: to the Irish Embassy to the Vatican (or, to use its official title, the Holy See). Oddly enough, a strong Northern Ireland theme ran through this posting also: the Vatican had marked sympathies at the time with Irish republican objectives, the No. 2 in the Secretariat of State having served in the Papal Nunciature in Dublin in the fifties.

From Rome I went to Bonn, then the capital of West Germany, on a five-year posting as Press Officer at the Irish Embassy. From a different perspective, Northern Ireland and Anglo-Irish relations dominated my work there. In that period (1978–83), Anglo-Irish relations came under particular strain as new leaders took over, Margaret Thatcher in London and Charles J. Haughey in Dublin, who were poles apart from each other on Northern Ireland for much of the time. The growing disenchantment between the two Governments, notably over the handling of IRA hunger strikes and the Falklands War, was of keen interest to the German media. Winning support for Irish Government thinking on Northern Ireland and Anglo-Irish relations was the major preoccupation of my years in Bonn.

MY LIFE AS A 'TRAVELLER'

I n July 1985, I returned from abroad to the Anglo-Irish Section in Dublin. It was in the throes of the negotiations which would lead to the Anglo-Irish Agreement, signed at Hillsborough Castle on 15 November that year by Garret FitzGerald and Margaret Thatcher.

This Agreement would transform the prospects for political progress in Northern Ireland. It would bring our Government for the first time into a serious policy engagement with the British Government on Northern Ireland. We would be able to present views and proposals for policies to address the deep-rooted problems of nationalist disaffection and alienation. And the British Government committed itself to making 'determined efforts' to resolve any differences with us. In other words, we were being brought into the governance of Northern Ireland in a formal and far-reaching way.

The unique partnership launched under the Anglo-Irish Agreement would lay the basis for the peace process, and its joint management, over the following decade. Without that partnership, indeed, the peace process could never have succeeded.

I arrived when the negotiations towards this Agreement were in their final stages. Michael Lillis, the head of the Anglo-Irish Section, had been closely involved with his British counterpart,

David Goodall, in developing the conceptual framework for it. Other senior actors on the Irish side included Dermot Nally, Seán Donlon and Noel Dorr, all working under close political direction from the Taoiseach, Garret FitzGerald.

My role was to assist in the negotiations with research and drafting of various kinds. In anticipation of the Agreement being successfully concluded, I was also to begin building up a network of contacts across Northern Ireland which would help us to contribute effectively to its implementation.

Previously, Irish Governments had contented themselves with largely rhetorical denunciations of British policies relating to Northern Ireland. They had never been in a position where they were expected, still less asked, to present specific proposals for reform. Now there would be formal intergovernmental machinery to enable just such an input. We wanted to use this to make detailed proposals across the full range of policies. To do this credibly, we had to up our game. We needed to increase rapidly both our technical expertise and our broader political understanding of the issues causing concern at local level.

It was particularly important to ensure that the representations the Government would make on individual issues, through the new Anglo-Irish Conference and its supporting Secretariat (in Belfast), would be based on solid evidence gathered from contacts at local level. Our colleagues in the Secretariat would not be in a position to assemble such evidence themselves. But Dublin-based staff could do so, travelling north regularly. It was for us to put together the best possible picture of what was happening on the ground and the best possible material, therefore, from which our Secretariat colleagues could work in presenting the 'views and proposals' expected of the Government under the Agreement.

I succeeded Dáithí O'Ceallaigh in this travelling role in mid-1985. From early 1986 onwards, I was joined by four or five additional colleagues. We were known colloquially in the department as the 'travellers'.

I had a foretaste of my new responsibilities even before the Agreement was concluded. In September 1985, I was asked to try to secure a meeting with a member of the Democratic Unionist Party (DUP). The Government wanted to know how hard-line unionists were reacting to media and other reports about the emerging agreement. Ian Paisley and the DUP were signalling vehement opposition to the role being contemplated for the Irish Government.

There had been hardly any contact previously between the Government and the DUP. I was chosen simply because I was the last person in and had the benefit of anonymity (at a time of rising loyalist tensions and, accordingly, heightened physical risks for Irish Government representatives).

I managed to arrange a meeting in Belfast with a DUP representative. It proved very worthwhile, alerting us in the clearest terms to the growing unionist fears about the Agreement and helping us to understand these. When I asked my interlocutor why he had agreed to see me, he told me, with disarming frankness: 'Because one day, down the road, we'll have to be dealing with you people.' That was 1985. It would be seven years before the DUP would have their first official meeting with the Irish Government, and 22 years before Ian Paisley, as First Minister, would sit down formally with Bertie Ahern as Taoiseach.

My specific brief over the next couple of years was to develop a range of contacts who would be relevant to the security, justice and rule of law aspects of the Agreement. Managed by Declan O'Donovan in the department, this was the policy area of greatest challenge and sensitivity; without serious reforms, there would be no prospect of ending nationalist alienation. We embarked on the Agreement with a full agenda and high expectations among nationalists about what the Agreement should deliver under these headings.

In September 1985, I had a memorable first encounter with Seamus Mallon, who as the SDLP's spokesman on these issues would become my single most important contact. Mallon had come down to Dublin with SDLP colleagues for a meeting with the Government. They were all having lunch in a Dublin restaurant when he suddenly collapsed. I was dining nearby in the same restaurant and rushed over to help lift him up from the floor. Not having met him before, I stuck my hand out in the process to introduce myself, and Mallon, despite his momentary weakness, shook it. It was a dramatic first meeting, which he often recalled later. Luckily, Dr Rory O'Hanlon TD was on hand to tend to Mallon; he was whisked off to St James's Hospital, where he recovered within a day or two.

As with others in the department, Mallon and I would go on to have a very close working relationship. I saw him regularly during the first two years of the Agreement. He was perhaps the pivotal player in terms of ensuring ongoing nationalist support for the Agreement and his views were of great interest to the Government. Our cooperation continued after he was elected MP for Newry and Armagh in 1986 and would last for a total of some 15 years, variously in London, Dublin and Belfast.

At the end of 1985, Michael Lillis and Dáithí O'Ceallaigh took up duty at the Secretariat in Belfast, newly opened in a building called Maryfield on the Palace Barracks compound. For staff transferring to Maryfield, the assignment would clearly be both prestigious and dangerous. Extra security was arranged for the homes of the senior colleagues and special allowances were set to compensate for the risks being incurred.

My own turn in Maryfield would come a decade later. I did, however, have an early taste of the 'Bunker' when I overnighted there a couple of times in the first weeks, experiencing for myself the extremely basic living conditions and the pleasures of all-night RUC patrolling immediately outside my bedroom window.

My routine as a 'traveller' during the years 1986–7 involved spending an average of three days a week travelling around the North. My primary focus was on the security situation in the most sensitive and disadvantaged areas. I was trying to establish what the most pressing concerns were for local nationalists and how the Irish Government could address these through the new machinery.

The issues in which we took particular interest in the early days included controversial practices such as that of Ulster Defence Regiment patrols operating without police accompaniment, the security forces' use of plastic bullets or reliance on 'supergrass' evidence for criminal prosecutions. We wanted, on the one hand, to gather from reliable sources the raw material which would support our work on these issues in the Secretariat (individual cases as well as general policy concerns) and, on the other, to be able to give prompt feedback at local level on the outcome of our efforts. Our hope was that we could show the Agreement working concretely for the benefit of the nationalist community and that this would translate over time into reinforced support for constitutional nationalism.

In an average week, I might call on people as diverse as trade unionists, lawyers or human rights experts, priests in housing estates in West Belfast and SDLP councillors in rural areas like Fermanagh or South Armagh. I built up a large network of contacts among the Catholic clergy. I also gradually extended my range to include senior Church of Ireland, Methodist and Presbyterian clergy and others who could interpret the mood within the unionist community, both on security issues and more widely.

This was necessarily discreet work which required careful planning. I prepared my own itineraries and took my own security precautions. In those days, given the various paramilitary campaigns, Irish civil servants seldom travelled to Northern Ireland. Indeed, it was rare to see any car with a Southern number plate north of the border. I generally used hired cars and stayed with trusted friends.

On a couple of occasions I narrowly avoided trouble. I once arranged to see a priest in the Divis Flats area off the Lower Falls Road in West Belfast. Using an enclosed pedestrian bridge over the motorway to get into that area, I found a group of local youths waiting at the other end of the bridge, brandishing some plastic tubing menacingly and clearly intent on denying me access. I turned round to find others with the same intent at the near end. I burst into a run, dashing past the latter and thankfully reaching safety. I rang the priest and asked him to come and collect me. When he arrived in his car a few minutes later, he burst out laughing: tall, neat-looking and in a jacket, I looked like an off-duty RUC officer, an extremely rare sighting for the Divis Flats and one which had presented too tempting a target for some local vigilantes. He hung the proverbial white flag out of his car window as he drove me to his home.

With phone-tapping not uncommon, another clerical contact suggested that I adopt an alias when ringing him to make an appointment. He would do likewise. I was initially sceptical but went along with this, agreeing at his request to pose in our next phone call as a vacuum cleaner salesman anxious to call on 'Mr

Brown' with a new model. This subterfuge hilariously fell apart when 'Mr Brown', not yet used to his new identity, told me that he unfortunately could not meet me at the time suggested as he would be saying Mass then. Despite this bungled start, we kept going with this elaborate cover for several months.

I relied on local people living in 'flashpoint' areas, such as SDLP or clerical contacts, to give us a sense of how particular security situations were developing. This would help us to decide what corrective actions needed to be sought through the Secretariat. On one occasion, I rang an elderly priest to ask if he would look out his window to report on a contentious parade that was passing by on the street below him. He replied that, though ill and confined to his bed at the moment, he would be happy to do so. The detailed account he provided was, indeed, of great assistance to us in monitoring a difficult situation. In departmental folklore, of course, much was made of the lengths to which 'travellers' such as myself would go to secure information, dragging dying priests from their deathbeds if necessary.

We did manage to build up over the first few years a comprehensive network of contacts spanning all parts of the North and all the policy areas covered by the Agreement. This helped the Government to contribute actively under all those headings and to present cogent and well-informed proposals for reforms.

The only problem was that Margaret Thatcher, having (as she saw it) gone out on a limb politically to give our Government its unprecedented role under the Agreement, felt she could not risk further offending unionism and right-wing Conservatism by agreeing to some of the more controversial reforms for which we were pressing. The structures of the Agreement were, in her view, already a major contribution on her part. Her commitment to actual delivery of its provisions was lukewarm. She also complained, in our view unfairly, that she was seeing inadequate results from the enhanced security and extradition cooperation which she had expected as part of the Agreement. Gradually a degree of disenchantment set in on her part.

We, in turn, felt that the failure of her Government to work the Agreement fully and grant the reforms which had been clearly contemplated when we negotiated it was eroding the Agreement's potential. Indeed, it risked exacerbating the very problems of alienation and instability which the Agreement was supposed to be addressing.

In the summer of 1987, there was a change of Government in Dublin. In came a Fianna Fáil administration headed by Charles J. Haughey. In Opposition he had been very critical of the Agreement and there was much speculation about how the new Government would handle things. This included rumours that the Foreign Affairs civil servants who had been operating the Agreement since November 1985 would be replaced. In the event, we all survived the transition, though some moved on voluntarily to new roles at that stage.

In my case, I was due a move abroad and I departed on a posting to the Irish Mission to the United Nations. I had been in New York only a few months, however, when the post of Press Officer at the Irish Embassy in London fell vacant and I was asked to fill it. Northern Ireland would be the almost exclusive focus of the post. Though it was unusual to be asked to change posts so soon, I had no hesitation in agreeing to a transfer to London.

I spent three years there, trying to achieve the best possible coverage in the British media for Irish Government policies on Northern Ireland and Anglo-Irish relations. Charles Haughey was back in office, Margaret Thatcher was still in No. 10 and the relationship between both leaders was as fraught as ever. We had a succession of security and legal crises which polarised the two Governments further.

I was engaged in a propaganda contest for much of the time. Northern Ireland policy was a battleground on which Britain's right-wing media could extol Thatcher's law-and-order credentials (with a swipe or two at our Government in the process). The few liberal or left-wing media, on the other hand, saw it as an opportunity to highlight the severe limitations of Thatcher's policy and the risks she was running in the way she treated her partnership with the Irish Government. It was a difficult era in Anglo-Irish relations.

3

THE PEACE PROCESS: BEGINNINGS

I n November 1990, Margaret Thatcher was ousted as Prime Minister and replaced by John Major.

Initially it did not look as if the new Prime Minister would prioritise Northern Ireland. A few months later, however, his press spokesman, Gus O'Donnell, told me that in fact Major planned to take a serious initiative on Northern Ireland. He wanted to see whether a basis could be created for multi-party talks with the aim of achieving a lasting settlement.

Peter Brooke, a genial Tory of Anglo-Irish stock, had been appointed Secretary of State for Northern Ireland in July 1989. Brooke brought a refreshingly open mind and pragmatic approach to the job. He indicated at an early stage that he could envisage the British Government talking to Sinn Féin if IRA violence were ended.

In a speech in November 1990, remembered today as the 'Whitbread' speech, Brooke declared that the British Government had 'no selfish strategic or economic interest' in Northern Ireland. This was a pivotal clarification which would be of enormous importance for the efforts, over the coming years, to end IRA violence and bring about an inclusive peace settlement. It confirmed John Hume's assertion that the British Government had no interests of its own to protect in Northern Ireland and was neutral on the latter's constitutional future. The SDLP leader's long-standing analysis had been that the British Government was not the problem. Rather, nationalists and republicans would have to win over unionists to their vision of a future Ireland. And this would be possible only by peaceful persuasion, not by coercion or violence.

The Whitbread speech was one of the earliest landmarks in what came to be known as the 'peace process'. What brought this process into being?

After over two decades of violent conflict, it was becoming clear that there would be no resolution in terms of a clear-cut military victory for either side. The IRA would not be able to defeat the British Army; and equally the latter would not defeat the IRA. The 'armed struggle' seemed likely to settle into a protracted stalemate. Linked to this, a degree of war weariness was becoming detectable. There was an appetite within Sinn Féin to explore a political alternative for the achievement of republican objectives.

Exploratory contacts began in the late eighties and continued intermittently. The Irish Government, first under Charles Haughey and even more when Albert Reynolds replaced Haughey as Taoiseach, actively pursued the opportunities for peace. John Major, more of a pragmatist than his predecessor, was a willing partner.

Peace would make an inclusive political settlement possible. The view was taking hold, more fundamentally, that we could achieve a stable settlement only through political negotiations which involved *all* protagonists to the conflict, with an absolute commitment to peace as the price of admission.

The Anglo-Irish Agreement had started from a different analysis: that a process involving direct Irish Government engagement and far-reaching policy reforms would make it possible to strengthen the nationalist middle ground in Northern Ireland and, in the process, undermine support for militant republicanism.

Several years into the Agreement, the results in this respect were a little mixed. The new machinery set up under the Agreement, and the close cooperation which had been launched between the two Governments on Northern Ireland, would be of lasting benefit to nationalists. However, there had been no significant shift in electoral preferences from Sinn Féin to the SDLP within the first few years. The middle ground had not been expanded to the extent hoped for.

Against this background, there was an increasing readiness to try a new strategy: that of building a political framework broad enough to include the extremes. Our goal was to achieve a consensus across all parties on shared values and objectives, drawing the extremes back in towards the centre. This could then serve as the basis for inclusive talks and a negotiated political settlement.

In March 1991, Peter Brooke set out a plan for multi-party talks which had been carefully coordinated with the Irish Government. The two Governments, he recalled, had always been ready to consider 'a new and more broadly based agreement' to replace the Anglo-Irish Agreement. This was indeed the case; that Agreement had always been intended as, in part, an incentive to the unionists to try to negotiate a more palatable alternative. Clearly, however, it would have to be something which nationalists would also find palatable. Irish Government statements preferred to speak of a new agreement which would 'transcend' the existing one.

Reflecting an analysis which John Hume had been putting forward for years, Brooke said that the talks would seek to achieve a new beginning for relationships 'within Northern Ireland, within the island of Ireland and between the peoples of these islands'. These would come to be known as the three 'strands': Strand One (internal), Strand Two (North/South) and Strand Three (East/West).

To facilitate the talks, Brooke continued, the two Governments had agreed to have a gap between meetings of the Anglo-Irish Conference. (This was a compromise between the need to maintain normal functioning of the Agreement, with regular ministerial meetings in this format, and the unionists' long-standing demand for removal of the Agreement, without which they would not sit down to talk.) The talks would begin with Strand One, which Brooke himself would chair, and move on 'within weeks' to the other two (at an appropriate moment which he would judge).

The process got under way a couple of months later. I returned to the department in June 1991 and joined what had now become the Anglo-Irish Division. Its new head, replacing Dermot Gallagher, was Sean O hUiginn.

O hUiginn, like his predecessor an old hand on Northern Ireland policy, would make a major personal contribution to the peace process over the next few years. He worked tirelessly to create a context in which an IRA ceasefire could take place and inclusive talks could lead to a comprehensive political settlement. He developed a clear conceptual framework and held consistently to this, even as crises of all kinds intervened. He was also a peerless drafter and led the drafting work we did on key documents. His effectiveness in challenging British Government policies which he considered misguided led over time to efforts by some on the British side to demonise him. Unionist suspicion of him was probably also a factor. But he did not allow himself to be deterred.

O hUiginn co-chaired with Quentin Thomas of the Northern Ireland Office (NIO) a Liaison Group which brought Irish and British officials together for regular consultations. This group, which met variously in London, Dublin or Belfast, kept all aspects of the peace process and the talks under close supervision. It was also the main mechanism through which the two Governments developed joint positions and papers for the talks. Thomas was a good match for O hUiginn, intellectually and temperamentally, and much groundbreaking work was done at those meetings under their joint leadership.

Having continuity at a senior level on both sides during those critical years was very valuable. The group also benefited from the involvement of other key figures on the Irish side, such as Fergus Finlay, Martin Mansergh and Seán Donlon, and from the contributions made by Jonathan Stephens and other talented British officials.

I worked closely with Sean O hUiginn for six years, acting in effect as his deputy over much of that period and supporting him on the developing peace process.

In the first instance, we had the so-called Brooke talks. In 1991, these got only as far as Strand One during the agreed gap between Conference meetings. In 1992, they became the Brooke–Mayhew talks, after Sir Patrick Mayhew succeeded Brooke as Secretary of State. They were facilitated by a further agreed gap between two Conference meetings which was progressively lengthened, lasting ultimately for almost seven months (from April to November 1992). During the 1992 talks we moved into Strand Two and there were also several Strand Three meetings.

The opening Strand Two meeting in London in April 1992 was the first occasion on which the Irish Government would be taking part in a multi-party talks process including the DUP. I remember some awkward initial encounters. John Chilcot, head of the NIO, hosted a reception for participants at which the DUP was represented by Peter Robinson, Sammy Wilson and Rhonda

Paisley. The Irish Government representatives at the event were Noel Dorr (then head of our department), Sean O hUiginn and myself. Given the DUP's policy of not fraternising with the Irish Government, the issue arose between us of whether we should proffer a handshake to them, a normal courtesy but one that we knew with near certainty would be refused. Two of us did so, while the third demurred; and, needless to say, it was declined. The next day, with David Andrews (the Minister for Foreign Affairs) in the Irish Government seat at the talks, Ian Paisley had a gruff but good-humoured exchange with Andrews as he walked past.

A Rubicon of sorts had been crossed. The DUP would now talk to us, in a negotiation context. When Strand Two moved back to Belfast, our delegation was led by John Wilson (as Tánaiste) and included also David Andrews and Padraig Flynn. A mild bonhomie developed there between Wilson and Paisley (as fellow Ulstermen). Flynn, in turn, showed enthusiasm for the artwork of Rhonda Paisley and bought one of her paintings. Our ministers developed a reasonably good rapport with Paisley senior.

There were light-hearted moments as well. The delegations all had lunch each day in the Stormont canteen, where the DUP representatives positioned themselves right at the kitchen door so that they could demand instant, and exclusive, service from the waitress who had to pass by them. As our own delegation was placed furthest away from the kitchen, this meant that no staff came near us, and our ministers got hungrier and hungrier, to the DUP's undisguised glee.

On substance, the 1992 talks did not get very far. They did, however, establish important concepts including the three-stranded basis for any agreement and the principle that 'nothing is agreed until everything is agreed'. In Strand One, some institutional models were discussed to which the parties would return in the

1996–8 talks. The Strand Two debates broke new ground in some respects, with the unionist parties and ourselves engaging in detail, and more or less for the first time, on our divergent views of Irish history.

This included our ministers hinting at a willingness on the part of the Irish Government to contemplate eventual change to Articles 2 and 3 of the Irish Constitution as part of a balanced settlement. The thrust of such change would be to reflect the principle (to which we had already subscribed in the Sunningdale Agreement and the Anglo-Irish Agreement) that any change in the status of Northern Ireland would come about only with the consent of a majority of the people of Northern Ireland. Known in shorthand as the 'principle of consent', this key commitment on the constitutional front would be a central feature of the various agreements reached over the coming years, culminating in the Good Friday Agreement.

The elements which might form part of a future agreement did at least become discernible in the 1992 talks. While the position of the Ulster Unionist Party (UUP) on North/South cooperation was generally minimalist, informal contacts with the party's representatives suggested a willingness to look at North/South institutions with some decision-making powers provided these were authorised by the respective legislatures.

The talks came to an end in November 1992. The Fianna Fáil–Progressive Democrat Government in Dublin was running into difficulty at that stage. The Government fell and an election took place. This led to a new coalition Government headed by Albert Reynolds, this time a Fianna Fáil–Labour combination.

While the talks launched by Peter Brooke had run into the sand, they had at least demonstrated to Sinn Féin the potential in a broadly based process of this kind where no issues were excluded from the agenda. Attention now turned to developing a framework of principles which might whet further the appetite of the republican movement for political engagement and provide a basis for an IRA ceasefire. The two Governments felt that there might now be an opportunity, if carefully managed, to achieve this objective.

4

LANDMARKS

E arly in 1993, the idea began to develop of a joint declaration which the Taoiseach and the British Prime Minister would issue. There had been a draft from John Hume in 1991 based on his contacts with Gerry Adams. More drafts and suggestions followed. The so-called Hume–Adams initiative grew, culminating in the Irish Government handing over a draft declaration to the British Government in mid-1993.

This was developed intensively by the two Governments over the subsequent months. A small group of Irish officials, working under the political supervision of Albert Reynolds and Dick Spring (Tánaiste and Foreign Minister), negotiated a joint text with their British counterparts. Given the Major administration's heavy dependence on UUP support at Westminster throughout this period, the British were anxious not to be seen to be responding, even obliquely, to a Sinn Féin initiative. Instead, there was much emphasis on achieving a document that would respect unionist concerns.

In December 1993, the text was agreed. The 'Downing Street Declaration', as it would come to be known, was unveiled in London by Albert Reynolds and John Major and their ministers. It would be of decisive importance for everything which came after: the IRA ceasefire of July 1994, the launching of an inclusive talks process and finally the Good Friday Agreement of 1998.

The Declaration, which had been significantly influenced by John Hume's ideas, struck a creative balance between self-determination and the principle of consent. It reaffirmed the right of the people of Ireland as a whole to self-determination. But, in line with what the two Governments had agreed in the Anglo-Irish Agreement, it made the exercise of this right subject to the consent of a majority of the people of Northern Ireland. The two Governments accepted, furthermore, that 'Irish unity would be achieved only by those who favour this outcome persuading those who do not, peacefully and without coercion or violence'. If in the future a majority of the people of Northern Ireland were so persuaded, both Governments would support and give legislative effect to their wish.

I remember some testing at the time of the proposition that the British Government should be an active 'persuader for unity'. There was no appetite for this in London, however, and we accepted this. Being a 'persuader for agreement' was as far as that British Government – and as it turned out, its successor – was prepared to go.

The Declaration made it clear that, in the event of a permanent end to paramilitary violence, 'democratically mandated parties which establish a commitment to exclusively peaceful methods' would be free to join a multi-party talks process with the two Governments. Among other key points, the Prime Minister made it clear that the British Government would 'encourage, facilitate and enable' the achievement of agreement among all the people of Ireland. The Taoiseach also confirmed that, in the event of an overall settlement, the Irish Government would, as part of a balanced constitutional accommodation, put forward and support proposals for change in the Irish Constitution which would fully reflect the principle of consent in Northern Ireland. He also signalled his intention to establish a Forum for Peace and Reconciliation on ways of promoting agreement between both traditions in Ireland.

The Declaration, painstakingly agreed over many months, provided a framework of principles designed to persuade those who were carrying out paramilitary campaigns to abandon violence and pursue their objectives instead through peaceful political means. It signalled to republicans that they would have access to a potentially far-reaching political process, with a 'level playing field' from a nationalist perspective, if the IRA's campaign of violence were to be ended. It did so, however, in terms which gave important balancing reassurances to unionists.

The Declaration was positively received on all sides. Sinn Féin did not formally welcome it but, as was their wont, sought 'clarification' on various points. We were willing to provide this; the British Government were slower to respond but eventually did so.

Eight months later, on 31 August 1994, the IRA announced their long-awaited ceasefire. It was clear to us that this was not a temporary stratagem but was intended to be permanent. However, the British Government became fixated for a while on the absence of the word 'permanent' from the IRA statement. The IRA were also grudging in their initial response, slow to demonstrate either in political outreach to Sinn Féin or in security policy reforms that they were taking the ceasefire seriously. And some early breaches did not help, fuelling British Government and unionist suspicions. But gradually the reality that the IRA's campaign was over took hold. And in October the loyalist paramilitary groups followed suit.

At the international level, a tangible response came in the form of generous political and financial support which the United States and the European Union pledged in the new context created by the IRA and loyalist ceasefires. I was heavily involved in developing these external dimensions.

Meanwhile, the two Governments had launched work on another document which we intended as a detailed prospectus for inclusive talks. On the Irish side, we saw little chance of those talks succeeding unless the Governments set out in advance a shared vision of what they should deal with. We needed an understanding between us of what a settlement might look like, spanning constitutional issues, institutional arrangements in the three strands, protection of rights and various other aspects.

This work took place mainly in the Liaison Group, beginning more or less in tandem with the negotiation of the Downing Street Declaration, and continued for roughly a year. It was difficult work, given the breadth and complexity of the issues to be covered and the balances required between them. We were anticipating, in many ways, the structure, substance and major fault-lines of the actual negotiations when they would finally get under way. Much consultation was required en route with the parties likely to be sitting at the table. There were also various disruptions to the work, including damaging leaks of drafts to both the Irish and British media.

The document built heavily on the Downing Street Declaration. Among its key provisions, it declared that the two Governments intended to 'promote and establish agreement', based on the principle of consent, and to work with the parties to achieve a comprehensive accommodation involving interlocking institutions across the three strands. It then spelled out what the latter would entail. For example, new institutions in Northern Ireland and North/South institutions would have to afford both communities 'secure and satisfactory political, administrative and symbolic expression and protection'. The British Government, for its part, pledged that, for as long as it exercised jurisdiction in Northern Ireland, it would do so 'with rigorous impartiality on behalf of all the people of Northern Ireland in their diversity'.

The two Governments also committed themselves to ensuring equitable political participation for whichever community found itself in a minority position by reference to the Northern Ireland framework or the wider Irish framework, following application of the consent principle. There were provisions to ensure that, in the event of the new institutions breaking down for whatever reason, the two Governments working through a continuing British–Irish Intergovernmental Conference would step in and take remedial action.

Sean O hUiginn led our drafting team for this document. My contribution was to coordinate views within the Irish Government system on the options for North/South cooperation and to suggest language for the North/South section.

The Joint Framework Document, as it was eventually called, was largely agreed by the end of 1994. It fell to the new Taoiseach, John Bruton, to issue it with John Major at a summit on 22 February 1995. On the same day, the British Government published a companion piece which outlined what Strand One of the prospective talks might cover.

The Downing Street Declaration and the Framework Document were landmark documents in the peace process. They were essential precursors to the all-party negotiations towards which all our efforts were directed. We hoped that the Framework Document in particular, which seemed broadly acceptable to the republican movement, would be a catalyst for early movement into those talks.

A number of pressures conspired against this, however. The document got a hostile reaction from the unionists, who took fright on seeing for the first time the detail of what might be on the agenda in Strand Two. This unsettled a British Government which, with mounting internal Tory dissent over Europe, was becoming increasingly dependent on UUP votes. John Major had, of course, shown commendable courage in presenting, with John Bruton, this best guess at what would be a fair and balanced outcome from the talks. But, as the UUP acquired more leverage over his Government, he preferred to distance himself from what had been agreed in the Framework Document.

5

THE DECOMMISSIONING STALEMATE

Against this background, the issue of the disposal of paramilitary weapons, never far from unionist minds, moved to centre stage.

This was one of the most sensitive issues of the entire negotiation process. The 'decommissioning' of paramilitary weapons – this term signalled that there might be options other than destruction – was, of course, something which both Governments wished to see. However, the Irish Government was quite clear that this would happen only voluntarily and in the context of a political settlement. Unless the organisation concerned decided of its own free will to dispose of its weapons, this would simply not happen. Even if a paramilitary group claimed to have got rid of all of its weapons, there was no way of establishing with certainty that this had actually happened. Significant arsenals could be held back; the group could dispose of some weapons in the morning but go out and purchase more in the afternoon; it could manufacture home-made explosives, and so on.

For these various reasons, therefore, we considered the unionist demand for decommissioning ahead of participation in talks to be unrealistic and misguided. It suggested an agenda focused primarily on blocking inclusive talks so as to defer the prospect of eventual power-sharing with Sinn Féin.

Republicans had their own objections to the demand: the IRA had not been defeated militarily – they had voluntarily declared a ceasefire – and now the unionists were requiring them, in effect, to come in with their hands up. The issue of the disposal of weapons had not been mentioned by either Government in the run-up to the IRA ceasefire decision. While we all abhorred paramilitary violence, and while unionist suspicions about an IRA refusal to decommission might be understandable (that is, that there could be a plan to retain weapons for future use if the ceasefire ever broke down), the approach of trying to coerce those in possession of the weapons into disposing of them was doomed to failure. The 'decommissioning of mindsets' would first be necessary, to use a formulation from that time. We had to create a political context in which such decisions might more easily be taken. And that meant clearing the way for inclusive talks.

Instead, under pressure from the unionists, the British Government erected a roadblock. In a speech in Washington DC in March 1995, Sir Patrick Mayhew set out three preconditions for Sinn Féin's entry to political talks. The party would have to be willing to 'disarm progressively'; there would have to be agreement on the modalities for achieving this; and 'the actual decommissioning of some arms' would be required as a confidence-building measure. With the latter requirement ('Washington Three', as it came to be known), the British Government impaled itself on a hook from which it would not be able to free itself for some time to come.

To impose decommissioning as a precondition before participants even reached the negotiating table was without precedent in other peace processes. This issue now stood a good chance of destroying ours. For the next 12 to 18 months, it would bedevil our efforts to get all-party talks under way. Sinn Féin saw

Washington Three as a perfidious move. With a weakened Major Government camped on Washington Three and insisting there could be no access for Sinn Féin to talks without this, republican confidence began to ebb away.

We worked to detach the decommissioning issue from the main business of the prospective talks so that it would not jeopardise the latter altogether. In November 1995, the two Governments announced a 'twin-track' approach to make progress in parallel on all-party negotiations and on decommissioning. An international body would be established to give an independent assessment of the decommissioning issue. This would consist of Senator George Mitchell, General John de Chastelain (a former Canadian general) and Harri Holkeri (a former Finnish Prime Minister).

Reporting in January 1996, Mitchell and his colleagues recommended that some decommissioning take place *during* the talks, rather than as a precondition for participation. They also recommended that the participants in all-party talks commit to six principles of non-violence. We saw acceptance of these 'Mitchell Principles', a formal demonstration of commitment to exclusively peaceful and democratic methods, as one way of overcoming the impasse on decommissioning.

The launch of this report in Belfast was my first encounter with George Mitchell, who impressed me hugely with his political acumen, tact and judiciousness. In contrast to the arrangements made for the 1991–2 talks, Mitchell came across as a genuinely independent chairman. Little did I, or he, realise that his mission to Northern Ireland would be prolonged well beyond this initial assignment and that we would all have reason to be grateful for his skills over the next 18 months and longer.

We hoped initially to get all-party negotiations launched by the end of February 1996. On 9 February, however, the IRA ceasefire collapsed with the Canary Wharf bombing in London. An IRA statement admitted responsibility and said the 'complete cessation of hostilities' they had ordered in August 1994 was at an end. Sinn Féin blamed British Government bad faith, claiming that they had been promised access to substantive talks within three months of that cessation.

The two Governments reacted by suspending political-level contact with Sinn Féin. Officials remained in touch, however; and, in addition, John Hume had his own contacts and there were other intermediary channels.

While it did not come as a major surprise, the collapse of the ceasefire was a profound setback nevertheless. It called into question all the achievements of the peace process to date. We would not accept, however, that this was the end of the process. We had to work all the harder to put it back on the rails. We had to try to ensure with the British Government that, as an incentive for the earliest possible restoration of the ceasefire, the door would remain open for meaningful and inclusive negotiations.

It was a dispiriting period as we worked to rebuild what had been destroyed. We had to create a positive way forward which would not impose any fresh roadblocks. At a summit on 28 February, the Taoiseach and the Prime Minister were careful not to add conditions to their simple call for a restoration of the ceasefire of August 1994. We knew, however, that a restored ceasefire would have to be credible and clearly permanent in intent.

The Mitchell report in January had also contained a suggestion that elections would be a confidence-building route into all-party talks. The unionists had been pressing for this, wanting parties to secure fresh mandates for participation in talks. The British Government supported them. We, the SDLP and Sinn Féin wanted to see talks directly convened and had various misgivings about an electoral route. However, as it was clear to us that the British saw elections as a face-saving way of obscuring Mitchell's rejection of Washington Three, we were willing ultimately to set these aside.

Another key confidence-building factor would be a firm date for the talks. At their summit on 28 February, John Bruton and John Major agreed that the talks would begin on 10 June 1996. Sinn Féin would be able to join them, it was made clear, if the IRA ceasefire were reinstated in the meantime.

The elections took place on 30 May 1996. These determined which parties would eventually sit around the negotiating table. The effect was to add to the existing five (the UUP, the SDLP, Alliance, the DUP and Robert McCartney's UK Unionist Party (UKUP)) two loyalist parties – the Progressive Unionist Party (PUP) and the Ulster Democratic Party (UDP) – as well as a new Northern Ireland Women's Coalition and a Northern Ireland Labour group.

We had regular contact with Sinn Féin at official level during this period. However, although they showed keen interest in the arrangements being negotiated for the all-party talks, no restoration of the IRA ceasefire came.

On 10 June, the talks opened in Belfast without them. The Taoiseach and the Prime Minister attended and gave opening addresses.

The two Governments had asked Senator Mitchell and his two colleagues to be the independent chairmen for the negotiations. The Irish Government strongly backed Mitchell as the chair of both the Plenary and Strand Two. We saw him as a person of impeccable competence, judgement and stature who would be ideal in the sensitive Strand Two role. We also felt his presence there would reassure Sinn Féin that the Strand Two negotiations would be serious and meaningful.

Our British colleagues, however, had initially considered

General de Chastelain. The UUP were unhappy with Mitchell for Strand Two, presenting him as someone close to Irish America who would have an inherent nationalist bias. The British reservation about him reflected this unionist concern but also, perhaps, a fear of their own that Mitchell would not be easily controllable in the Strand Two role.

United States officials strongly supported Mitchell, however. And David Trimble, the UUP leader, indicated in due course that he was personally open to Mitchell and recognised his qualities. After trying for a while to qualify the Senator's role, the British agreed to issue an invitation to the three men to act collectively as independent chairmen for relevant parts of the negotiations.

On 10 June, when nominations for the posts of chairmen were reached, the DUP and the UKUP objected strongly to these nominations, claiming a lack of consultation with the unionist parties on them, and refused to accept Senator Mitchell. Unsettled by this move, Trimble indicated that he had reservations about some of the powers contemplated for the chairmen.

The stand-off dragged on all afternoon and evening and for the whole of the next day. The two Governments were agreed that, if we could not get Mitchell installed, there would be no talks.

Various procedural solutions were explored. With tempers rising, there were farcical scenes on the evening of 11 June, when Cedric Wilson of the UKUP parked himself in the chairman's seat for a while so that Mitchell could not occupy it.

Finally, a compromise of sorts was found which saved face for the unionist parties and enabled the three independent chairmen to be appointed. Mitchell took the chair of the Plenary, while de Chastelain would chair Strand Two and a Business Committee. (When, a few months later, de Chastelain preferred to concentrate on his decommissioning role, the two Governments proposed

Mitchell once again for Strand Two and the Plenary, and eventually this was agreed.)

There was also a prolonged row over the rules for the negotiations. We wanted to ensure that decommissioning could not be used to block progress in the wider talks. The British Government agreed in due course to a proposal from us that this would be handled in a separate sub-committee, to be chaired by de Chastelain. We also agreed to establish an International Commission on Decommissioning.

In the wake of the stand-off over the chairmanships and the rules, we had to get the opening Plenary back on track and completed so that we could move on to the substantive negotiations. Much time and energy were spent on devising a choreography which, on the one hand, would show the decommissioning issue being 'addressed' in that meeting (as per the Mitchell report) but, on the other, would pass it on without delay to a separate sub-committee for detailed attention.

The real world intervened starkly when that year's 'marching season' arrived. Disastrous handling of two of the most controversial Orange parades caused deep unhappiness within the nationalist community, fuelled sectarian tensions and led to a crisis of confidence in the talks process. The Chief Constable of the RUC had originally banned a parade in Portadown from Drumcree church down the mainly nationalist Garvaghy Road. Later, under Orange pressure (though he would claim a public safety motivation), he reversed his decision. This was followed by several days of loyalist mayhem and intimidation of Catholics. There was also a highly contentious parade on the Ormeau Road in Belfast, another well-known flashpoint.

The impact on the talks was considerable. Nationalist attitudes hardened and there was much less willingness to cooperate with the unionist parties. With opinion now deeply polarised, there was little chance of agreeing a way forward. All that could be done before the August recess was to agree a date in September for the resumption of the talks.

For all the difficulties, the talks remained the only game in town. As one colleague remarked at the time, we were like slow-bicycle riders, trying desperately not to fall off during the months of interminable squabbling over procedures or decommissioning – or, more usually, the interplay between them. No substance was being addressed. Procedure – political in its own way, of course – had become a proxy for substance.

Our priority that autumn was to get the remaining procedural matters dealt with as quickly as possible. We believed that key elements of the republican leadership were keen to restore the ceasefire and that that decision might be taken if they saw that there would be no decommissioning blockage in the talks.

More and more, however, the shadow of the forthcoming general election in the UK was falling over the talks and affected all calculations. Major's position was weakening, dissent within his party was growing and it was not clear how long this state of affairs could continue. His Government was less and less likely to take the political risks needed for a restoration of the IRA ceasefire. Conversely, it was less and less likely that republicans would put their faith in this administration and restore the ceasefire while Major was in office. Efforts by John Hume to get a restoration continued behind the scenes but were thwarted by this shrinking room for manoeuvre. We became less confident that a serious effort to reach a balanced overall settlement would be made, or could succeed, under this British Government.

In late January 1997, the opening Plenary finally managed to agree the remaining procedural matters. The next stage would ordinarily have been to get agreement on a substantive agenda. However, with the election campaign effectively under way and parties sniping at each other, the conditions were not conducive for this. So, with 1 May 1997 tipped as the election date, the two Governments decided to 'park' the talks in early March for a three-month period. We wanted to be able to pick them up promptly after the election, preserving the (admittedly modest) degree of agreement reached to date. The talks were therefore adjourned on 5 March and would resume on 3 June. A general election was also due in our own jurisdiction, with speculation focusing on a June date.

Many of us felt that only an incoming British Government with a comfortable majority – in the range of 30–50 seats – would have the latitude to resist the unionist demands on decommissioning, achieve a restored ceasefire and offer a genuinely level playing field in the next round of talks.

6

BUNKER DAYS

will step back at this point and describe where I was living and working during this period.

In the summer of 1995, I was promoted and transferred to Belfast as the Irish head of the joint secretariat that the two Governments had established 10 years earlier.

The Bunker, as we called it, was not actually a bunker. It was a nondescript, somewhat dilapidated two-storey civil service building, bearing the name Maryfield, which the British Government pressed into service in 1985 as the premises for the new Secretariat. Situated on the periphery of the Palace Barracks campus near Hollywood, Co. Down, it had the advantages of privacy and good security. These considerations were uppermost on the minds of both Governments, particularly in the face of the mass unionist protests about the Anglo-Irish Agreement and the creation of the Secretariat. In the period after the Irish staff moved into Maryfield, there were constant large-scale demonstrations at the Secretariat's gates, with one protester, Cedric Wilson (of chair-grabbing fame later on), occupying a caravan there for many months.

Little had changed by the time I got there in 1995. I had of course been a frequent visitor in the intervening years. But now I would be arriving to live and work there for a four-year period. While there had been some modest improvements in the living accommodation over the years, Maryfield was still essentially as I had known it from the day I first set eyes on the building in December 1985. It was part of a military-police compound and you could not easily forget this. Visitors coming up the driveway from the forbidding metal entrance gates were still given a disconcerting instruction, on the first signpost, to discharge their firearms into a sandbox provided nearby. There was still the familiar rat-tat-tat of gunfire from an RUC rifle testing range located within a few feet of our offices. (In the early days, staff assigned to Maryfield would hold up their phones to this cacophony for the benefit of bemused colleagues in Dublin; however, the novelty value quickly faded.)

It was, as I have said, a joint secretariat. The British side occupied the ground-floor offices, while our side was billeted on the first floor. The Irish staff had small bedrooms in addition, as for security reasons we had to live there. There was also some communal space for joint meetings and hospitality. Our side consisted of the Irish Joint Secretary (myself from 1995 to 1999), about eight Foreign Affairs staff (diplomats plus administrative support) and two senior colleagues from the Department of Justice.

Local staff incurred a certain amount of risk working for the Secretariat. In the early days one staff member would often come to work lying at the back of a station wagon under a coat to avoid being seen by protesters at the entrance. We had huge regard for the courage and devotion demonstrated by such colleagues.

As getting catering assistance from the local community was problematic (given the Secretariat's location close to a unionist heartland), it was necessary to bring our own cook with us. We also had a local housekeeper; both were vital members of the team.

There was no question of family accompanying those who were assigned to the Secretariat. It was a claustrophobic and spartan environment with few diversions. We took all our meals together.

Exercise mainly took the form of walks around the perimeter of the building (though occasional walks along a coastal path towards Bangor were also possible). Travel outside Maryfield was limited and only RUC vehicles were used.

The Irish staff had, on the whole, excellent working relations with our British colleagues. Nevertheless, we had to assume that all our electronic communications were being monitored. I was amused from time to time if I found a British colleague repeating back to me, inadvertently, a precise phrase I had used in a report transmitted a few days earlier. If necessary, the Irish staff would have guarded conversations outside or chat to each other in Irish (though this was hardly a hermetic code). Sometimes we would deliberately transmit messages which, for one or other tactical reason, we wanted our British colleagues to pick up.

The whole experience, with its emphasis on daily routines, self-discipline and continual security precautions, resembled a military assignment. We were living and working together all day, in close proximity, and had to plan everything as a team.

In my first few months there, the security atmosphere in Belfast was more relaxed because of the previous year's IRA ceasefire. This led to a point where we could venture forth on occasional group outings to carefully selected pubs in Belfast. The Canary Wharf bomb in February 1996 brought such excursions to an abrupt halt. We all went back below the parapet for the next year and a half. I felt at times like the captain of a submarine, who would raise the periscope occasionally to see if the coast was clear for a brief trip to the surface (and usually find that it was not).

The ability to move around more freely during the 1994–6 ceasefire period had personal consequences for me. During that time I received, and was able to accept, invitations to represent the Irish Government at various public events in Belfast. This meant that I had a higher public profile than my predecessors, who had operated under the stricter secrecy of the pre-ceasefire years. My greater visibility meant in turn that, when the ceasefire collapsed and we had to revert to the status quo ante, I became an easier target for loyalist paramilitaries.

I was fortunate in having a British counterpart, Peter Bell from the Northern Ireland Office, who was well disposed towards Ireland and favoured close Anglo-Irish cooperation. A classical scholar and former British diplomat, Bell was an unconventional figure within the NIO. He was highly intelligent, a witty conversationalist and excellent company. He was also a shrewd commentator on current political developments. Happily, from my perspective, he was not always guarded in his comments on events and people. Our conversations, frank and frequent, helped me to assess, and to report on, current thinking in the British Government on the peace process. Bell and I developed an easy rapport which, while not precluding occasional stern words on behalf of our respective Governments, helped both sides to manage the constant challenges thrown up by the process and to have a better understanding of each other's problems.

Bell was a gregarious individual and, like me, wanted to strengthen the Secretariat's outreach work. In the early years, contacts were deliberately confined to officialdom. As time passed, however, both sides of the Secretariat saw advantage in cultivating jointly a broader range of contacts. We wanted to improve our understanding of the political, security, economic and other agendas we were dealing with. So a wide range of interlocutors – ministers, senior officials, religious leaders, top Army or RUC figures and so on – were invited to lunch or dinner in Maryfield.

Here the Irish side's cooks were a great asset. Building on the standards set by my immediate predecessor, Declan O'Donovan, we managed to build up Maryfield's culinary reputation to the point where it was dubbed the 'second best restaurant in Belfast after Roscoff's' (then the city's premier eatery). Despite the unpromising environment, one of our cooks would use his downtime to enhance his patisserie skills to award-winning standard. While it might have been expected that an invitation to our controversial premises would scare off some potential visitors, generally we found that we had no trouble attracting our target guests. The same applied to larger-scale receptions which we hosted from time to time.

Despite sustained efforts on our part, unionist guests – in the sense of UUP and DUP party members – remained conspicuously absent. I had been asked by the Taoiseach, John Bruton, when calling on him before taking up my post, to do my utmost to reach out to unionists and to assuage their suspicions of Maryfield. The leaderships of both the UUP and the DUP had ordained, however, that there was to be no contact of any kind with this reviled institution. Bell and I did manage to bring in one or two guests with UUP connections but, for the most part, we had to make do with proxies of various kinds.

Apart from our exchanges on day-to-day political developments, our responsibilities as Joint Secretaries included a wide range of issues flowing from the Anglo-Irish Agreement. Many of these related to the security situation on the ground in Northern Ireland. The greatest challenge each year was how the marching season would be policed and how sectarian confrontation and violence could be avoided at particular flashpoints (such as the Garvaghy Road in Portadown).

I also developed good working relations with the RUC Chief Constable, initially Hugh Annesley and later Ronnie Flanagan. I had many discussions with both about individual parades and how our Government felt these should be handled. They knew that, in talking to us, they were engaging at one remove with nationalist opinion on the ground. Each year saw intensifying crises at Drumcree and elsewhere, which the RUC had to handle, and the Secretariat was an important channel for dialogue and communication about these.

Unionists, however, were suspicious of any RUC contacts with us. They imagined that the Irish Government was succeeding in having dozens of Orange parades rerouted each year. Nationalists were, of course, hoping that we had a success rate on that scale. On the most sensitive parades, we were rarely able to change RUC minds to the degree that unionists feared or that nationalists hoped for. Indeed, there were several occasions during my time in Belfast when we were bitterly disappointed with decisions taken on individual parades. Nevertheless, unionists believed that I and my colleagues were wielding sinister influence over the RUC.

Our security situation at Maryfield was always a headache. Three or four times while I was there, the Loyalist Volunteer Force (LVF), who were led for a time by Billy Wright (aka 'King Rat'), issued a statement which named me and gave me 48 hours in which to leave Northern Ireland, failing which I and my colleagues would be treated as 'legitimate targets'. In the past, there had been generalised threats against the Secretariat but staff had not been named. (This was assisted by the Irish Government's practice of not listing the staff concerned in its directories and by the willingness of the Irish media, over many years, to support this secrecy.) Each threat against us was taken very seriously by the RUC. There were, however, limits to what could be done to enhance our security. Forms of transport (air, road or rail), timings and access routes could be varied but the scope for variation was not endless. My own height, furthermore, did not exactly make me inconspicuous.

My colleagues were resilient and philosophical about the assignment. They balanced the physical risks and uncomfortable living conditions against the attractions of working in a uniquely challenging and sensitive post. Many went on to very distinguished careers in the diplomatic service; one of them, Joe Hackett, is the current Secretary General of the Department of Foreign Affairs.

During the talks from 1996 on, the ministers and senior officials who were representing the Government there often stayed with us at Maryfield. Hugh Coveney, Liz O'Donnell and John O'Donoghue were regular visitors, cheerfully putting up with the limitations of the place. John O'Donoghue would go for bracing walks along the coastal path, his RUC minders barely able to keep up with him.

Over the years we became very attached to the drivers, cleaners and other support staff who made our lives bearable at Maryfield. One driver used to lay on informal tours of notorious trouble spots in West Belfast for our visitors. As he was from a unionist background, his idea of what constituted safety in that part of the city was diametrically opposite to the nationalist view. After nervously driving visitors up and down the Falls Road, all the while regaling them with blood-curdling accounts of various atrocities, he would turn off with a great show of relief into Tiger's Bay, a loyalist stronghold which would have terrified most nationalists.

In April 1998, it was agreed by Tony Blair and Bertie Ahern during the Good Friday Agreement negotiations that the Maryfield Secretariat would close by the end of the year. This was confirmed to David Trimble in a side letter on Good Friday. The successor institution, the British–Irish Secretariat, would be housed elsewhere.

In the event, we overshot the deadline for closure by a few weeks. The two Governments found premises for the new Secretariat in an office block in central Belfast, Windsor House (felicitously named from a unionist perspective). We moved there in February 1999.

I hosted a farewell party in Maryfield to mark the closure of the Bunker after 13 eventful years. We brought back many of the staff, Irish and British, who had toiled there over those years. There were many bittersweet memories of an institution which was truly unique.

A few nights later, I overnighted alone in Maryfield, the place by then completely empty. When the gates closed behind me on my departure the next morning, the days of the Maryfield Secretariat were over. I heard later that it was to be turned into a convalescent home for disabled RUC officers. The UUP's Ken Maginnis, I was told, arrived a few hours after me to inspect the premises – and, no doubt, to check that we were definitively gone.

New accommodation had to be found for our staff, who were all transferring to the British–Irish Secretariat. We found two apartment complexes in central Belfast and moved everyone in there.

After years of incarceration in the Bunker, the relocation was a slightly disorienting experience. We eased it by bringing our cook with us and continuing with old habits – communal eating and transport – for a transitional period. We also provided ourselves with vague cover stories to deflect any questions about the sudden appearance in the new apartment blocks of a group of new tenants with Southern accents. We abandoned such efforts, however, when, within 10 minutes of arrival, one of the groups was greeted with a breezy 'Are youse all from Maryfield, then?' In Belfast very little stayed secret for long.

7

THE STARS ALIGNED

I n the summer of 1997, changes of administration in Dublin and London created a new dynamic which would transform the prospects for peace and a comprehensive political settlement. The formation of Governments headed by Bertie Ahern and Tony Blair respectively, each with a comfortable majority, had the effect of renewing republican confidence and led very quickly to a restoration of the IRA ceasefire. This paved the way for Sinn Féin to be readmitted to the talks process.

Tony Blair arrived in office first. On 1 May 1997, the Labour Party won a landslide victory in the British general election. Blair became Prime Minister, with a huge parliamentary majority. Two months later, following an Irish general election on 26 June, Bertie Ahern succeeded John Bruton as Taoiseach, heading a Fianna Fáil–Progressive Democrats coalition Government.

Ahern and Blair had been preparing for their potential roles for a couple of years already. They had had a first private meeting, as Opposition leaders, in the Gresham Hotel in Dublin in 1996. This was followed by several further meetings in London and Dublin. At one meeting in the spring of 1997, they agreed that, if or when they formed Governments after the respective elections that year, they would make a serious and concerted effort within the first 18 months or so to achieve a Northern Ireland settlement.

They also agreed that, ahead of the elections, Ahern would explore the prospects for getting a restoration of the IRA ceasefire, while Blair would try to prepare the ground politically with the unionist parties for inclusive talks following a resumed ceasefire. While the Irish Government had suspended all political-level contacts with Sinn Féin after the Canary Wharf bomb in 1996, Ahern had some informal contacts with Gerry Adams while in Opposition to emphasise his own continuing commitment to the peace process.

The close working relationship that he and Blair had developed from 1996 onwards laid a vital foundation for what they hoped to do together in office. Both were straightforward, pragmatic types. In contrast to some of their predecessors, neither had heavy ideological baggage. They each wanted to achieve a settlement. They were close in age and political outlook, coming into office at the same time and enjoying solid parliamentary majorities. There was excellent personal chemistry from their first meeting – assisted, as Ahern has remarked, by a mutual interest in football. They had a good understanding of each other's political needs. Most of all, they trusted each other.

As they faced into the multiplying demands of trying to get the ceasefire reinstated and keeping the talks process on track, the two men were in constant, almost daily, communication with each other. They started a practice of having direct phone calls, without officials listening in (traditionally a feature on the British side). During their terms in office, they would have significantly more regular and direct contact than their predecessors ever had. There was also intensive contact between the senior advisers in No. 10 and Government Buildings.

Blair, it rapidly became clear, was ready to give the Northern Ireland issue an unprecedented degree of priority for a British

Prime Minister. The partnership on which he and Ahern now embarked, and the personal friendship which would grow from it, would endure for the next decade and beyond.

One key difference, of course, was that Blair was coming into 10 Downing Street without any previous experience of Government. Ahern, on the other hand, had served in a number of Irish Governments and in a variety of ministerial posts. He was an astute and experienced negotiator, having honed these skills notably during his time as Minister for Labour with trade unions. I remember one occasion during Easter Week in Castle Buildings when Blair suggested to Ahern that the UUP, who had just made a concession of some kind, be immediately rewarded for this. Ahern cautioned against this, reminding Blair that there was something more important which the Governments still needed from the UUP and that it would be better to delay the reward until this had been secured. Blair took the point; it was a telling example of Ahern's longer experience as a negotiator.

I had first met Tony Blair myself in 1990. We had a mutual friend, Derry Irvine, who would become the Lord Chancellor in Blair's first Government. Irvine, who in the mid-seventies had given Blair a pupillage post in his barrister's chambers (where Blair met Cherie Booth, a fellow pupil), was a kind of political mentor to both Blairs as well as a close family friend. In the summer of 1990, the Irvines invited my wife and me to spend a weekend with them at their Scottish retreat. Tony and Cherie Blair were the other guests. Although at that time Blair was merely the social security spokesman for Labour in Opposition, it was obvious that he was destined for great things in the party. He was a star performer on the front bench; he was personable and telegenic; and, as an Englishman who had been educated in Scotland, he had a broad geographic appeal within the party which would count in his favour whenever the Scot John Smith stepped down as leader.

During that weekend with the Irvines, we struck up a good rapport, helped by a football match involving Blair, me and our respective sons, and by my wife accompanying him and his children to Mass in the local church. I had an opportunity for a chat with him about the Northern Ireland situation. However, possibly because of his responsibilities as social security spokesman, it was clear that he had not yet engaged with the issue in any detail. He was well disposed towards Ireland generally, his mother's Donegal Protestant background and the family holidays in Rossknowlagh in the sixties no doubt contributing to this, but the challenge of a Northern Ireland settlement did not yet appear to be on his radar.

We saw each other occasionally over the next few years. When he won the 1997 election and became Prime Minister, the first topic of conversation whenever we met (including at Hillsborough Castle during Easter Week) would tend to be Derry Irvine – and, increasingly, the political controversies which attended Irvine as Lord Chancellor.

It seems that, as the 1997 election approached, Blair decided that pursuing a Northern Ireland settlement would be one of his Government's top priorities. This required a major gamble on his part. But, with a very safe parliamentary majority, he could afford to take risks.

A fortnight after the UK election, Blair made his first visit to Northern Ireland as Prime Minister. In a speech at the Balmoral Show, his first speech anywhere as Prime Minister, he set out his perspective on Northern Ireland in terms that tilted more clearly in a unionist direction than previous Labour leaders would have done. He was signalling a break with previous Labour orthodoxy.

The new Government's agenda would not be Irish unity, he said. Nor would it be a persuader for unity. A political settlement would be based on the principle of consent and would not be 'a slippery slope to a united Ireland'. Blair 'valued the Union' and doubted we would see a united Ireland in the lifetime of anyone present, 'even the youngest'. He would, however, abide fully by the consent principle on the basis set out by the two Governments in the Downing Street Declaration.

It was clear that, after several decades of a Northern Ireland policy based on support for Irish unity by consent and solidarity with Irish nationalism, Blair wanted to rebalance the Labour Party. He saw the need to reach out to both traditions if there was to be any chance of achieving a balanced overall settlement.

Bertie Ahern understood the considerations underlying the Balmoral speech and was relaxed about it. There were several important things in it from his perspective, notably an assurance that Sinn Féin could have a place at the talks if an 'unequivocal ceasefire' were restored and they committed themselves to exclusively democratic means. The key thing was that no decommissioning precondition on the lines of Washington Three was being attached. We would go forward on the basis of the Mitchell report, which merely involved an undertaking to 'consider' some decommissioning in parallel.

The talks were due to resume on 3 June 1997. It was likely that they would then be adjourned to accommodate the Irish general election. The hope was that conditions could be achieved for a restoration of the IRA ceasefire in July and that Sinn Féin could enter the talks quickly thereafter, committing to the Mitchell Principles at the outset. The talks would then be adjourned and would resume in early September with, hopefully, the launch of substantive negotiations at that point.

On 16 June, however, two RUC policemen in Lurgan were killed by the IRA. At a time when a de facto ceasefire had seemed to be in operation, this caused widespread dismay and created a major crisis. There were suspicions of a power struggle between the militant wing of republicanism and those backing the political alternative. The British Government responded by suspending the official-level contacts with Sinn Féin that it had resumed on taking office.

At the same time, there was a concern to show that the two Governments were still in control of the agenda and that the talks would go ahead on the basis we had planned. To keep alive the prospect of a restoration of the ceasefire, the two Governments finalised on 23 June a joint paper on the handling of decommissioning in the talks. Based largely on an Irish draft, this paper sought to allay republican fears that decommissioning would monopolise the talks, trapping Sinn Féin in a situation in which they could be expelled if there were no decommissioning during the talks. We also wanted to dispel any idea that the unionists would have a veto over the move into substantive negotiations. We hoped that this would reassure the republican movement, strengthen the political wing and create the basis for an early restoration.

We tabled this paper in a Plenary session on 25 June. There were predictably apoplectic reactions from the DUP and the UKUP, that day and also a week later. They tried in every way possible to make life difficult for the UUP leader over this paper. However, David Trimble remained cautious, voicing a series of concerns about it and seeking clarification but keeping his options open. This was an important pointer for how he would act when faced with a crucial fork in the road just three months later.

Following the Irish election on 26 June, Bertie Ahern replaced John Bruton as Taoiseach.

From the moment he took office, Ahern's top priority was to achieve a restoration of the IRA ceasefire. In early July, he and Blair sent out signals emphasising the opportunity which republicans now had. There were more confidence-building factors in place, from a republican perspective, than ever before. They would probably never again have as promising a route into political engagement. This time, however, the ceasefire would have to be definitive and final: there could be no third ceasefire.

One issue was how to provide certainty that Sinn Féin could join the talks by a given (and early) date, assuming no breaches of a renewed ceasefire. Blair had indicated in May that, if the IRA ceasefire were to be restored by July, there would be a six-week 'testing period' and Sinn Féin could then be into talks straight away. This timing took account also of August being a holiday period. Ahern, taking office in July, backed a scenario involving the admission of Sinn Féin on 1 September.

On 1 July the new Irish Government was represented at the talks for the first time. The new Minister for Foreign Affairs was Ray Burke, who established a good rapport with his British opposite number, Mo Mowlam. Burke was accompanied by John O'Donoghue, the new Minister for Justice, and by Liz O'Donnell, the new Minister of State at Foreign Affairs.

In the Plenary a week later, George Mitchell secured agreement to a timetable involving completion of the rest of the opening agenda at a subsequent meeting, the launch of the three-stranded negotiations on 29 July (and establishment of the Independent Commission on Decommissioning) and adjournment of the talks from then until 15 September.

Once again, however, the handling of Orange parades dealt a severe blow to the prospects for the talks. Acting on RUC advice, Mo Mowlam allowed the Drumcree parade down the Garvaghy

Road on 6 July. This convulsed the nationalist community, causing widespread anger and bitterness. As in the previous summer, I was heavily involved in efforts through the Secretariat to avert this outcome. The decision, which sparked displays of unionist triumphalism and was followed by several days of disturbances, was an inauspicious beginning to Mo's tenure as Secretary of State. It almost sabotaged the moves to get the IRA ceasefire restored.

On 18 July, Sinn Féin issued a statement saying that Gerry Adams and Martin McGuinness had provided a detailed report and assessment to the IRA and had urged the latter to restore the cessation of August 1994. They felt that the commitment on the part of the two Governments to inclusive peace talks which they had been seeking was now in place. Sinn Féin's own commitment to 'significant and substantive change' and to issues of equality and 'demilitarisation' was now shared by the Irish Government, the SDLP and Irish-American opinion (a nod to the pan-nationalist consensus which the party had long championed).

On the following day, 19 July, the eagerly awaited statement came at last. The IRA announced a 'complete cessation of military operations' with effect from midday on 20 July. They had ordered the unequivocal restoration of the ceasefire of August 1994. In subsequent press comment, Gerry Adams made it clear that a pivotal factor had been the assurances given that decommissioning would not be allowed to block the negotiations.

The two Governments' efforts had paid off at last. On 21 July, Sinn Féin representatives visited Castle Buildings and met our Government and other delegations. British and Irish officials were in touch with the Sinn Féin leadership and there was talk of the British resuming political-level contacts also. On 25 July, in a deliberate echo of the meeting Albert Reynolds had had with

Hume and Adams when the first ceasefire was declared, Bertie Ahern welcomed Adams and Hume to Government Buildings.

The mood at the talks was less welcoming, however. On 23 July, the UUP closed ranks with the DUP and UKUP and voted against the Governments' paper on the handling of decommissioning. We responded with a deliberate reiteration of our commitment to the launching of substantive negotiations on 15 September. The DUP and UKUP withdrew from the talks that day, denouncing the British Government's surrender to 'IRA blackmail', and did not return.

The IRA's failure to use the word 'permanent' in their 1994 statement had bothered the Major Government. On this occasion, Tony Blair contented himself with a low-key reference to the need for careful assessment of the ceasefire to ensure that it was 'genuine in word and deed'. On 29 August, having satisfied herself to this effect, Mo Mowlam wrote jointly with Ray Burke to invite Sinn Féin to join the talks as from 9 September.

With the DUP and UKUP gone and Sinn Féin about to join, the UUP needed some cover if they were to stay on at the talks. They sought responses to the concerns they had raised about our paper, including confirmation that the Irish Government supported parallel decommissioning during the talks. We began work, therefore, on a procedural agreement which would give them a basis for staying.

8

ALL IN AT LAST

On 9 September 1997, the Plenary resumed. Sinn Féin arrived, signed up to the Mitchell Principles and delivered opening remarks which acknowledged the historic nature of the occasion.

The UUP were not yet there, however. Drafting a procedural motion to facilitate their return was a difficult exercise for the two Governments. We had to find a balance which would satisfy the UUP's needs but would not lose Sinn Féin, the SDLP and other delegations in the process.

On 15 September, the substantive talks were convened formally for the first time. The UUP did not appear; however, David Trimble sent positive signals, citing a joint statement by the two Governments on consent and decommissioning which he had found reassuring. Having also secured a mandate from his party's Executive, he indicated that his party was getting ready to join the talks over the coming days.

This happened finally on 24 September. The UUP appeared and, at a Plenary meeting that evening, we all reached agreement on the procedural motion (except for a negative Sinn Féin vote on one section of it). Separately, it was agreed that George Mitchell, John de Chastelain and Harri Holkeri would act as joint chairmen of Strand Two and that de Chastelain would be appointed chair of the Independent Commission on Decommissioning. (In practice, Mitchell would be the main chair of Strand Two.)

This was the most significant move forward since the talks process had begun in June 1996. At last, we had crossed the threshold and substantive three-stranded talks could begin, with everyone at the table. John O'Donoghue commented that this agreement cast 'a ray of light' across Ireland.

It could not have been taken for granted that David Trimble would resist the DUP and UKUP pressure and stay at the talks. It was always possible that the UUP leader would baulk at the last moment and decide that he did not have enough political cover to stay. Public criticism of him for staying came from two of his own party's MPs, Willie Thompson and Willie Ross. There were reports, indeed, that seven of the ten MPs were, to a greater or lesser extent, opposed to the UUP being involved in talks with Sinn Féin.

Ultimately, however, Trimble appears to have decided that it was part of his mission as UUP leader to take this historic opportunity for a settlement. The Governments, it is true, gave him significant assistance via the procedural motion. But there can be no denying the political courage which Trimble showed at this moment. He faced down taunts, accusations of selling out and threats of electoral annihilation from Paisley and McCartney. It was a fork in the road. Had he yielded to this intimidation, the inclusive talks which we had all worked so long to put in place would have been stillborn. However trying he was to prove as a partner for the road ahead, there would have been no Good Friday Agreement at the end of that road without Trimble.

Beginning in his Opposition years, Bertie Ahern had made very deliberate efforts to develop a good relationship with David Trimble. In 1995, he visited the UUP's Glengall Street offices, the first Fianna Fáil leader to do so, and had a first meeting with

Trimble. They met again at a British–Irish Association conference in Oxford in September 1996 and in Armagh in early 1997. In November 1997, with Ahern now in office as Taoiseach and the talks under way, they met in London with full delegations. They had a further meeting in February 1998.

Over time, these contacts paid off. I remember Trimble mentioning in public on a couple of occasions that he trusted Bertie Ahern and felt he could work with him. In informal weekend meetings from time to time, they worked through the political challenges each was facing and forged a relationship which was open and robust enough to withstand occasional turbulence.

My own relationship with David Trimble got off to a rockier start. In September 1995, we were both attending a conference in Cambridge. Trimble, who had just become the UUP leader, joined a group of which I was part. When one of our number introduced me to Trimble, making a jocular reference to the Maryfield Secretariat (where I had taken up duty a couple of months earlier), the UUP leader turned to me and made it clear, in the plainest of terms, that he considered my work in Belfast unhelpful. The background, I sensed, was unhappiness at Irish Government interventions on parades issues, notably Drumcree, during that summer. Trimble was no fan of the Secretariat, that much we all knew, and was generally of the view that officials of both Governments wielded too much influence and were bent on undermining the Union. The terms he used were a little startling but I made allowances for the fact that there had been a particularly difficult marching season, and some suspicions or animosities would inevitably linger. I did not take it personally; he had never liked Maryfield as an institution so his criticism did not in itself come as a complete surprise, merely its vehemence.

It was a defining moment when we achieved the breakthrough on 24 September 1997. The stage was now set for the long-delayed negotiations on the content of a three-stranded settlement.

There was a sense of great expectancy and promise. I vividly recall the relief all round that the process was at last moving forward, after a year of procedural stalemate and skirmishing about decommissioning. All going well, we might be able to achieve a settlement involving all key players within a matter of months.

Although the 24 September breakthrough was cathartic, it in fact took a long time for the talks to get going. It took several weeks to settle organisational arrangements (for example, the frequency of meetings, the size of delegations and the designation of representatives for the different strands) and to get the supporting mechanisms up and running.

On 10 October, Bertie Ahern and Tony Blair had a brief meeting in Strasbourg to take stock. Ahern marked Blair's cards clearly: we would need North/South institutions with executive powers if we were to have any chance of winning a referendum involving changes to Articles 2 and 3. Blair took this point but warned that the unionists would need cover in Strand Three if they were being asked to sign up to significant North/South structures. He accepted, however, the need for North/South structures on the lines set out in the Framework Document.

On a visit to Belfast three days later, Blair told our delegation that he was convinced that the UUP leader wanted a settlement – and indeed would not otherwise have joined this process. He also had a 15-minute meeting with Gerry Adams. This was the first time in 76 years, we were told, that a British Prime Minister had met a republican leader. Much media interest concentrated on whether or not Blair would shake hands with Adams (he did). Adams told us afterwards that he had a sense of genuine engagement on Blair's part when he outlined key republican concerns.

Unionism was unsettled by the ease with which Sinn Féin could get access to the new Prime Minister. Blair took pains, therefore, to give Trimble at least the same degree of access. Indeed, it was to become a standard complaint of the SDLP and other delegations at the talks that Sinn Féin and the UUP seemed to have almost unlimited access to 10 Downing Street and Government Buildings throughout the negotiations.

Seamus Mallon, in particular, lamented the ability of Adams and Trimble to press their cases directly at Head of Government level and win concessions there, bypassing the constraints of collective negotiation in Castle Buildings. Noting that the Governments regularly described the latter talks as the only show in town, his colleague Mark Durkan warned that 'they shouldn't make it seem as if other shows are more valuable'. The Taoiseach and Prime Minister were, of course, ready to receive any other party leaders as well. There was nevertheless a view among some delegations that the real business of the talks was being transacted in the visits paid to them by Adams and Trimble.

On 9 October, Ray Burke resigned after being embroiled in corruption allegations. He was replaced by David Andrews, who made his first appearance at the talks on 14 October. Andrews had, of course, been involved in the 1991–2 talks, knew many of the current participants well and got down to business straight away. He met David Trimble, who wanted to see the complete deletion of Articles 2 and 3 from our Constitution and gave a strikingly pessimistic prognosis for the talks, speculating that they would not last beyond Christmas in their current format. Trimble also indicated that his party would have no direct discussions with Sinn Féin.

From the moment the UUP found themselves at the negotiating table with Sinn Féin, they declined all direct engagement with the latter. Trimble and his colleagues evidently saw this as a quid pro quo for their willingness to stay at the talks. They felt a need to insulate themselves from the taunts of the DUP and the UKUP and indeed from some grassroots unease within the UUP. They resisted, accordingly, all efforts by Sinn Féin to draw them into direct dialogue, though they were willing to respond through the chair to questions put to them.

Others, however, recognised that there was simply no alternative to direct dialogue, however unpalatable the interlocutors. I remember Seamus Mallon remarking bleakly to me on the fact that he was now expected to talk to a particular UDP delegate who in an earlier paramilitary career had murdered one of Mallon's closest friends. Yet talk to him Mallon did, if they found themselves together, for example, in the coffee queue, because the UDP had a legitimate mandate and this delegate, having paid his debt to society, was legitimately there. There was a need for what was sometimes called 'strategic forgetting'.

We all had to make adjustments. At my first meeting with David Ervine, a former Ulster Volunteer Force member who had served a prison sentence for bomb-making offences, Ervine cheerfully informed me that I had been on the UVF's list of targets a few years earlier. This did not prevent us from going on to have an excellent working relationship, assisted by Ervine's engaging personality and acute political skills. There were several other loyalist politicians who were similarly impressive.

9

SOME OF THE PLAYERS

A word at this point about the people who flanked Tony Blair and Bertie Ahern and about the other participants in the talks.

Blair had appointed Mo Mowlam as Secretary of State for Northern Ireland. This came as no surprise: Blair had already decided on this two years earlier, Mo told me. Mo was a strong Blair supporter and part of his inner circle. In 1994, he had given her the shadow spokespersonship on Northern Ireland, in succession to Kevin McNamara. I had known Mo for several years, having first met her at a Labour Party conference in 1989. She impressed me immediately as a bright, lively and unconventional MP. She was highly thought of by the Labour leadership, and a ministerial career clearly beckoned. She was not long back from a period spent at an American university which had imbued her with strong liberal/left values.

Initially appointed as a deputy to Kevin McNamara, she was asked to balance the party's traditional Irish nationalism by building up its contacts with unionism. This she did conscientiously, cultivating people such as Ken Maginnis, Willie Ross and Peter Robinson and regularly travelling to Northern Ireland over the next few years. At the same time, she stayed close to John Hume, Seamus Mallon and other SDLP figures.

Mo's refreshingly direct style went down well in some circles but not in all. Those of more conservative mindset in Northern Ireland found her exuberance and lack of inhibition a little intimidating. Other complaints related to her regular use of earthy vocabulary.

Mo was always very good company, ebullient and personable. Her informality was apparent in her habit of kicking off her shoes regularly (and then failing to find them again). She had a down-to-earth and uncomplicated style which endeared her to many. As one small example, I think of an occasion during the talks when the two Governments and the chairmen had something to celebrate. Mo, who was hosting us, had her private secretary bring in a bottle of whiskey and a large box of jelly babies. We found ourselves toasting whatever minor victory it was with a glass of whiskey each and a generous helping of jelly babies – to astonished looks from Senator Mitchell and his fellow chairmen.

Mo was, in short, a one-off. Most people found her instantly appealing. She was warm, compassionate and independent-minded. She also had considerable political skill and courage, a good example being her decision to visit loyalist prisoners in the Maze prison on 9 January 1998 to seek their support for the talks process. Public affection for Mo grew as it became known that she had a life-threatening brain tumour. She would wear a blonde wig to conceal the hair loss from her chemotherapy but would cheerfully toss it aside at private meetings. (She was undergoing daily therapy even during Easter Week 1998.) Most of the delegations at the talks had great respect and admiration for Mo, in particular because of her dogged determination to press on towards agreement, even while in frail health, during that final week in Castle Buildings.

Mo was impatient with protocol, frank in her language and sentiments and endearingly unselfconscious. However, unionists disliked her, and this was a political liability. She, for her part, did not hide her lack of empathy with most unionist politicians. Her relaxed banter with people such as Martin McGuinness and David Ervine created an uneasy contrast. She believed strongly that the British Government had to reach out to republicanism and to loyalism and this inevitably ended up alienating many traditional unionists.

David Andrews was Mo's opposite number during the negotiations leading up to the Good Friday Agreement and beyond. (She also dealt with our Minister for Justice on some aspects of her portfolio.) In Foreign Affairs for the second time, Andrews brought a lot of valuable experience with him as well as an instinctive grasp of the needs of constitutional nationalism. He and Mo built up a good relationship with each other. She was keen to have regular joint press conferences and statements (partly for the added profile this gave her on her own side). In the later stages of the negotiations, with Tony Blair and No. 10 steadily increasing their involvement, displays of partnership with the Irish Government became all the more important to Mo as a means of protecting her role and relevance.

Liz O'Donnell was David Andrews' highly competent, energetic and articulate deputy at the talks. Incisive and fearless in her interventions, she made a very significant contribution. Paul Murphy, a quiet and amiable Welsh Catholic, was Mo's deputy and Liz's opposite number. John O'Donoghue and Michael Smith (the Minister for Defence) were also involved in the early stages of the negotiations.

We had a strong team of officials on our side, headed by Paddy Teahon, Dermot Gallagher and Tim Dalton. Paddy Teahon had been the Secretary General in the Department of the Taoiseach for several years. He had worked on Northern Ireland policy under

Albert Reynolds, John Bruton and now Bertie Ahern. A shrewd and genial Kerryman, Teahon was the main interlocutor with Blair's advisers in No. 10.

In the summer of 1997, Sean O hUiginn departed for Washington DC to take up the post of Irish Ambassador there. Dermot Gallagher returned from Washington to replace O hUiginn as the head of the Anglo-Irish Division in Dublin. 'Dag', as we knew him internally (a reference to his full name in initials), had strong tactical skills, a wide range of contacts among the Northern parties and a deal-making instinct which came into its own in the final phase of the negotiations. Always close to his Leitrim roots, he had been involved with Northern Ireland policy since the Sunningdale Agreement and was now back in charge of it, for the second time, in Foreign Affairs.

Tim Dalton, Secretary General in the Department of Justice, and a Kerryman who had been Paddy Teahon's contemporary at school in Killarney, had extensive knowledge of Anglo-Irish security issues. He was also more familiar than most with republican thinking and concerns.

The chemistry between Teahon, Gallagher and Dalton worked very well. They operated as a closely knit team throughout this period. Even after the umpteenth brick wall had been reached, they would keep working together behind the scenes to find some alternative way forward.

My own role, at the Secretariat in Belfast, was to handle day-to-day contacts with the British Government on all developments. The pace was generally intense; we were at the mercy of fast-moving events, whether in the political or security domains. I would usually give an initial Irish Government response to issues as they arose, working through my British opposite number or other senior officials in the Northern Ireland Office. There might be follow-up from Dublin with more detailed instructions as the Taoiseach and ministers were consulted. I would give our view, for example, of speeches or interviews given by British Ministers or of British drafts for position papers in the negotiations. Conversely, I would be asked about Irish Government interventions of various kinds. My work laid the groundwork for meetings of the Liaison Group, now co-chaired by Dermot Gallagher and Quentin Thomas, which became more frequent as the negotiations developed. In the final months of the talks, there was also much direct phone contact between senior officials, in particular between the Department of the Taoiseach and No. 10.

A key figure within our team was Martin Mansergh, an adviser to successive Taoisigh who had begun his career as a Third Secretary in the Department of Foreign Affairs (in, as it happens, my own cohort). A historian by background and temperament, Mansergh had engaged in the initial contacts with Sinn Féin in the late eighties. He had an unrivalled understanding of the republican movement and made a vital contribution through his ongoing contacts as well as his ability to interpret republican concerns and intentions.

In Foreign Affairs, Dermot Gallagher was supported by a number of talented officials in the Anglo-Irish Division who served as the engine room for the Government's involvement in the negotiations. He set up a dedicated talks team in September 1997. David Cooney, who would later serve as the Irish Ambassador in London and as the department's Secretary General, played a key role, as did Tim O'Connor, who would go on to lead the North–South secretariat established under the Good Friday Agreement. Other members of the team who were heavily involved and made outstanding personal contributions were Rory Montgomery, Ray Bassett and Eamonn McKee.

Between them, the group provided essential expertise on issues ranging from potential policy areas for North/South bodies to the scope for constitutional change, human rights enhancement, options for electoral systems and the potential for security reforms in Northern Ireland. They drafted position papers and speeches, carried out research and analysis and liaised continuously with the parties. Some dealt intensively with the SDLP or Sinn Féin, some with the UUP (though Dermot Gallagher himself had perhaps the closest contacts, going back to the early seventies). David Cooney kept in touch with the loyalist parties and the other smaller parties (the 'smalls', as Mo Mowlam affectionately referred to them). He and I liaised with the chairmen and their staff. Tim O'Connor and Rory Montgomery were closely involved in Strand Two work, especially in the final week; Eamonn McKee specialised in security policy and, with Rory Montgomery, contributed also on constitutional issues; and Ray Bassett had expertise in a range of areas. We all took on multi-tasking, inevitably, as the daily pressures of the talks built up. Dan Mulhall, the department's Press Counsellor, also provided important support.

In London, Ambassador Ted Barrington and Philip McDonagh, the Political Counsellor, maintained a wide range of contacts which were invaluable for the negotiations. Similar contributions were made by Sean O hUiginn and his colleagues in Washington. In the Department of the Taoiseach, Wally Kirwan brought to the table experience which stretched back to the Sunningdale Agreement. In the Department of Justice, Paul Hickey was expert on prisons policy, decommissioning and many other issues. All played a vital role in the team effort which delivered the Good Friday Agreement.

The main British officials we dealt with during this period were Quentin Thomas, Jonathan Stephens, Peter Bell, David Hill, David Cook and David Lavery. These were all from the Northern Ireland

Office, though some came originally from the Home Office and others from the Ministry of Defence. (Virtually all were English, as it happens; the Northern Ireland departments, with Northern Ireland-born staff, came into their own only after the conclusion of the Agreement.)

Paddy Teahon's opposite number in 10 Downing Street was John Holmes, a Foreign Office official who had been seconded to the post of Private Secretary for Foreign Affairs under John Major and who continued in this role under Blair. Blair's closest adviser on Northern Ireland, however, was Jonathan Powell, also a former diplomat who had joined the Labour leader's team while they were in Opposition. Alastair Campbell, whom I had known in his days as a *Mirror* journalist, was another key adviser to Blair. He was ably matched on our side by Joe Lennon, the Government press secretary. Blair and his small team knew each other well and, even in the stressful conditions of Easter Week 1998 (or perhaps because of them), engaged in a fair amount of banter and joking, with schoolboyish mimicry also playing a part.

Overseeing the talks process were the three chairmen: George Mitchell, John de Chastelain and Harri Holkeri.

George Mitchell was the undisputed primus inter pares. He had demonstrated abundantly during the 1995–7 period his qualifications for this role: remarkable political instincts accompanied by scrupulous impartiality and an air of quiet authority and gravitas. He had superb chairmanship skills. And he distinguished himself also by a precision of language which was unusual among American politicians, by a lawyerly respect for procedure and by almost superhuman levels of patience.

There were other aspects which might not have been suspected. Beneath Mitchell's unfailing personal courtesy lay a steely determination and tough-mindedness. In the summer of 1996, he was asked by Bill Clinton to help prepare the President for TV duels with Bob Dole, the republican challenger for the Presidency. I heard from a staffer at the time that the Senator was so ruthlessly effective in playing the part of Dole, with a no-holds-barred interrogation of the President on his private life, that Clinton begged for mercy and called the whole thing off after five minutes. Later Mitchell would recall that, over dinner before the session, the President spent the entire time quizzing him about Northern Ireland, to the detriment perhaps of the job in hand.

Mitchell also showed steely resolve when an article in a British newspaper in late 1996 made an unfounded claim about a romantic involvement between his senior aide, Martha Pope, and Gerry Kelly of Sinn Féin. While privately furious about this effort to sabotage the peace process by undermining him in his chairmanship role, Mitchell would not allow himself to be distracted. He avoided all comment and stayed single-mindedly focused on his immediate responsibilities.

Martha Pope, an astute political operator, had been Sergeant at Arms in the Senate when Mitchell was the Majority Leader. She accompanied him on his Northern Ireland assignment and won the respect of all who dealt with her. Even Ian Paisley paid her the occasional public compliment, adding with gruff good humour that he never thought he would find himself welcoming a Pope to Northern Ireland.

While there was initial speculation that Mitchell and de Chastelain were the preferred candidates of the Irish and British Governments, respectively (with Holkeri as an agreed neutral), the truth was more complex. Mitchell indeed came from an Irish-American background but had little in common with Irish-

American stereotypes and was very much his own man, unbiddable by either Government.

General John de Chastelain, for his part, seemed to have at first sight impeccable British credentials. He came from a Commonwealth country; he had been educated in Britain; he had a military background; and his parents had seen wartime service with British intelligence. In practice, however, de Chastelain was much more independent-minded than these factors might suggest. He was able, for example, to develop an excellent personal relationship with Martin McGuinness, building a level of trust which made its own contribution to the eventual resolution of the decommissioning issue. There was a sense that the invitation from the British and Irish Governments came at a good time for him personally. As chief of staff of the Canadian armed forces, he had had to carry some of the responsibility for misconduct by Canadian military personnel in Somalia. He threw himself with enthusiasm into his Northern Ireland role, first with the independent body on decommissioning, then with the talks and later as chair of the Independent Commission on Decommissioning. De Chastelain, who was assisted by several Canadian staff, would spend a total of some 15 years on successive Northern Ireland assignments.

Harri Holkeri, a former Finnish Prime Minister (and future President of the UN General Assembly), challenged some of the conventional assumptions about Nordic politicians. He was genial, relaxed and gregarious. And, while occasionally despondent about the lack of progress in the talks, he would put up with the frustrations with good humour and patience. If not a central player, Holkeri was nonetheless popular and affable.

The eight political parties fielded impressive delegations for the negotiations. In the SDLP, John Hume and Seamus Mallon were formidable spokesmen for nationalism, providing a depth of experience and a quality of analysis which set them apart from most other participants. They were ably supported by Mark Durkan, Bríd Rodgers, Seán Farren, Denis Haughey, Alex Attwood and others.

The Sinn Féin team, led by Gerry Adams and Martin McGuinness, were hard-working, well prepared and invariably 'on message'. Adams and McGuinness had contrasting negotiating styles but worked very effectively as a team. Other members included Pat Doherty, Gerry Kelly, Lucilita Bhreatnach, Bairbre de Brún, Siobhán O'Hanlon, Aidan McAteer and Rita O'Hare. The Sinn Féin delegation were known for their assiduous note-taking and the preparation of extensive policy positions on those topics which interested them.

In the UUP, David Trimble was flanked by John Taylor, Reg Empey, Ken Maginnis, Jeffrey Donaldson, Peter Weir, David Campbell, Steven King, Anthony Alcock and others. The dynamics within the UUP delegation were more opaque. With different people turning up to different meetings, it was less clear who was covering what and what continuity there would be from one meeting to the next. The tone could vary on issues, one day indignant and the next more relaxed (often a function of who was representing the party that day). Some days the entire UUP delegation would arrive for a meeting, while on others David Trimble might come on his own. We had the impression that Trimble took many key decisions either on his own or in a very small circle.

The Alliance Party was led by the forceful and articulate John Alderdice. A trained psychiatrist, Alderdice had a penchant for political diagnosis which drew on his professional experience. While his analysis of trends in the negotiations was useful, it was qualified somewhat by the sympathy he regularly displayed for unionist concerns. Strong on procedural issues, he would become the first Speaker of the Assembly created by the Good Friday Agreement and would later be elevated to the House of Lords. Among his delegation colleagues were Seamus Close, Seán Neeson, Eileen Bell and David Ford.

The two loyalist parties brought a fresh perspective to the table: that of working-class unionism. The Progressive Unionist Party were linked to the Ulster Volunteer Force while the Ulster Democratic Party were close to the Ulster Defence Association. The PUP's leading lights, some of whom had served sentences for paramilitary offences, were Hughie Smyth, David Ervine, Gusty Spence, Billy Hutchinson, 'Plum' Smith and Dawn Purvis. The UDP's senior representatives were Gary McMichael, John White and David Adams. Common to both parties was a trenchant analysis of the concerns of their communities. Many of them had come from grassroots activism at local level along the sectarian interfaces in Belfast. Shaped by these various background factors, they were noticeably more relaxed about political dialogue and cooperation with Sinn Féin than UUP traditionalists. They made a very positive contribution.

The Northern Ireland Labour group was usually represented by Malachy Curran, a former SDLP member who tended to align with SDLP positions.

The Northern Ireland Women's Coalition (NIWC) had a powerful impact on the negotiations. Led by the dynamic Monica McWilliams, they came with a new agenda in Northern Ireland politics which challenged traditional stereotypes and demanded higher standards of governance. Bronagh Hinds, Pearl Sagar, Jane Morrice, Avila Kilmurray and Kate Fearon were other members of the NIWC team. Engaging actively with all other delegations, they worked hard to ensure that the talks were conducted on a basis which was fair, inclusive and transparent. Their zeal not being shared by every delegation, they had to muster considerable patience and resilience along the way. The Coalition were, in a sense, the conscience of the negotiations. We found them flexible and creative in their thinking and determinedly positive at all times. The success on Good Friday 1998 was in no small measure due to their constructive influence.

10

THE NEGOTIATIONS BEGIN

What kind of agreement were we setting out to achieve? Our Government's view was quite clear. It would have to be broadly on the lines indicated in the Framework Document. That is, a comprehensive agreement covering structures within Northern Ireland, North/South institutions and East/West structures as well as balanced constitutional change, measures to protect rights and a range of other provisions.

We expected that the structures within Northern Ireland would involve an Assembly with an Executive which would exercise powers devolved from Westminster and would operate on the basis of cross-community agreement.

For the North/South component, we envisaged a Ministerial Council which would bring together Irish Government ministers with their Northern counterparts. This body, established under Westminster and Oireachtas legislation, would have delegated 'executive', 'harmonising' or 'consultative' functions. It could carry out its work through a number of subsidiary agencies (which in due course we termed 'implementation bodies'). And there would be a supporting secretariat.

The East/West structures would involve a standing Intergovernmental Conference established under a new British–Irish Agreement. This would carry forward the role which the

Irish Government already had under the Anglo-Irish Agreement, while excluding the policy areas which would be devolved to the presumed new Assembly. This conference would also keep the operation of the new agreement under review and – a very important point for nationalists – intervene if any of the new institutions were not functioning properly.

These new institutions would be accompanied by human rights measures and reforms in areas such as policing, security policy and the economic and cultural domains. There would be constitutional change in both jurisdictions; in our case, this would involve the amendment of Articles 2 and 3 to implement the commitments we had made in the Downing Street Declaration.

The agreement which emerged from the negotiations would be put to both electorates, North and South, for approval in referendums held on the same day. John Hume had long advocated this approach. In this way, the Irish people, North and South, would be exercising their right to self-determination for the first time since 1918. This was a point of critical importance for the republican movement. Sinn Féin saw the all-Ireland general election in 1918 as the last occasion on which the people of Ireland had been able to carry out an act of self-determination. They had done so and it had yielded clear support for Irish unity. In the Downing Street Declaration, we had, of course, accepted that the exercise of this right was subject to the principle of consent.

We saw consent as a two-sided coin. On the one hand, we accepted that there could be no change in the status of Northern Ireland without the consent of a majority of the people there. But on the other, nationalists in Northern Ireland had not consented to the latter's existing status and their consent would have to be obtained for whatever new arrangements were agreed in these talks. There had to be an entirely new beginning across the three core relationships. The future in Ireland would have to be based on agreement between the two main traditions rather than on domination of one by the other, whether through force or otherwise. There could be no going back to the injustices of Stormont majoritarian rule.

With substantive all-party negotiations finally launched, the Framework Document was the key point of reference for the Irish Government. We saw it as the road map for the settlement we all hoped to achieve.

The British Government were in principle of the same view. While the document had been agreed with us by the Major Government, Blair and his ministers had no difficulty with its contents. However, they worried more about their ability to sell the document to unionists, given the UUP's unrelenting hostility to it. In private, the new Government would assure us of their complete commitment to the Framework Document; in public, they preferred to equivocate about it.

We found it odd that a new Government with a very comfortable majority at Westminster should find it necessary to distance itself publicly from this text. It had, after all, been agreed with us by a minority Conservative administration that had been wholly dependent on unionist support for its survival. While the UUP had not liked it then and still did not like it, the document was in fact carefully balanced between unionist and nationalist sensitivities. We also warned that the constitutional changes flagged in it were predicated on the balancing provisions being delivered in their entirety.

Mo Mowlam was conspicuously lukewarm about the Framework Document. It was 'a useful basis for discussion', she acknowledged in Strand Two on a number of occasions. But it was only one possible way of balancing the various concerns

– and she was ready to look at any others which might attract support.

Differences over the relative weight to be given to the Framework Document were to become a significant fault-line in the negotiations. The Irish Government, the SDLP and Sinn Féin insisted on absolute fidelity to it and were supported by most of the smaller parties. The UUP and the loyalist parties, on the other hand, opposed the document and received tacit support from the British Government.

Overall, the Irish and British Governments functioned well together as the motor of the negotiation process. We succeeded in agreeing a series of joint positions over several months which gave direction and impetus to the talks. To the Irish Government, it was clear that a steering role of this kind was not just desirable but essential. The talks would rapidly run into the ground without this. The key protagonists were very unlikely to move of their own accord off their opening positions. They would do so only if put under pressure by one or other Government. The two Governments had to take charge and to create a context in which compromises and trade-offs would eventually become possible.

This responsibility, however, was viewed with a certain hesitation in London. The new Government preferred the posture of 'neutral' bystander, waiting passively in the wings to see whether the Irish Government, the UUP and the SDLP could agree something among themselves, especially in relation to Strand Two. And, even though Blair had declared that his Government were ready to be 'persuaders for agreement', they were reluctant to accept that they might have any role to play in encouraging unionism towards agreement with nationalism.

There was also a tendency in parts of the British system to ignore the logic of all-party talks and to see an agreement reached between ourselves, the UUP and the SDLP as the primary objective. This was clearly influenced by the UUP's deep-rooted reluctance to contemplate sharing power with Sinn Féin. NIO officials would claim from time to time that the Irish Government was working with undue zeal on behalf of Sinn Féin in the talks and that the SDLP's interests were being neglected. This was a familiar unionist mantra. We were, of course, highly active in the support we were providing for SDLP interests, notably in Strands One and Two. But the British colleagues were going along with a unionist script which sought to marginalise Sinn Féin and to disrupt the prospect of broad nationalist consensus in these talks.

The SDLP and Sinn Féin did differ on some fundamental aspects. In Strand One, the SDLP were active participants, contributing in detail to the negotiations on the future internal arrangements for Northern Ireland. However, Sinn Féin largely stayed away, unwilling to imply any acceptance of the legitimacy of Northern Ireland as a political construct. Both parties had a keen interest in Strand Two but the SDLP engaged more closely with the detail, including the legal foundation for the North/South bodies and the policy areas which the latter would cover. Sinn Féin's major interests in the talks were less the detailed institutional arrangements and more the need for generous prisoner release arrangements, serious reform of policing and the administration of justice, 'demilitarisation' of security policy and action on a range of equality and identity issues.

This, then, was the broad context in which the all-party talks got under way.

On 7 October 1997, the opening sessions of all three Strands took place at Castle Buildings: Strand One in the morning, Strand Two in the afternoon and Strand Three in the evening. Over the following six months, there would be a pattern of meetings taking place in at least two of the Strands most weeks. Various subsidiary groups were also created to handle, for example, cross-strand issues, confidence-building measures or decommissioning.

The Irish Government were usually represented by two ministers (most often David Andrews and Liz O'Donnell) and by a supporting team of officials. The ministers had a constant round of contacts with all parties, as well as the British Government and the chairmen, while in Belfast.

Let us begin with the Strand One negotiations. Though not a participant, we were kept fully informed of all developments there by the British Government (usually Paul Murphy, who chaired Strand One) and by the SDLP.

The plans announced by the Blair Government for legislative devolution to regional Assemblies in Scotland and Wales were an important part of the backdrop. The new Government had no difficulty in promoting a devolved Assembly and Executive for Northern Ireland as well. And it was psychologically easier for unionists to accept this devolution model, as they did eventually, when it was being applied at more or less the same time in Northern Ireland, Scotland and Wales.

An initial British Government paper proposed a set of principles to underpin new institutions in Northern Ireland. Among these were the need for any new arrangements to secure 'sufficient consensus' among the parties and to give appropriate expression to the identity of the two main traditions. ('Sufficient consensus', drawn from the South African peace process, was a rule which required majority support for key measures within both the unionist and nationalist blocs.) They should also uphold and apply the principles of equality of opportunity, equity of treatment and 'parity of esteem' between unionism and nationalism. The new arrangements should incorporate checks and balances sufficient to command the confidence of both main traditions.

Much of the content of Strand One, in the sense of fundamental principles and potential institutional models, had already been broached in the 1991–2 talks. In addition, loosely agreed proposals coming out of those talks had been incorporated in the Strand One document which the Major Government had published in February 1995 alongside the Framework Document. So there was a raft of ideas already available as Strand One got under way. Further British Government papers asked a series of questions aimed at identifying some common ground.

The UUP made clear at the outset, however, that they did not feel bound by any agreements reached during the earlier talks. They were clearly holding back from endorsing a model for legislative devolution which could see them in a power-sharing Cabinet alongside Sinn Féin. They promoted instead a model for 'administrative' devolution only, under which executive responsibility for devolved policy areas would be exercised not by ministers but by the chairmen of Assembly committees corresponding to Northern Ireland's six departments. The chairs and vice-chairs of these committees would be 'Heads of Department' who would implement Assembly decisions in devolved areas. They would be nominated on the basis of the so-called d'Hondt method (a formula for proportionate distribution devised by a nineteenth-century Belgian mathematician).

The SDLP's strong preference, however, was for a cross-community Cabinet-style Executive, which would operate on the basis of collective responsibility. We worked closely with them as they prepared their input to Strand One. We suggested possible institutional models and electoral systems, including options in relation to weighted majorities and other safeguards.

In early December, the SDLP presented proposals for a 100-member Assembly, elected by proportional representation.

Of these, 90 would be elected from 18 five-member constituencies (reflecting the current 18 Westminster constituencies) and the remaining 10 would be elected from party lists. The policy matters that had been transferred under the 1973 Northern Ireland Constitution Act (i.e., the responsibilities of Northern Ireland's six departments) would be devolved to the Assembly. The party did not envisage justice and policing matters being devolved initially but wanted agreement reached on a timescale for their devolution once an agreed programme for change (i.e., for reform of the policing system) had been completed.

The SDLP saw a Cabinet-style Executive being elected by the Assembly. They wanted as the threshold for this a qualified majority involving (a) 60 per cent of the total membership of the Assembly and (b) majorities of those representing both the unionist and nationalist communities. They envisaged that, on election, Assembly members would make an optional declaration of community identification.

The Executive, as the SDLP saw it, would be headed by a First Minister (borrowing from the models recently agreed for Scotland and Wales) and a Deputy First Minister. It could include eight other ministers. A limited number of junior ministers might also be appointed. The composition of the Executive would depend on 'whatever combination of parties might find it possible to work together and to agree a common programme'. (Later, this was refined to formation of an Executive under the d'Hondt system.) There would also be a system of committees to scrutinise the work of the Executive, with chairs nominated on a proportionate basis.

The Executive would provide the Northern leg of whatever North/South structures were agreed in the negotiations. Participation in these structures would be a duty of service for all members of the Executive (a key point for the SDLP, who wanted to guard against unionist abstentionism or selectivity in the area of North/South cooperation).

Ultimately, it was the SDLP's model which very largely prevailed in the deal which was done in Strand One on the final night of the negotiations.

Holding that Northern Ireland was a failed political entity after five decades of Stormont rule and systematic discrimination against nationalists, Sinn Féin proposed an all-island approach which at the same time would recognise the island's economic and regional diversity. They favoured a single all-Ireland Government which would be supplemented by a system of decentralised structures involving community, district and regional councils. They envisaged 15 regional councils covering the whole island (including West, East and South Ulster and one for Belfast). Sinn Féin were on their own with this proposal, however; all other parties favoured an Assembly for Northern Ireland.

A further issue in Strand One was the need to ensure that decisions taken by the Assembly would be in conformity with international human rights protections. The British Government had already committed itself to incorporating the European Convention on Human Rights (ECHR) into domestic law. Most of the parties backed this and a number also proposed a supplementary Bill of Rights for Northern Ireland.

Sinn Féin sought the immediate incorporation of the ECHR by both Governments (though we saw less need for it given the extensive protections already afforded under the Irish Constitution, which corresponded to, or in some cases exceeded, those provided by the ECHR). They also favoured an all-Ireland Human Rights Commission to oversee a charter or covenant on measures to protect the rights of 'everyone living in Ireland'.

The UUP supported incorporation of the ECHR. While ready

to agree to comprehensive arrangements for the protection of minority rights, they maintained that arrangements could be devised which would not challenge existing borders. Dermot Nesbitt, one of the UUP negotiators, pointed to the Council of Europe's Framework Convention for the Protection of National Minorities – which both Governments had signed but not yet ratified – as a model for such an approach. (Nesbitt's all too regular references to this Convention would lead Martin McGuinness to remark sourly on the UUP man's 'unique ability to drag us all to the further reaches of Eastern Europe'.) In Strand Two, where several of these issues resurfaced, we countered by pointing to the Helsinki Final Act's provision for peaceful border change (as had happened in Germany).

These were the broad parameters of the Strand One discussions. The real battleground, however, would be Strand Two.

11

STRAND TWO

The first meeting of Strand Two took place on 7 October 1997, under Senator Mitchell's chairmanship. With delegations submitting a series of papers on individual aspects, the early debates followed predictable lines.

The SDLP pointed to the principles for a satisfactory North/ South accommodation which had been set out in the Downing Street Declaration and to the political structures which had been proposed by the two Governments in the Framework Document. The party wanted to see significant North/South bodies with executive powers. They argued for a North/South Council of Ministers supported by a permanent Secretariat. Equality of allegiance would have to be addressed in Strand Two as much as in Strand One, Seamus Mallon warned. A 'limp and anaemic' Strand Two would be totally unacceptable to nationalists. If unionists did not take nationalist requirements seriously, there would be knock-on implications for agreement in Strand One. Mallon recalled that the Sunningdale Agreement, supported by the major unionist party of the time, had involved a Council of Ireland with executive powers greater than those proposed in the Framework Document.

Sinn Féin offered a trenchant analysis: partition had failed and the conflict could be resolved only in an all-Ireland context. A sovereign all-Ireland state was Sinn Féin's objective. Martin

McGuinness recognised, however, that unionist agreement and participation would be essential in devising the structures of Irish unity. The Framework Document had signposted the way forward. Although Sinn Féin would from time to time hint that this document did not represent the full extent of their ambitions, it was clear to us that they were broadly content with it as the basis for negotiation in Strand Two.

Alliance and the Northern Ireland Labour group wanted to see practical and accountable institutions for North/South cooperation. The Northern Ireland Women's Coalition put forward a detailed proposal for a North/South body to develop 'structural synergies' between the two parts of the island.

For the UUP, John Taylor insisted that North/South cooperation must be based on mutual respect and recognition and should not weaken the Union. The UUP attached greater importance to East/West cooperation; indeed, it could contemplate North/South bodies only as a by-product of an expanded East/West relationship. They must also be strictly subordinate to a future Assembly.

When Seamus Mallon asked at one meeting if unionists accepted the need to establish and develop relations with people in the rest of the island, Jeffrey Donaldson replied that they did not feel compelled to do so. While they would like to have good-neighbourly relations, they would not agree to abandon their British citizenship so that nationalists in Northern Ireland could have their Irish citizenship.

Donaldson asked nationalists to accept that an 'island of Ireland' framework would deny unionists the expression of their identity and allegiance. For this, they looked to the wider framework of 'the islands' and the European Union. (It was striking during these negotiations, given the position which the DUP would take 20 years later on Brexit, that the EU was still considered a benign dimension by Donaldson and other unionists.)

Recalling an SDLP characterisation of the Council of Ireland in 1974 as a means to bring about Irish unity, Donaldson emphasised that unionists would not agree to all-Ireland institutions with executive powers whose purpose was to achieve Irish unity. When Mallon asked if the UUP could accept all-Ireland institutions with executive powers which were *not* for the purpose of achieving Irish unity, Donaldson responded that they would consider that as the negotiations evolved; the context would be very important.

The UUP's general line at this stage was that it was in favour of North/South cooperation but saw no need for an all-Ireland body with executive powers to achieve this. Other parties highlighted the many practical benefits which institutionalised North/South cooperation would give people in both parts of the island. The British Government noted the potential for ever deeper North/South cooperation in the context of the EU membership of both countries.

The UUP tactics in Strand Two were somewhat incoherent. Our sense was that they recognised privately that they would ultimately have to concede ground on the North/South structures, and probably significant ground, as part of an overall agreement. In particular, the tangible gain from their perspective of changes to Articles 2 and 3 of our Constitution would not be delivered without this. David Trimble acknowledged to the SDLP at one point that there would have to be 'substantial North/South arrangements'.

Despite this, however, the UUP persisted for many weeks with a tactic of presenting any future Strand Two arrangements as subordinate to Strand Three, i.e., East/West institutions. At one point, they refused to discuss Strand Two until they had clearer indications of what they could expect in Strand Three. In effect, they were trying to conflate Strands Two and Three in order to avoid, or at least defer, the compromises required of them in Strand Two. A corollary was that they declined until a relatively late stage to flesh out the detail of their thinking in Strand Two.

The UUP tried, with some success, to recruit the British Government to their position. However, there was never any hope of winning the support of the Irish Government, Sinn Féin, the SDLP or most of the other parties for an approach which was not only at odds with the agreed three-stranded basis for the talks but also ignored the nationalist need for politically significant North/South institutions (all the more so in the context of constitutional changes which would have to be approved by referendum). We saw significant North/South institutions as the trade-off for the constitutional changes; the unionists were being a little ambitious, we felt, in looking for significant East/West institutions as an additional incentive. The UUP eventually backed down and, in the end game, moved into more realistic territory.

It was very important for nationalists that the new North/South structures should not be subject to oppressive control by a hostile unionist majority in the Assembly. They wanted them to be equipped with executive powers and, though accountable to the Assembly and the Oireachtas, to operate in practice with a large degree of autonomy and right of initiative. These new bodies should have political weight and profile and take major policy decisions for the benefit of both parts of the island. They were not to be mere talking shops or remote satellites of the administrations North and South.

The unionists had a much more modest vision for them. They were correspondingly allergic to any suggestion that the North/South bodies might resemble an embryonic all-Ireland government, a third form of government on the island alongside the administrations in Belfast and Dublin.

When David Andrews in an interview at the end of November made comments which appeared to go in that direction, there was uproar in unionist ranks. The minister made it clear that he had been misunderstood. The new North/South structures he had in mind would not be free-standing but accountable in Northern Ireland to a devolved Assembly and in the South to the Oireachtas. They would not in any sense amount to the creation of a third source of power in Ireland.

Mo Mowlam and Paul Murphy supported the minister in light of this clarification. A difficult day followed nevertheless in Castle Buildings. An irate David Trimble protested the remarks, and the unionist media, the loyalist parties and even the Alliance Party echoed this protest. The SDLP and Sinn Féin, on the other hand, lent Andrews strong support.

Andrews' expression of regret for how his remarks had been interpreted, combined with a recognition by others of their broad consistency with the Framework Document, helped to defuse things. An honourable man, he apologised to Trimble privately. He also briefly contemplated resignation. Within a couple of days, however, the controversy was over. Bertie Ahern emphasised in the Dail on 2 December that we did not perceive the envisaged North/South Council as 'a vehicle to take over the government of Northern Ireland against the wishes of a majority'. Rather, it would serve as a focus for practical action at the all-island level as well as institutional expression of the identity of Northern nationalists.

12

STRAND THREE AND ONWARDS

Strand Three dealt with East/West structures. At its heart were the creation of two institutions.

First, a Council to bring together the British and Irish Governments with representatives of the new devolved administrations in Scotland and Wales and the existing administrations in the Isle of Man and the Channel Islands. We had already recognised in the Framework Document the need to provide for cooperation between the two Governments 'and both islands' on a range of East/West issues. With the UUP and the loyalist parties demanding a 'Council of the British Isles' to promote cooperation on the East/West axis, it was clear that something on these lines would have to form part of an overall agreement. Unionists regarded such a Council as a necessary counterweight to the North/South institutions which nationalists wanted.

We had no fundamental difficulty with this. We understood the need for unionists to see their identity given institutional expression. We recognised also that they would need some cover for participating in the North/South structures. However, we made it clear that we envisaged the East/West Council having a largely consultative role. If scope emerged for decisions on practical cooperation between individual members, fine; we did not, however, see it going significantly beyond exchanges of information and experience.

Second, there would be a standing Intergovernmental Conference to facilitate bilateral cooperation between the British and Irish Governments on matters which would not be devolved to a future Assembly in Northern Ireland. (By a 'standing' conference we meant a mechanism for permanent interaction between the two Governments.) This would replace the Anglo-Irish Conference through which we had cooperated for the previous 12 years under the Anglo-Irish Agreement, with the Maryfield Secretariat as its most visible manifestation.

The Framework Document had already set out in detail the role we envisaged for a new Conference in a post-devolution context, including the continuing institutional expression it would provide for 'the Irish Government's recognised concern and role in relation to Northern Ireland'.

We had also agreed that the future Conference would have a review role in relation to the workings of the new agreement and we had indicated remedial action which could be taken. (This was always a point of great concern to Seamus Mallon, who recalled bitterly what had happened to the Sunningdale Agreement.) Another key point was the British Government's acceptance that, in the event of a collapse of the institutions and the reimposition of direct rule, 'other arrangements' would be made to implement the commitment to promote North/South cooperation at all levels. These 'failsafe' provisions were required to reassure nationalists that the new arrangements could not be sabotaged. Not surprisingly, they were resisted for a long time by the unionists.

Such arrangements gave us some leverage, of course, in ensuring that the unionists took Strand Two seriously. It would not be in the unionist interest to precipitate situations in which the remedial mechanisms would have to be activated. Their biggest fear was of action taken by the two Governments over their heads. This was how they viewed the Anglo-Irish Agreement, which they were now seeking to replace. Strand Three was an important negotiating weapon for the two Governments in encouraging full unionist engagement in Strand Two.

The participants in Strand Three were, formally speaking, just the two Governments. In practice, we ensured regular liaison with the parties to keep them abreast of our deliberations and to give them an opportunity to express views. We prepared a series of joint papers as the basis for these liaison sessions, which started in October 1997.

Bertie Ahern and Tony Blair, meanwhile, were keeping a close eye on all developments in the talks. They met regularly, usually on the margins of European Council meetings, to review the progress being made (or lack of it).

Meeting in Luxembourg in late November, they looked at issues such as the contribution to be made by the release of paramilitary prisoners to a settlement and the need to get the UUP and Sinn Féin into direct dialogue with each other.

In December, a Sinn Féin delegation led by Adams and McGuinness had a meeting with Blair in London. Another milestone: the first time in a quarter of a century that Sinn Féin representatives had entered 10 Downing Street.

Meeting again in Luxembourg on 12 December, Ahern and Blair took stock of the progress made in Strand Two to date. Reiterating our need for a North/South Council with executive powers and implementing agencies, Ahern made it clear that he would be unable to get an agreement through his own party without these. People were already wondering if the implementation bodies would be sufficient compensation for changing Articles 2 and 3.

Adams and Hume would have to be able to say that such structures could develop over time.

Blair, for his part, gave an upbeat account of his recent meeting with Sinn Féin in No. 10. He had told Gerry Adams that he hoped Sinn Féin were serious and meant it when they said they were committed to the peace process. Adams' response had been firmly positive. Ahern reported also on an encouraging conversation he had had himself with Adams and McGuinness a few days previously in West Belfast.

There was, however, constant friction around this time between Sinn Féin and the unionists, exacerbated by the UUP's refusal to engage directly with Adams and his colleagues. David Trimble claimed that our Government was being too indulgent towards Sinn Féin (though he exempted the Taoiseach from this criticism, finding Ahern receptive to unionist concerns at a meeting they had had recently in Dublin).

The tension between Sinn Féin and the unionists was not in itself surprising. On the one hand, Sinn Féin was jittery, with the leadership under constant pressure to demonstrate to sceptics within the republican movement tangible benefits from the party's participation in these talks. And on the other, unionists were beginning to face up to the uncomfortable implications of an inclusive talks process and the likely requirement to share power with Sinn Féin if it succeeded.

By early December, there had been much discussion in the three Strands but little real engagement. As Mark Durkan put it, delegations were only 'surfing' the agenda. We were nowhere near 'negotiations' in the normal sense. The meetings were primarily occasions for grandstanding, for presentations aimed at the gallery and the media outside. There was a dispiriting stalemate.

The two Governments felt that, unless we could find some means of injecting momentum, the talks were in danger of collapsing altogether. With the chairmen, we decided that an effort should be made to have the participants agree on the broad parameters of a settlement. If so-called Heads of Agreement could be approved, it might be easier to draw up work plans to agree the detail in each area (though we knew that this detail would be fiercely contested). A Heads of Agreement approach would also enable participants to see the wider balances and trade-offs needed across the full spectrum of the negotiations. It might be easier to get the thornier individual issues resolved if people had a reasonably clear picture of the likely overall outcome.

Senator Mitchell proposed, therefore, to the Plenary on 2 December that an informal working group be set up which would prepare an agreed list of issues to be resolved in the talks and report back by 15 December.

This was agreed. Liz O'Donnell and Dermot Gallagher represented the Irish Government in the working group. However, with the atmosphere between the UUP and Sinn Féin becoming increasingly fractious, the effort to agree a list of key issues ultimately failed. Against this background, the chairmen issued a statement on 16 December which sought to end the talks on as positive a note as possible as we entered the Christmas recess.

There was inevitably a feeling of disappointment and deflation. We had achieved practically nothing after three months of talks. The chairmen had originally hoped to be able to announce agreement on a format for carrying forward the negotiations but even this eluded them. George Mitchell was quite dejected. 'If we cannot get people even to agree on what the problem is,' he remarked, 'how can we ever get them to sort it?' But there was no alternative to pressing on and hoping that there would be better prospects for agreement when we returned in January.

By now we had a settled time frame for the talks. The two Governments had agreed that the referendums should be held no later than May 1998. Counting back, this meant reaching an agreement by Easter (early April 1998). From January on, therefore, we would have only a few short weeks in which to get down to serious business.

So the two Governments started working privately on a Heads of Agreement draft, for agreement with the parties in January, which we hoped would kickstart the talks process. We had to find ways of nudging the participants out of their comfort zones and into engagement with each other.

There were, it must be said, conflicting schools of thought about this. On the Irish Government side, we feared that the UUP and Sinn Féin would refuse to sign up to a detailed outline of the settlement – which would mean, inevitably, painful compromises and trade-offs – until the final stages of the negotiations. There was a risk of destabilising them if we presented such an outline too early. But some on the British side, including the Prime Minister, saw a risk of the negotiations collapsing altogether unless we got into detail very soon.

The Taoiseach agreed to go ahead. We built on a checklist of key issues which George Mitchell had prepared. On 24 December an Irish draft was handed over to our British colleagues and they responded with one of their own.

A few days later there came a stark reminder of the proximity of paramilitary violence and the ever-present threat this posed to the talks process. On 27 December, the LVF leader, Billy Wright, who was serving a sentence in the Maze, was murdered by Irish National Liberation Army prisoners. This precipitated a number of revenge attacks on Catholics. With sectarian unrest mounting, there were rumours that the loyalist parties might pull out of the talks.

The two Government teams pursued their work on a Heads of Agreement paper, through the Secretariat mainly but also in the Liaison Group and in phone contact between No. 10 and Government Buildings. We also consulted closely with the SDLP and Sinn Féin, while the UUP kept in close touch with British officials.

As to its status, the British, under unionist pressure, initially shied away from presenting it as a joint paper. They wanted ideally to say that the UUP and the Irish Government had been able to agree something between them and they were simply supporting this. We argued, however, that the main value of such a paper would reside in its being something to which both Governments had clearly signed up. Our approach prevailed.

Following a phone conversation between the Taoiseach and the Prime Minister, the paper was finally agreed between the two Governments just in time for the resumption of the talks on 12 January 1998. It bore the somewhat cumbersome title 'Propositions on Heads of Agreement'. (In practice, we called it simply the 'Heads of Agreement' and that is how I will refer to it here.) It would be a significant milestone on the road towards the Good Friday Agreement.

13

HEADS OF AGREEMENT AND THE AFTERMATH

The Heads of Agreement document, just over one page in length, set out what the two Governments considered to be the main building blocks for a settlement:

- Balanced constitutional change in both the Irish Constitution and British constitutional legislation, based on commitment to the principle of consent.

- Northern Ireland institutions which would include an Assembly elected by proportional representation and exercising devolved executive and legislative responsibility over at least the responsibilities of the current six Northern Ireland departments.

- A new British–Irish Agreement to replace the Anglo-Irish Agreement. This would embrace, in Strand Three, (i) an Intergovernmental Council dealing with the 'totality of relationships' (to include representatives of the British and Irish Governments, the Northern Ireland administration and the devolved institutions in Scotland and Wales); and (ii) standing intergovernmental machinery between the two Governments covering issues of mutual interest, including non-devolved issues for Northern Ireland.

- In Strand Two, a North/South Ministerial Council to bring together those with executive responsibilities in Northern Ireland and the Irish Government in particular areas. Each side would consult, cooperate and take decisions within the mandates of, and be accountable to, the Assembly and the Oireachtas, respectively. All decisions would be by agreement between North and South, and implementation bodies would be established for policies agreed by the Council (in 'meaningful' areas and at an all-island level).

- Provisions to safeguard the rights of both communities in Northern Ireland (with steps to ensure an equivalent level of protection in the Republic).

- Measures to establish and consolidate a peaceful society, dealing with issues such as prisoners, 'security in all its aspects', policing and decommissioning of weapons.

This document was our preliminary sketch of what should go into the Good Friday Agreement.

On the constitutional issues, we had been pressed by the British to include an explicit reference to the envisaged changes in Articles 2 and 3 but we declined. In Strand One, Sinn Féin would have preferred no explicit reference to an Assembly but were ultimately willing to accept this in exchange for strong Strand Two language; we achieved the latter.

A decommissioning reference of some kind was inevitable. The British had sought mention of a 'commitment' to decommission and for this to happen within a fixed period of the agreement being concluded. We got this pared down, however, to a minimalist reference at the end of the paper. We also got in references to prisoners and other issues of major concern to Sinn Féin.

In return, we made some minor presentational concessions to the UUP. One of these was the way in which the word 'executive' was used in the Strand Two part (describing ministerial responsibilities rather than the Council as such). Another was a re-ordering of the institutional sequence which put the British–Irish Council ahead of the North/South structures. (This was congenial to the unionists but in itself insignificant, as all of this came under the heading of the British–Irish Agreement, whose detailed content we would ultimately be determining.) The British Government preferred to promise 'equity of treatment' between the two communities rather than the more demanding standard set in earlier formulations such as 'equality of opportunity and advantage'.

The paper was accompanied by a joint statement from the two Governments which presented it as our best guess at what might be a generally acceptable outcome. We included some additional clarification about the institutions and also clarified that the constitutional changes could include changes to Articles 2 and 3 as well as to Section 75 of the Government of Ireland Act of 1920. The Governments asked the parties to proceed to detailed negotiations and to reserve judgements on the overall package until later.

On 12 January 1998, the Heads of Agreement paper was tabled by the chairmen on behalf of the two Governments. Its substance – as distinct from some presentational aspects – was, in our view, evenly balanced between unionist and nationalist concerns and this could be objectively demonstrated. However, Trimble and the UUP talked it up as if it were a major victory for unionism. In this they were assisted by British Government briefing and advance leaking.

There was, of course, a wider political background here. The Framework Document had been hailed as a huge advance for nationalism and republicanism. Unionists had rejected it from the word go and the British Government, both the Blair administration and its predecessor, had been feeling the pressure. The unionists needed something which they could claim tipped the scales back in a unionist direction. It is arguable, indeed, that allowing the UUP to make exaggerated, or inaccurate, claims about this paper helped in the short term to stabilise unionist involvement in the talks and ultimately served the best interests of the process. The Blair Government, stung by constant UUP criticism that they were unhelpfully 'neutral' (in contrast with the Irish Government's perceived zeal on behalf of Sinn Féin), would have been content to go along with these unionist claims.

Trimble welcomed what he represented as the paper's demonstration of commitment on the part of all parties to an Assembly and placing of the North/South Council within an East/West setting. He brushed aside suggestions that the Council would have executive powers, noting that the paper did not actually say this.

The SDLP preferred to highlight the paper's clear recognition of the three sets of relationships which needed to be resolved. Seamus Mallon deduced from it, furthermore, that the North/South bodies would stand apart from the East/West structures.

Predictably, the DUP and UKUP rubbished Trimble's claims about it. Dismissing the proposed British–Irish Council as a 'valueless sop' and noting what seemed to be a calculated avoidance of the term 'executive powers', Robert McCartney described it as the Framework Document 'wearing a wig and a false beard'. Trimble, on the other hand, held that it was 'vastly different' from the Framework Document – after one of his MP colleagues, Willie Thompson, had claimed that the two documents were virtually identical.

Sinn Féin then began to turn sour on the paper.

Having initially given it qualified support in public, they came back to us to report an adverse reaction to it at grassroots level. It had gone down 'like a lead balloon' with republicans, Martin McGuinness told David Andrews, because they saw its references to a Council of the British Isles, a Northern Assembly and changes to the Irish Constitution as a sell-out to unionists. McGuinness complained that there was no sense of a dynamic which could be presented as having the potential to lead on to a united Ireland. Sinn Féin had come into the negotiations on the basis that they would be based squarely on the Framework Document and that this could be built upon.

Andrews pointed out that, in a letter sent to McGuinness the previous day, he and Mo Mowlam had said that the two Governments 'naturally remain committed to the positions set out in the Joint Declaration and in the Framework Document'. He pointed also to the clear commitment to a strong North/South Ministerial Council with executive powers. Agreement to such a body would be necessary if the Government were to propose any amendment to Articles 2 and 3.

Dermot Gallagher and Paddy Teahon added that, far from giving in to the UUP on this paper, we had blocked UUP efforts to delete references which they disliked. They observed, furthermore, that there would have to be an Assembly as the Northern point of reference for the North/South Council; the latter could not work without it.

As we saw it, the Heads of Agreement paper would inevitably contain pluses and minuses for everyone – 'parity of comfort and of discomfort', as Andrews put it when addressing the Plenary. To have it accepted on all sides, we had to make minor adjustments of language and presentation. Nothing in it, however, was inconsistent with the positions the two Governments had set out in the Downing Street Declaration and the Framework Document. In fact, in some respects it went further than the latter, extending the agenda into issues of importance to Sinn Féin such as prisoners, security and policing. It also had the merit that it had got unionists to sign up to key concepts in the Framework Document, even if labelled differently.

We did, however, recognise that the Heads of Agreement had had an unsettling effect on republicans and that some mending of fences in the latter direction would be needed. Trimble's enthusiastic public reaction to the paper did not help. Indeed, it may ultimately have been self-defeating from a unionist perspective as it created a clear need for the Governments to rebalance things, in the next joint declaration and otherwise.

Bertie Ahern suggested to Tony Blair that they both act over the coming period in ways that would be sympathetic to republican concerns. In particular, he recommended that Blair accept the need for an independent inquiry in relation to Bloody Sunday and that early release dates be set for the so-called Balcombe Street Four. The latter were members of an IRA active service unit that had been responsible for a spate of bombings in England in the mid-seventies and had been caught, tried and imprisoned following a siege in Balcombe Street in London. They had by then spent longer in jail in Britain than any paramilitary prisoners in Northern Ireland.

Building on the work done on the Bloody Sunday issue by the previous Irish Government, Ahern told Blair that everyone in Ireland wanted to see a new inquiry. He subsequently ratcheted up the pressure on Blair to the point where the latter told him in a resigned fashion: 'If I don't do this, when will you ever speak to me again?' (Never, Ahern responded, tongue in cheek.) On 29 January 1998, and with the anniversary of Bloody Sunday imminent, the

Prime Minister announced the establishment of a new inquiry. As for the Balcombe Street Four, they were transferred from their English prison to Portlaoise in Ireland four months later and in 1999 were released under the terms of the Good Friday Agreement.

As regards the handling of the talks from then on, Ahern also proposed to Blair that the two Governments work privately to flesh out the Heads of Agreement paper into a full draft agreement. We should prepare this overall draft now and decide later how and when to table it. In addition, the Governments should prepare detailed joint drafts under each of the paper's broad headings for tabling in the talks.

Under Dermot Gallagher's direction, the small team of officials in the Department of Foreign Affairs had already been working on sections of an overall draft since November. The intention was to have material ready for early discussion with the British.

Sinn Féin, meanwhile, continued to voice unhappiness about the Heads of Agreement paper. In the *Irish News* on 19 January, Gerry Adams said that his party considered the Heads of Agreement document to be unbalanced. Unionists were perceived to have secured an Assembly and were blocking progress on the equality agenda, demilitarisation and other fronts. At the same time, they were refusing to deal directly with Sinn Féin. It seemed they were now being rewarded for this. If confidence was to be restored, the two Governments would have to create a level playing field.

Two days later, an ominous IRA statement repeated some of Adams' key points and said the leadership of Óglaigh na hÉireann did not regard the Heads of Agreement paper as the basis for a lasting peace settlement. Yet another British Prime Minister had 'succumbed to the Orange card'. The responsibility for undoing the damage done, the statement warned, rested squarely with the British Government.

14

THE LONDON AND DUBLIN MEETINGS

The action then moved to London, where a three-day session of the talks took place from 24 to 26 January 1998.

For some time, there had been a view on the part of the two Governments, shared by the chairmen, that a change of venue would be beneficial. This was primarily because of the severe limitations of Castle Buildings in Belfast. If ever there was a building designed to discourage human interaction, this was it. A cheerless and featureless prefab from the sixties, it had a maze of narrow corridors, each indistinguishable from the other, and very few communal areas or facilities.

This meant that delegations were effectively confined to their own dreary quarters. All contacts had to be arranged by phone. There was hardly any scope for bumping casually into someone in the corridor or having a quiet word in the corner, the means by which agreements have been reached and deals done the world over. Spontaneity was ruled out. Not even a walk in the grounds was possible: the building had a small strip of tarmac in front of it, a high fence separated it from the rest of the Stormont Estate and that was it in terms of grounds. Inside, there was very little natural light, prompting bleak comparisons with the Castlereagh interrogation centre. All in all, it was a 'dead' building; sometimes the only issue on which those of us who were incarcerated there for several years could agree was how much we detested it.

No wonder, therefore, that people longed for a more congenial alternative. Before Christmas, consideration had been given to moving the talks abroad for a few days, to a 'neutral' country such as Austria or Finland. A secluded setting in one of these countries would reduce pressures on participants and help to keep external influences, including the media, at bay.

However, cost considerations arose, along with a worry, particularly in the UUP, that the impression of a 'travelling circus' would harm the process and play into the hands of its opponents. It also became clear that, for reasons of internal party management, the UUP did not favour a remote venue which would cut them off from their base. There had been grassroots criticism of the political cost paid by the party for its involvement in negotiations in 1973 in the isolated conditions of Sunningdale. The unionists were willing to exchange Castle Buildings for short periods of concentrated negotiation elsewhere. But these would have to be other locations within the British Isles, not further afield, and there would have to be scope to hold party consultations nearby. Although the purpose of a move away from Castle Buildings would actually have been to create a more relaxed atmosphere conducive to agreement, the unionists feared the opposite: that they would find themselves in a 'pressure-cooker' situation designed expressly to force them into an agreement.

We settled, therefore, for a politically balanced combination which involved the talks moving to London for a three-day period in late January and to Dublin for a similar period in mid-February. This followed a precedent set in the 1992 talks. The Taoiseach and the Prime Minister wanted the move to take place only after there had been some significant achievement in the talks; the agreement on the Heads of Agreement paper was deemed to be this milestone.

In preparation for London, Irish and British officials met on 22 January. It had been agreed that we would present a joint paper on Strand Two issues as the basis for discussion at the London meeting. Differences surfaced once more, however, over the extent to which the Framework Document should inform this paper. Our colleagues held that a paper based solely on the Framework Document would guarantee unionist rejection. They wanted to present a range of options instead. We replied that, if we were to do that, it would be logical to include options upstream of the Framework Document. This, of course, would polarise opinion and not move things forward.

The British indicated they would be ready to present a paper of their own if necessary. We warned them that a unilateral British Government paper, which would signal to nationalists that the British had retreated from the Framework Document, could have a disastrous impact on the entire talks process.

With the London meeting due to begin on 24 January, we explored with our colleagues a possible compromise approach. This would invite the parties to present ideas of their own while making it clear that the two Governments' position remained as set out in the Framework Document. The Governments would suggest a list of issues to be addressed in London. A paper to this effect was agreed between us in outline. We were also able to agree a further paper listing current and potential future areas for North/ South cooperation.

But trouble was brewing on another front. The rules governing the talks, as we have seen, required an absolute commitment on the part of all participants to the Mitchell Principles of non-violence. If a party was linked to a paramilitary organisation which was found to have been involved in violence, that party had to pay the price of exclusion from the talks for a period.

The UDP found itself in this situation when the Ulster Freedom Fighters (UFF), an offshoot of the Ulster Defence Association with which the party was closely associated, was judged by the RUC Chief Constable to have been responsible for the killing of three Catholics in the aftermath of the murder of Billy Wright in late December 1997. On 22 January, the Chief Constable issued his finding. On the following day, a UFF statement said that recent violence by the Irish National Liberation Army had made a 'measured military response unavoidable', that that response was now over and that the UFF remained committed to the search for a peaceful political settlement.

As we all gathered at Lancaster House for the opening of the London meeting, the scheduled agenda had to be put to one side while the implications of this development were worked through. Under the agreed rules, it fell to the two Governments to issue a 'joint determination' on whether or not the UDP was guilty of a breach of the Mitchell Principles. A 'representation' to this effect would first need to be made; if one or other Government would not do this, the SDLP or Alliance was willing to oblige. We were on the horns of a dilemma, as Liz O'Donnell remarked: we had to balance our commitment to the Mitchell Principles, and our fundamental moral convictions, against our desire to protect the talks process from disintegrating. We were also, of course, alive to the possibility that representations could potentially be made against others and to the need for clarity and consistency in how the Governments responded to all such allegations. (As it happened, we would be dealing with allegations in relation to Sinn Féin within a matter of weeks.)

The meeting in Lancaster House opened with an exchange of views around the table which revealed general support for the expulsion of the UDP. The idea of a voluntary withdrawal was canvassed privately with the latter; this would facilitate consultations with a view to securing an unambiguous reconfirmation of the UFF ceasefire. Gary McMichael and his colleagues were initially not keen. At a special Plenary, they stressed their own unequivocal commitment to the Mitchell Principles and the efforts they had made, and would continue to make, with the UFF. They could not, however, control the UFF and had been unaware of its decision to go back to violence.

Meeting in the early afternoon, the two Governments drew up a joint determination which expelled the UDP from the talks. However, we held out the possibility of their rejoining if a complete and unequivocal UFF ceasefire were demonstrated and found to have been fully and continuously observed over 'a period of weeks'.

Anticipating this decision, the UDP withdrew of their own accord in mid-afternoon. On the assumption that the process would conclude by Easter, they hoped for readmission within a few weeks. A period of four to six weeks in what we christened the 'sin bin' was on the cards but in the event this was truncated. When a similar controversy relating to Sinn Féin erupted in mid-February and that party received a fixed term of expulsion, the UDP drew attention to this difference in treatment. They were duly invited to rejoin as of 23 February.

Such episodes caused real harm to the process. They were unavoidable in the sense that the Mitchell Principles were the admission ticket to the talks and no breaches could be tolerated if we were to maintain collective trust in the process. We had all agreed to a procedure for the handling of alleged breaches and this had to be followed, regardless of whatever progress we might be making in the talks at that particular time. It meant, of course, that, when such allegations or 'representations' were made, the entire process ground to a halt until the matter had been dealt with. The talks were held hostage to events outside and were robbed of vital momentum. The impact of each of these controversies was profoundly divisive, with most parties lining up to one degree or another against the accused party and mutual suspicion deepening.

The procedure was a political one, as George Mitchell often reminded us, not a legal one. But the Governments had to go into quasi-judicial mode regardless, taking great care, for example, to say nothing which might appear prejudicial while the joint determination was being prepared. We also found ourselves in the uncomfortable position of being prosecutor, judge and jury simultaneously (by virtue of the agreed rules). All in all, while we recognised that such proceedings were politically, and indeed morally, necessary, they were also serious distractions from the real business of the talks at a crucial moment.

A couple of weeks later, it was Sinn Féin's turn. On 12 February we heard that the Chief Constable had concluded that the killings of Brendan Campbell and Robert Dougan a few days earlier had been sanctioned by the Provisional IRA leadership. Campbell had been a known drug dealer and Dougan had been a member of the UDA/UFF who was suspected of involvement in recent sectarian murders.

To the intense frustration of the delegates, therefore, the three-day meeting planned for Dublin Castle from 16 to 18 February 1998 had to be devoted entirely to the issue of whether Sinn Féin should be expelled in consequence. It rapidly became clear that no business would, or could, be done in the Strands until this matter was disposed of. This was all heavily ironic in circumstances in which Sinn Féin had been the most vocal advocate for having a Dublin session of the talks in the first place. It did not escape attention that this unexpected turn of events also had the benefit for unionists of averting, or at least delaying, the showdown over Strand Two which had otherwise been looming.

The proceedings opened on the morning of 16 February in Dublin Castle. Mo Mowlam, with David Andrews' support, asked Mitchell to arrange a special Plenary to consider this matter. This eventually met at 2 p.m. on the following day. After statements from the two ministers, Martin McGuinness followed for Sinn Féin with a lengthy rebuttal of the British case on several grounds. He also dwelled on the litany of murders committed by loyalists and, with heavy use of anecdote, on his personal efforts in the cause of peace. ('People I've known for 30 years called me a "traitor" yesterday on my arrival at Dublin Castle.')

In the subsequent debate, David Trimble noted that there had been no IRA denial of involvement in the recent killings – nor had Sinn Féin condemned them. Claiming that Sinn Féin and the IRA were inextricably linked, he recalled Gerry Adams saying in 1986 that 'armed struggle is a necessary form of resistance; and if at any time Sinn Féin decides to disown the armed struggle, they won't have me as a member'. Sinn Féin seemed more wedded than ever to the armed struggle, he charged, given the IRA's refusal to decommission weapons, Sinn Féin's refusal to recognise the principle of consent, their failure to present any proposals relevant to the issues under discussion in the talks and their consistent ignoring of the existence and rights of unionists.

In a forceful intervention the following day, Seamus Mallon said that each 'indictment' episode so far had 'eaten into the soul of the process', undermined mutual trust and 'devalued all of us'. He intensely disliked this procedure. He anticipated sourly that, if an offender had 'pressing business like St Patrick's Day', it could find itself back in less than three weeks. (This, of course, proved an accurate forecast, with Sinn Féin indeed returning from the 'sin bin' in time to attend the St Patrick's Day festivities in Washington DC that year.) But, Mallon continued, we had all agreed rules, and these would have to be applied on a basis that was fair and consistent.

After several hours of acrimonious debate, John Hume appealed for these proceedings to be wound up ('three of the most wasted days of my life'). Gerry Adams delivered final remarks which underlined his party's commitment to a pluralist Ireland and to 'making peace with the unionists'. He also emphasised the importance of Sinn Féin's role in the peace process ('We, with all our faults, are the best chance you have').

The meeting then ended and delegations left Dublin Castle. The two Governments finalised the joint determination over the next few days. They concluded, on the basis of the information available to them (which in our case meant an assessment by the Garda Commissioner), that there had been IRA involvement in the two killings and that, as the IRA were linked to Sinn Féin, Sinn Féin could no longer participate in the talks. Emphasising their aim to maintain an inclusive talks process, as well as their commitment to the timing already indicated for its completion, they went on to say that, subject to events on the ground and to a complete and unequivocal IRA ceasefire being fully and continuously observed, they expected that Sinn Féin could return to the talks on 9 March.

This date had been the subject of consultations between the two Governments up to the level of Bertie Ahern and Tony Blair. Ahern had favoured setting a date in the first few days of March, Blair preferred mid-March and 9 March was the compromise. With the joint determination issuing on 20 February, this would mean an absence of only about two-and-a-half weeks.

The expulsion of Sinn Féin from the talks came as the process was nearing its conclusion. It had a destabilising effect within the republican movement, and to some extent outside it as well. A shadow fell over the prospects for achieving an inclusive settlement, towards which all of our efforts had been directed. But everyone recognised that this was a temporary hiatus only. Political and official channels remained open. With sensitive management all round, and above all no recurrence of IRA violence, the conditions were there for the return of Sinn Féin to the process within a couple of weeks.

15

BACK TO BUSINESS

W hile these episodes were disruptive and unsettling, the talks still managed to make some progress in January and February. We inched forward in the three Strands with a succession of papers which sought to narrow divergences and to identify common ground.

The London meeting in January got round to some discussion of substance once the UDP issue had been dealt with. This was based on the Strand Two paper which the two Governments had agreed a few days earlier. Emphasising nationalist dismay at the British ambivalence about the Framework Document, we had insisted on describing the Governments as 'firmly committed' to this document. After some hesitation, the British agreed to this.

The joint paper was tabled and introduced by Liz O'Donnell and Mo Mowlam. Welcoming it, Sinn Féin asked questions designed to establish its consistency with the Framework Document. Most other delegations saw it as a helpful basis for getting into detailed Strand Two negotiations. The UUP were critical of it, unsurprisingly, and Jeffrey Donaldson tore up a copy at a press conference.

The UUP's Reg Empey, however, made a noteworthy contribution to the debate which moved beyond argument over this document and onto the broader plane of relationships between unionism and republicanism. By way of response to Sinn Féin's renewed complaint about unionist non-engagement, Empey said that unionists resented Sinn Féin's failure to acknowledge their existence and rights. 'We're a blot on the landscape for them, to be driven into the sea.' With a claim that 'a significant part of the Army Council' was in the room, he said that the deaths of Robert Bradford and Edgar Graham (two prominent UUP victims of IRA violence) had been one example of 'engagement' with the UUP. Acknowledging the 'inalienable' right of republicans to put forward proposals, and accepting the sincerity of their views, he asked Sinn Féin nonetheless to recognise that the proposals they had put forward for regional councils had no prospect of winning UUP support – and, therefore, of featuring in any settlement. The UUP were there to get a settlement, furthermore, and were not interested in any transitional arrangements. Neither these Sinn Féin proposals nor the Framework Document were acceptable to unionists. Acknowledging that mistakes had been made on all sides, Empey observed that nonetheless 'we are where we are'.

In a paper circulated that day, Sinn Féin had put forward their proposal for a system of regional councils in the context of a unitary 32-county state. The point about transitional arrangements went back to the republican doctrine of a militant struggle with various phases and Gerry Adams' emphasis on getting transition arrangements which would move things forward towards 'an agreed, or a new, or a united Ireland'.

Replying to Empey, Martin McGuinness said he understood the unionist community was hurting at present, as it feared for the future. But the nationalist community had been victims of discrimination and domination; nobody had a monopoly on suffering. What was needed was direct dialogue and engagement; ultimately, the UUP would have to listen to Sinn Féin's views on what was wrong with Ireland.

In earlier remarks, McGuinness had appealed to the UUP for direct engagement. A brief exchange he had just had with David Trimble outside the room had given him a sense, he said, that the UUP leader wanted to engage. Now, addressing Trimble directly, McGuinness renewed Sinn Féin's offer of a bilateral meeting. 'People like you are beacons of light, genuinely,' he continued – and added lightly that Trimble probably got more praise in the nationalist community than in his own. (To which David Ervine delivered the acerbic riposte: 'That's why you should desist from doing it!')

There was an impassioned intervention from Seamus Mallon. Flatly rejecting a Sinn Féin claim that his party supported a partitionist settlement, Mallon demanded greater sensitivity to the concerns of others in future. The SDLP, he pointed out, represented the greater part of the nationalist community in the North of Ireland. Its position was based on what the two Governments had agreed in the Framework Document. As part of this, he wanted to see structures set up in the North which would involve 'Irishmen and Irishwomen administering the part of Ireland I live in'.

In a powerful contribution, Monica McWilliams of the NIWC observed that we had all 'done terrible things to each other'. There had been 'real hurt' in Reg Empey's remarks. More generally, the process had been damaged by a lot of 'spinning' on all sides over the previous fortnight. Congratulating the two Governments on that day's paper, she looked forward to 'stopping the spinning and starting the negotiations'. (This elicited the characteristically droll observation from Mark Durkan that, as the SDLP had done no spinning of its own but had merely reacted to the spinning of others, 'we are a party more spinned against than spinning'.)

That evening, Tony Blair visited Lancaster House to meet the delegations. At the meeting our ministers had with him, David

Andrews observed that, with Sinn Féin and the UUP having respectively rejected the last two papers (the Heads of Agreement paper and that day's joint paper on Strand Two), it was fair to speak of a 'parity of pain'. It should, we hoped, be easier to convince all sides that there was a level playing field in the talks. Paul Murphy, accompanying the Prime Minister, agreed but remarked that, 'like a seesaw, it's never easy to get it exactly level!'

When the Strand Two debate resumed on 26 January, John Hume developed a position modelled closely on the Framework Document. Gerry Adams did likewise. He supported North/South arrangements capable of advancing 'the national process of reconciliation and unity on the island' which would have a strong executive element, be dynamic and have functions designated from the outset. He also acknowledged Reg Empey's contribution of the previous day as a sincere effort to articulate a unionist understanding of the republican position. 'I know republicans have inflicted hurt and unionists have suffered, as we all have, as a result of this conflict.' Sinn Féin, for its part, wanted to see a pluralist Ireland and was willing to address unionism's legitimate fears.

In one of the few light-hearted moments during this London week, someone got a good racing tip, a syndicate of enthusiasts was formed (from the SDLP, the PUP and the Irish Government delegation) and the horse won, to the delight of all.

In the following week, the talks resumed in Belfast in all three Strands.

The UUP continued to present Strand Two as a subset of Strand Three. The North/South Ministerial Council, they insisted, would have to be subordinate to the British–Irish Council. On this basis, they argued, there would be no need to give executive powers to the North/South Council: the British–Irish Council would itself not have, or ever need, executive powers and therefore what David

Trimble termed the 'North/South element within the British Isles Council' would not require such powers either. When it was put to him in an interview that there could be no agreement without executive powers for cross-border bodies, Trimble said that there were numerous cross-border cooperative arrangements in various European contexts and that these were all 'essentially consultative'.

The UUP position was roundly criticised by the SDLP and Sinn Féin. More widely, it was judged to be an entirely unrealistic negotiating stance, involving ideas which the UUP must know stood no chance of being acceptable across the board.

An optimist might have read this as the UUP leader moving to protect his flank in the run-up to the Dublin meeting, which everyone was expecting would be the moment for key decisions – and compromises – on Strand Two. In the event, the Dublin meeting (16–18 February) was completely dominated, as we have seen, by the moves to exclude Sinn Féin in the wake of the Campbell and Dougan killings.

In early February, Mo Mowlam had visited Dublin to take stock ahead of the Dublin meeting. Bertie Ahern proposed that work continue quietly between us towards a single draft agreement which would develop the Heads of Agreement paper, the British Government's Strand One document and our joint papers in Strands Two and Three. It could be a single text but with a lot of square brackets, he suggested. We should take whatever time was needed to get it right; he did not want to find himself again under the pressure he and Tony Blair had faced when they had to finalise the Heads of Agreement paper over a weekend by phone (with Blair in Tokyo).

Mo agreed. Conscious of the risk of leaks, she preferred to avoid a single document for now ('keep it in segments'). She asked that neither Government pass texts to any of the parties.

We detected a continuing nervousness on the British side about the two Governments appearing too obviously to be in the driving seat. Mo and her officials wanted to play down our joint stewardship of the talks, even though it was obvious to all and centrally important for several of the participants. They wanted instead, in deference to unionist sensitivities, to emphasise the invitation to the parties to put forward proposals of their own.

At a press conference after her meeting with the Taoiseach, Mo made this point strongly. Her response, when asked about suggestions that the two Governments were preparing a draft agreement, was to note vaguely that we were, of course, 'looking at options for the future'.

We could go along with this reticence to some extent, for short-term tactical reasons. We knew, however, that ultimately it would be for the two Governments to present the draft of an overall agreement, and to use our full influence and authority in support of this, if the talks were to reach a successful conclusion. There would no doubt be substantial divergences to be overcome, especially in Strand Two, and our draft could undergo significant revision in the end game. But we knew we would not get to that end game unless the two Governments reached a joint view on what would be a fair and balanced outcome and presented a draft agreement which reflected that. The impetus, it was clear to us, would have to come from above.

Attention was beginning to turn now to the overall timing for a political agreement and for its aftermath: the referendums to endorse it, the anticipated election to a new Assembly and the legislation which would be needed to put the agreement into effect in both jurisdictions.

Blair had reaffirmed, on taking office, a May 1998 deadline for completion of the negotiations which had been set by the previous

British Government. However, when we took account of the annual marching season (which would peak in early July) and the need to keep the referendums and Assembly election campaign well clear of that, we realised that we would need an earlier completion date. A three-week referendum campaign and a three-week period to pass the consequential legislation would have to be allowed for. Mo had suggested to the Taoiseach, and he agreed, that we would need to have an agreement by the end of March.

George Mitchell favoured setting an Easter deadline. David Trimble told the British Government that he could go along with that. Easter Sunday that year would be 12 April and Thursday 9 April came into focus as the target date.

On this basis, Mo Mowlam favoured 7 May as the date for the referendums. Both Governments wanted to move with all possible speed to the referendum stage, profiting from the momentum of a political agreement. However, our Government's preference was for a slightly later date, primarily to deny those opposed to changing Articles 2 and 3 an opportunity to claim that our electorate was being 'bounced' into this difficult decision with a rushed referendum. We also had to consider Referendum Act provisions and the Oireachtas timetable. Our preference, therefore, was for 22 May. Mo tried to split the difference, floating 15 May, but in due course 22 May was agreed.

As for the Assembly election, the British Government wanted this to follow quite soon after the referendums, by 25 June at the latest.

Speculation about various electoral scenarios and timings was now rife. Our sense was that the parties were beginning to recognise that a deal might indeed be on the cards and that its aftermath would need careful preparation. The few remaining weeks leading up to Easter would be crucial.

After the Dublin meeting, the talks resumed in Belfast on 23 February. Sinn Féin were absent but the reverberations from their expulsion lingered. Reg Empey held that it was not a real expulsion, given its short duration and the fact that the party would be seeing the Taoiseach, and possibly the Prime Minister as well, over the coming days.

On 26 February, Bertie Ahern and Tony Blair met at No. 10 to review developments. With the 9 April deadline only six weeks away, they had to consider tactical issues around the deployment of the overall draft agreement on which the two Governments were working.

Blair feared that to table a complete draft in the short term would trigger a UUP walkout. He preferred an incremental approach: the two Governments would work up between them agreed language on the individual parts of the prospective agreement but would hold back for now from agreeing, let alone tabling, a single document. He was clearly anxious to be able to deny to the UUP that any joint draft existed. We were in any event still some distance away from agreeing some parts of that draft, in particular Strand Two.

Ahern was broadly of the same view. He knew that at the end of the day a single draft agreement would have to be put on the table by the two Governments, working through George Mitchell. No other approach was conceivable if this process was to succeed. But now was not the moment.

He was willing in the meantime to have the Governments work up agreed language on an issue-by-issue basis. A drafting exercise of this kind, using square brackets as necessary, would be a useful way of clearing our minds on the issues. Ultimately there were deep interlinkages between all of them. Nothing would be agreed until everything was agreed; we might reach provisional understandings with the British in some areas but these would all be dependent on satisfactory outcomes in others. And the parties would also have to make their judgements about the trade-offs between one issue and another.

Blair suggested that the Governments start by identifying the dozen or so issues which were separating us at that point and work on those.

He and Ahern already had a good sense that Strand Two would probably be the most contentious area. A major unionist concern was to ensure that the North/South Ministerial Council would not be a free-standing body. They could accept the proposed implementation bodies, the Governments sensed, but only if these did not appear to be autonomous. From his own contacts, Ahern sensed that the unionists were hoping to avoid having implementation bodies prescribed, or 'designated', from the outset. This would not be acceptable to us, he told Blair, nor could we sell this to others. We would need some of these implementation bodies to be designated initially, to proof them against unionist veto, as well as a capacity to establish more of them over time.

What were the key issues which separated the two Governments, and behind them the individual parties, at that point in the negotiations?

In Strand One, there were differences over the extent of power to be devolved, the nature of the Executive to be formed and the checks and balances which should operate (for example, whether some form of weighted majority should be stipulated for certain decisions).

In Strand Two, there were differences over whether there should be a connection between the North/South structures and the East/West institutions; what kind of powers the North/South Ministerial Council should have (executive v. consultative);

whether there should be an initial designation of functions for implementation bodies; and whether the Assembly should have a role in relation to the establishment of the latter.

In Strand Three, there were differences over the extent to which representatives of the Executive should be involved in the future British–Irish Intergovernmental Conference; or whether the latter should have an overall power of oversight and intervention to remedy difficulties encountered in the workings of the new agreement.

As regards the anticipated constitutional changes, there were competing pressures on the Governments from the nationalist and unionist perspectives, respectively. There were also divergences between us over policing reform; reform of the justice system; the release of paramilitary prisoners (pace and extent of early release); decommissioning (the degree of specificity in the commitments to be made – the Blair Government agreed with us that decommissioning could only be a voluntary process but was still anxious to give the unionists more support in this area); treatment of the Irish language; and several other equality and rights issues.

All of this was predicated, of course, on an assumption that any agreement would be based broadly on the Framework Document and the Heads of Agreement paper and would not fall below the level of ambition set in these two documents (in which case there would have been more fundamental differences between the two Governments).

George Mitchell supported the work we were embarking on and backed the incremental approach. At the same time, he recognised that a single comprehensive draft covering the entirety of the negotiations would have to be put on the table eventually. The desired compromises and trade-offs across the Strands and the various thematic issues would not be achieved unless delegations had a single paper setting out all the building blocks for the settlement. There could, if necessary, be options to cover the most difficult points (an approach he also favoured as an insurance policy against leaks, which seemed almost inevitable).

With 9 April rapidly approaching, Mitchell estimated that this single overall draft would be needed by the last week of March.

16

THE PACE QUICKENS

On 6 March 1998, Irish and British officials met in the Liaison Group in Dublin. Taking stock generally, Dermot Gallagher expressed concern that, with constant public emphasis on the certainty both of a new Northern Ireland Assembly and of changes to Articles 2 and 3, and with little sign of serious UUP engagement so far on North/South structures, things were tilting very much in a unionist direction at present. This was causing disquiet among Northern nationalists and in the South. Quentin Thomas took this point but suggested that the pendulum might tilt back towards nationalism shortly (with a planned British Government announcement on human rights issues and some forthcoming prisoner releases).

That day, and only a fortnight after Sinn Féin had been expelled from the talks, the two Governments announced that they were now satisfied that a complete, unqualified and unequivocal IRA ceasefire was being observed. Accordingly, and 'subject to events on the ground', they invited Sinn Féin to rejoin the talks as from Monday 9 March. While this timing had been broadly agreed by the two Governments, our emphasis on republican disquiet probably advanced the announcement by a day or two.

Over that weekend, Gerry Adams used an article in *Ireland on Sunday* to ventilate much of this unease. Even full implementation of the Framework Document would be hugely challenging for Sinn Féin, Adams insisted. It accepted this document only as a 'basis for discussion' and would view any agreement reached 'in this phase' as merely part of a process of transition to Irish unity. He then listed under such 'transitional arrangements' Sinn Féin's familiar set of requirements covering North/South structures, constitutional change, equality and security policy reform.

With a maximalist presentation of this kind, the Sinn Féin leadership was essentially covering its flank as it prepared to re-enter the talks. There had been some indications of wavering republican commitment to the political strategy. As the latter's leading champion, Adams needed to signal that Sinn Féin would be rejoining the talks not as an end in itself but in order to demand, and work for, the right kind of agreement. This was a message which he wanted to bring to the Taoiseach and the Prime Minister at the outset.

Sinn Féin were officially free to return as of 9 March. However, they did not actually appear at the talks again until after Adams and McGuinness had been able to secure meetings with Ahern and Blair. Allowing also for the exodus of all parties and the two Governments to Washington for the St Patrick's Day festivities, this meant a delay of a fortnight. Trimble, keen to present the UUP and the SDLP as the key players as we advanced towards an agreement, chose to represent this as Sinn Féin boycotting the talks for a fortnight.

On 24 March, Adams, McGuinness and other senior Sinn Féin representatives turned up at Castle Buildings where, in a special Plenary session, they reaffirmed their commitment to the Mitchell Principles and were formally back in the talks. Adams said he and his colleagues wished to move with all possible speed into substantive negotiations on the core issues. They were welcomed back by the chairmen, the two Governments and several of the parties.

However, the UUP chose to be represented by an observer only and the loyalist parties stayed away from the meeting. All three were registering their disapproval of what they judged to have been too early a readmission for Sinn Féin. They maintained that the killing of a Lurgan man, Kevin Conway, on 18 February, as well as recent bombings in Moira and Portadown and a mortar attack in Armagh, had been the work of the Provisional IRA and that this warranted the renewed exclusion of Sinn Féin. However, neither Government had any evidence that these had been authorised IRA operations.

The SDLP, whom Trimble had been courting assiduously during Sinn Féin's absence, marked out their own ground. Interviewed on 23 March, Seamus Mallon accused the UUP of trying to make the SDLP 'the anvil upon which they and Sinn Féin hammer out their own particular antagonisms'. However, the SDLP would not allow that to happen. They would press on with their own policies and strategy and would not be deflected by anyone. As for Sinn Féin, they seemed to be moving towards SDLP positions and language on key issues, Mallon observed with grim satisfaction.

Addressing the Ulster Unionist Council on 21 March, David Trimble had emphasised meaningful engagement between his party and the SDLP as the essential path to an agreement. Citing the Heads of Agreement document and the UUP's own proposals for the talks, he said that the UUP had entered negotiations to reach a political settlement. But it would not 'buy peace at any price'. It would not agree to any form of North/South bodies which would establish 'an embryonic all-Ireland government'. Furthermore, it would not engage with 'Sinn Féin-IRA' for as long as the latter did not recognise the principle of consent or the right of unionists to define themselves as British. Trimble was clearly intent on reassuring the unionist grassroots as the UUP entered the final stretch of the talks, even if there was little in his speech to suggest that the party faithful were being prepared for the difficult decisions which were inevitably coming.

In Washington a few days earlier, the Taoiseach had briefed President Clinton in the White House on the latest developments.

Much has been written about Clinton's contribution to the peace process and to the negotiations which would deliver the Good Friday Agreement. From the moment he took office, we were stunned by the depth of his interest in the issue and the ease with which he commanded its detail. This was attributed to various factors, including a strong identification with his Irish roots on his mother's side and the emergence of the 'Troubles' while he was a young Rhodes Scholar at Oxford.

I remember the amazement on our side when Albert Reynolds had his first meeting with the new President. Expecting to find that generalities about Northern Ireland would suffice for the conversation, Reynolds discovered that Clinton was already familiar in detail with the political scene in Northern Ireland – to a degree never previously encountered with an American President.

Clinton later took the bold step of granting Gerry Adams a visa to visit the US. He succeeded in building trust with nationalists and unionists alike, throwing the doors of the White House open to both. On excellent terms personally with both Ahern and Blair, he was to prove a uniquely important asset both in the run-up to the Good Friday Agreement and for years afterwards as we faced up to successive implementation challenges.

Ahern told the President that the overall shape of an agreement was emerging. However, we still had to work through a few key areas which were highly sensitive. Our Government was prepared to introduce constitutional changes; and Sinn Féin, he believed, were moving towards acceptance of an Assembly in Northern Ireland. Both of these would be big gains for unionism. The quid pro quo would have to be the establishment of meaningful North/South bodies with executive powers. These would of course have to be underpinned by movement on the equality agenda.

Listening sympathetically, Clinton asked what he could do to help. Ahern asked him to focus on getting Adams and Trimble – the President would be meeting both in Washington that week – to move on the issues of greatest sensitivity for them (for Adams, the Assembly, and, for Trimble, the North/South bodies). For our part, we were ready to move on the Irish Constitution. But we would be unable to sell the changes involved unless we got strong North/South bodies.

The only way to get a sustainable settlement, he continued, would be to have Sinn Féin on board. From a unionist perspective, furthermore, an agreement without Sinn Féin would mean that they would be making concessions without any guarantee of greater stability in return. Anything Clinton could do to bring these points home to Trimble would be appreciated.

If Trimble moved on the North/South bodies, Ahern went on, it was likely we would get an agreement. If he did not, the current opportunity would be lost. The lesson of Sunningdale was that it could take over 20 years to pick up the pieces, losing a whole generation in the process. The unfortunate reality was that there were plenty of young people in Northern Ireland ready to opt for violence and simplistic 'Brits out' solutions if the process collapsed.

With all party leaders congregating in Washington for the St Patrick's Day festivities, there was no formal session of the talks in Belfast during that week. Clinton assured all his visitors of his strong personal commitment to a successful outcome and his readiness to do whatever he could to facilitate and support that. There was talk that he might visit Northern Ireland shortly, though this was likely to be after the talks had concluded (in May when he had to visit the UK for a G8 summit).

I remember an overall feeling I had at that time, around mid-March, that the odds on our getting an agreement by 9 April were at best even. I was frankly not optimistic. I did not yet sense a mood in Castle Buildings to seize the moment and go for a historic deal. The negotiating atmosphere had been soured by growing polemics between the unionists and Sinn Féin, nothing of substance had been 'banked' and time was running out.

17

CONSTITUTIONAL ISSUES

I t had always been accepted that a balanced constitutional accommodation would be central to the comprehensive settlement we were aiming for. This meant that the constitutional concerns of the two main traditions in Ireland, nationalism and unionism, would have to be addressed in an even-handed way.

Unionists had been campaigning for years against Articles 2 and 3 of the Irish Constitution and what they saw as a 'territorial claim' which was being asserted through them. In the Brooke–Mayhew talks of 1991–2, they had pressed hard to establish what might potentially be on offer in relation to these Articles as part of an overall agreement. As no such agreement was on the horizon at that stage, and changes to our Constitution could be contemplated only in that broader context, we had no basis for engaging on the issue at that point.

Over the next couple of years, the Downing Street Declaration and the Framework Document articulated a relatively detailed joint position of the two Governments on constitutional issues. This included a foretaste of what the Irish Government would propose by way of changes to our Constitution in the right context. Not the exact terms, clearly, but the broad thrust of what we had in mind. Equally, the British Government signalled some constitutional changes it would introduce.

The key undertakings were the following. In the Framework Document, the Irish Government indicated that, in the context of an overall settlement, it would introduce and support proposals for changes to the Irish Constitution to reflect fully the principle of consent. And the British Government would take similar steps in relation to British constitutional legislation defining the status of Northern Ireland. In addition, the two Governments would set out an agreed understanding of these constitutional issues in the opening article of a new British–Irish Agreement. (We had envisaged all along that, in addition to whatever emerged from the multi-party talks, there would be a new agreement between the two Governments which would replace the Anglo-Irish Agreement and set out the new institutions and arrangements agreed between us.)

By the time we got to the 1996–8 negotiations, therefore, much was known, at least in outline, of the Governments' intentions. Some of the heat had, accordingly, gone out of these issues. Though regularly brought up by the unionists with us, they no longer dominated the discourse in the way they had done over many years. Constitutional issues were in practice handled separately from the main business of the negotiations.

Our Government had to tackle two main challenges. First, we had to devise language which might replace the current Articles 2 and 3 of the Irish Constitution (subject to popular approval in a referendum). And second, we had to agree with the British Government the terms of Article 1 of a new British–Irish Agreement.

Constitutional matters were strictly speaking for the Governments only. Our proposals in relation to Articles 2 and 3, we made clear, would not be negotiated with the parties but would arise organically from the nature of the settlement on offer. There was a deep interconnection between our achieving a far-reaching accommodation that would give tangible expression to nationalist aspirations and what we might be ready to propose to our electorate by way of balancing constitutional change.

We were, of course, ready to listen to the views of all the parties on constitutional issues and we kept them briefed on our intentions, initially in general terms and later in precise detail. The normal setting for this was either Strand Two or the liaison mechanism which gave the parties an opportunity to debate Strand Three issues with the two Governments.

When Strand Two got under way in October 1997, most parties indicated that they were broadly content with the presentation on constitutional issues in the Framework Document, in particular the emphasis on the centrality of the principle of consent. Seamus Mallon, for example, made it clear that nationalists did not object to changes in the Irish Constitution designed to remove perceived threats to the unionist identity; however, they would expect that their own right to be part of the Irish nation would receive full constitutional expression.

For the UUP, John Taylor held that, under international law, there 'are and ought to be' no constitutional issues between the two sovereign states on the island and that the law and practice of each state should reflect this. Unionists rejected the Framework Document but welcomed its acceptance that the principle of consent should apply to the future arrangements for Northern Ireland. The removal of Articles 2 and 3, he suggested, would unlock the other issues to be discussed in Strand Two.

The SDLP, supported by Sinn Féin, took issue with some of Taylor's remarks. They complained about a unionist reluctance to address the implications of an absence of nationalist consent for the present arrangements. The SDLP totally accepted the consent principle; that did not mean, however, that there were no further constitutional issues to be addressed.

The PUP's Hughie Smyth wanted to see the Irish Government taking action on Articles 2 and 3 ahead of the negotiations, for general confidence-building purposes. Our position was clear, however: there was no possibility of securing our electorate's approval to constitutional change unless and until there was a comprehensive balancing agreement which would give satisfactory expression to nationalist aspirations. Amending Articles 2 and 3 would be an act of seismic proportions from a nationalist perspective; as John Hume described it to Tony Blair around this time, it would be like abolishing the monarchy in Britain.

In response to a direct question from Taylor about our intentions, David Andrews made it clear that there would be no changes to the Irish Constitution in advance of substantive negotiations. We would, however, be willing to look at the two Articles when we got to that stage. Taylor reacted sourly, inferring that we would be willing to address this issue only at the very end of the negotiations. Saying that his party would have to withdraw to reflect on the minister's comments, he led his team out of the room. Most parties reacted with strong disapproval to this walkout, which seemed linked to an impending UUP party conference. We offered the UUP a written text to clarify the Government's position and this facilitated the party's return to the room a couple of hours later.

As there had been some media leaks about the changes which the Government was supposedly contemplating, unionists kept up the pressure to see actual language. Andrews and Liz O'Donnell indicated we would not be getting into specifics in this regard until unionists became specific in terms of agreeing to North/South institutions with executive powers. O'Donnell compared this reciprocal relationship to 'synchronised swimming'.

In November 1997, we began preliminary work within the Irish Government system on our two main challenges: what might replace Articles 2 and 3 and what should go into the opening article of a new British–Irish Agreement. Martin Mansergh, Bertie Ahern's adviser on Northern Ireland, played the lead role. He was actively supported by Jim Hamilton, the head of our Attorney General's Office, who kept David Byrne – the Attorney General – fully briefed. Rory Montgomery in the Department of Foreign Affairs also made a significant contribution, as did Eamonn McKee.

Drawing on formulations used in the Downing Street Declaration, the Framework Document and other key texts, Mansergh and his colleagues proposed various redrafts of Articles 2 and 3 for consideration at the political level. The challenge was to find language which would address the unionists' concerns about what they termed the 'territorial claim' but without doing anything to weaken Northern nationalists' sense of belonging to the wider Irish nation. The language should at the same time avoid any implication that we regarded unionists as automatically part of that nation. Unionists did not wish to be included in the nation against their will and this had to be respected.

The approach proposed was to focus on a definition of the Irish nation rather than of the 'national territory'. Going beyond (but not entirely losing) the territorial frame of reference, we envisaged a new Article 2 which would declare that every person born on the island of Ireland was entitled by right to belong to the Irish nation, in all the diversity of its identities and traditions. It would be spelled out, additionally, that anyone born on the island was entitled to hold Irish citizenship.

In revisions to Article 3, which would be divided into two parts, it would be declared to be the 'firm will' of the Irish nation that all the people of the island be united in harmony and friendship, while recognising that a united Ireland could only be achieved by peaceful means and with the consent of a majority of the people, voting by referendum, in each of the jurisdictions on the island. (The phrase 'firm will' hailed from the 1968 Oireachtas All-Party Committee on the Constitution and was also very similar to language in the 1949 Basic Law of the Federal Republic of Germany.) Pending the achievement of a united Ireland, the laws enacted by the Oireachtas would apply in the 26 counties only. There would be an additional provision, however, to authorise the prospective implementation bodies (which would operate in all or part of the island).

There would also be an amendment to Article 29.4.4 of the Constitution to allow for approval of the overall agreement. And, catering for the possibility (however unwelcome) that the referendums might yield approval of the agreement in the South but not in the North, we had to ensure that the proposed changes would only come into effect if the referendum passed in Northern Ireland. A special mechanism would be needed to make it clear that the changes were being sought on this conditional basis. (David Byrne, as Attorney General, would be closely involved in devising this mechanism, the constitutionality of which was subjected to a happily unsuccessful High Court challenge a few days before the referendums).

As regards British constitutional legislation relating to Northern Ireland, Section 75 of the Government of Ireland Act of 1920 had bluntly affirmed the authority of the British Government over Northern Ireland without any further qualification. To be consistent with the Anglo-Irish Agreement, the Downing Street Declaration and the Framework Document, this would now need to be superseded by a declaration making it clear that Northern Ireland's constitutional future would depend on the consent principle. This declaration would note (a) the possibility that the people of Ireland could exercise their right of self-determination on the basis of consent, freely and concurrently given, North and South, to bring about a united Ireland, and (b) the commitments the British Government had entered into in this connection. The British Government made it clear to us that they were ready to bring in new legislation incorporating this understanding. This would repeal all that remained of the Government of Ireland Act and would also supersede the Northern Ireland Constitution Act of 1973 (though some technical provisions of both would have to be retained in the new legislation).

Sinn Féin wanted the British to go a step further and repeal the Act of Union as well. On 6 April 1998, Mo Mowlam told Gerry Adams that in Britain new legislation was regarded as automatically displacing old. However, given the concerns Sinn Féin had raised about the Act of Union, they would make it clear in the new legislation that nothing in any earlier Acts would be an obstacle to Northern Ireland ceasing to be part of the UK and becoming part of a united Ireland on the basis of consent. Sinn Féin also explored the possibility of our Constitutional changes spelling out that the Act of Union had been superseded. However, as there was no legal need to do this and there was also a risk that it might inflame extremist opinion, the idea was not pursued.

As regards Article 1 of the new British–Irish Agreement, we on the Irish side envisaged that this would make several key points, drawing on language used in the Anglo-Irish Agreement, the Downing Street Declaration and the Framework Document.

First, there would be a reference to self-determination, balancing and complementing the consent principle which would now be enshrined in our Constitution. The two Governments would make it clear that it would be for the people of the island of Ireland alone, without external impediment, to exercise their right of self-determination on the basis of agreement between them and of consent freely and concurrently given, North and South.

Second, the two Governments would recognise the legitimacy of whatever choice was freely exercised by a majority of the people of Northern Ireland – whether they preferred to support the Union or a united Ireland. (As in the earlier documents, only this binary choice was contemplated.)

Third, we would recognise that the present wish of a majority was to maintain the Union.

Fourth, we would acknowledge that a substantial minority legitimately wished for a united Ireland.

Fifth, we would affirm that, if the people of the island ever exercised their right of self-determination to bring about a united Ireland, it would be a binding obligation on the two Governments to introduce and support legislation in the respective Parliaments to give effect to this wish.

Sixth, whether the wish of the people of Northern Ireland was for no change or for a united Ireland, the sovereign Government in question would exercise its powers with rigorous impartiality on behalf of all the people of Northern Ireland and with full respect for the identity and aspirations of both communities.

And *seventh*, we would recognise the birthright of all the people of Northern Ireland to identify themselves and be accepted as Irish or British, or both, and confirm their right to hold British or Irish citizenship or both. (The 'Irish or British or both' concept came from a draft report of the Forum for Peace and Reconciliation, on whose staff Rory Montgomery and Tim O'Connor had served.)

These were the elements we wished to see in the new Article 1. In January 1998, work began in earnest on this between the Irish and British teams. We discussed this in the Liaison Group and there was also much correspondence through the Secretariat and other channels. We found that the British thinking was in the same general region as our own. An Irish draft was considered at a meeting of the Liaison Group on 6 March, which looked also at issues such as the relative merits of 'equity' and 'equality' and the sequence in which the references to consent and self-determination should be placed.

We consulted regularly with Sinn Féin as this work progressed. (The SDLP did not follow it quite as closely.) And we had no doubt that the UUP, not short of lawyers within its ranks, would be in regular contact with the British Government about it. Gradually the distance narrowed between the two Governments and by 20 March we had broad agreement on the new Article 1.

In the meantime, work within the Irish Government on the language to replace Articles 2 and 3 intensified during February and March. This also involved preparing the ground domestically for the changes which were coming. Bertie Ahern, assisted by Martin Mansergh, had to sell the planned amendments to Fianna Fáil and overcome potential resistance. Fianna Fáil support would be absolutely essential if a referendum was to succeed. This was a major political challenge but gradually, through a series of internal party consultations, they built up the necessary consensus.

We kept our British colleagues informed of progress and exchanged drafts regularly. As the weeks went by, we briefed the parties in steadily fuller detail on our plans (bearing in mind, of course, that our drafts were in a state of constant refinement and revision).

As we came into the home stretch of the negotiations, the two Governments tabled on 24 March a joint paper setting out their views on what a 'balanced constitutional accommodation' would require. This acknowledged a fundamental absence of consensus between the two traditions in Ireland, and the two communities in Northern Ireland, on constitutional issues. At the same time, we recognised that there was a growing convergence between the positions of the two Governments on many of these issues, and in particular on the questions of self-determination and consent. We then mentioned the separate undertakings made by each Government as well as, broadly, what we intended to say jointly in Article 1 of a new British–Irish Agreement. These three elements, we noted, would be needed for an overall political agreement between the two Governments and the parties.

Under unionist pressure, the British wanted to see the parties more fully involved in the constitutional work on all three fronts. From early March on, the UUP began to press us for the text of our proposed constitutional amendments. John Taylor, in particular, demanded this on a weekly basis, claiming on one occasion that the amendments would not be satisfactory to unionists and that his party, under pressure to agree to substantial North/South bodies in return for the promised removal of the 'territorial claim', was being lured into a trap by the Irish Government.

The UUP used some lawyers close to the party to try to explore the kind of amendments the Government might be considering. On 12 March, Martin Mansergh and Jim Hamilton had a meeting in London with two such lawyers, Austin Morgan and Jeremy Carver, at the latter's request. Morgan and Carver handed over UUP suggestions both for the new Article 1 and for the amendment of Articles 2 and 3. Hamilton wrote to Morgan a few days later to say that several of the changes sought were unacceptable to us for one or other reason, while others were more appropriate for a wider Constitution review process which was under way. The UUP no doubt saw advantage in trying to influence the final content of the amendments. However, the informal route they chose for this (lawyers who were outside the negotiations) suggested that this issue would not be of decisive importance in terms of unionist support for the agreement.

On 30 March, Peter King (another UUP lawyer) and Morgan met the Attorney General, David Byrne, in Dublin. Byrne told them what the Government's proposed amendments to Articles 2 and 3 would be. The UUP visitors did not exactly agree with these, Byrne recalled later, but neither did they oppose them. King said he did not oppose or reject what he had heard. It was also clear to Byrne that, while Morgan said he had no instructions to accept our proposals, the visitors had no legal issues with the latter. King went on to indicate that, if the Strand Two negotiations produced agreement, there would be no problem with what the Government was proposing on Articles 2 and 3. Byrne's clear impression from the meeting was that the amendments to the two Articles were unlikely to cause a problem during the negotiations in Belfast the following week.

The 'constitutional issues' section of the draft overall agreement that George Mitchell circulated on 7 April, and then of the Agreement as finalised three days later, consisted in essence of the new Article 1 and an endorsement of it by all the participants.

The constitutional changes envisaged in the respective jurisdictions were also finalised in the last week or two running up to Good Friday. The two Governments circulated these to the parties and also agreed that their precise terms would be annexed to the agreement.

In the British case, the clauses which the British Government intended to incorporate in legislation involved a declaration that (i) Northern Ireland remained part of the UK and would not cease to be without the consent of a majority of the people of Northern Ireland (voting in what has since become known as a 'border poll'); (ii) if the wish expressed in such a poll was for Northern Ireland to cease to be part of the UK and to form part of a united Ireland, proposals to that effect would be laid before Parliament; and (iii) the Government of Ireland Act was repealed.

A provision would be added – much invoked in the interim since Brexit – for the Secretary of State for Northern Ireland to direct the holding of polls 'if at any time it appears likely to him that a majority of those voting would express a wish that Northern Ireland should cease to be part of the United Kingdom and form part of a united Ireland'. The British initially envisaged a 10-year interval before a poll on this subject could be repeated. We argued for a shorter period and for language which would give the Secretary of State more discretion on timing. This came down eventually to 'not earlier than seven years'.

Sinn Féin wanted us to confirm that 'a majority' would mean a simple majority and, if so, to say why this could not be spelled out in the agreement. Rory Montgomery reassured them that, if the term was not qualified in any way, it automatically meant a simple majority. The generally spare language of this section reflected a concern not to frighten unionists with too much detail; for example, it is taken for granted that the Irish Government would be consulted by the Secretary of State in relation to this decision, but this is not explicitly stated.

As for our own Constitution, we envisaged, finally, a new Article 2 that would declare it to be the 'entitlement and birthright' of every person born on the island of Ireland to be part of the Irish nation and a citizen of Ireland. (The word 'entitlement' arose in discussion between Martin Mansergh, Eamonn McKee and others; it was an important addition, legally tighter than 'birthright' and signalling also to unionists that citizenship would not be imposed on them but was an elective matter.) Furthermore, there would be a warm reference to the Irish nation's special affinity with people of Irish ancestry living abroad. There would also be a new Article 3.1 on the lines indicated above (and with a phrase about the 'diversity of their identities and traditions' added). A new Article 3.2 would provide authority for the implementation bodies. And for technical reasons, Article 29.4.4 would be amended in the manner indicated above.

These constitutional changes were not part of the negotiations proper. They were agreed between the two Governments in London and Dublin rather than in Castle Buildings. They were, however, part of a vital political calculus that underpinned the new Agreement and were in themselves of profound significance for Anglo-Irish relations.

18

THE LAST FORTNIGHT

With the finale rapidly approaching, the chairmen and the two Governments had to consider how the remaining work of the talks would be managed.

There was by now a lot of frustration among delegations about the state of the process. With very little time to go, real engagement and negotiation between the parties had still not happened. Nobody could say with confidence that a deal would be achieved by Easter. Or if it would be reached at all.

One thing was clear in terms of the structure of the talks. From now on, only bilateral meetings (or occasionally trilaterals or larger informal groupings) would offer any prospect for moving things forward. Formal collective meetings enabled parties to play to the gallery and to avoid serious engagement. Whatever limited value such gatherings might have had in the past, they had exhausted their usefulness. The deals and trade-offs which were now urgently required would be done only in informal settings. It would also be necessary to create additional time for the talks, for example by extending working hours into the evenings. The current schedule of three days a week was far too leisurely.

We also considered a possible change of venue within Northern Ireland for the final week. However, with the UUP continuing to hold out against any move, and time running out anyway, the idea was dropped.

Access to the media was seen by many as a threat to the success of the talks at this stage. The Alliance Party suggested that all delegations observe a self-denying ordinance in relation to media briefing for the final couple of weeks; the chairmen might instead be authorised to make daily press comments on behalf of the participants. This suggestion was, however, blocked by the UUP.

The issue of the UUP's refusal to engage directly with Sinn Féin had been simmering for months. Sinn Féin had initially seemed more relaxed about the unionists' avoidance of direct engagement. They no doubt expected that, after a couple of weeks of this policy, realism and common sense would take over and exchanges, both at the table and outside, would quietly begin. I remember Gerry Adams on several occasions trying to lure David Trimble into inadvertent direct dialogue across the table. With the UUP stipulating that all remarks to them should be directed through the chair, Adams would begin with a cheery observation to the latter about some important point made by Trimble at an earlier meeting. He would then, in his enthusiasm about this point, lean across and make a direct overture to the UUP leader to get further elaboration. Trimble would stare grimly ahead, determined not to fall into this trap.

On one occasion, however, it happened that John Taylor was in the UUP seat. Adams went through the same motions, enthusing about a point made by Taylor the previous week and inviting him directly to expand on it. Taylor responded with a wink to the Sinn Féin leader, to the effect that no seduction of this kind was going to work with him either. At this point, the lights in the room suddenly went out. When they went back on five minutes later, Taylor was gone. It transpired later that the generator in Castle Buildings had broken down. But, for a brief and surreal moment, the coincidence of timing suggested to the more conspiratorially minded among us that someone in Glengall Street (the UUP's headquarters) had decided on desperate measures to stave off a direct exchange between Taylor and Adams.

As the weeks went by, however, such levity as there was in Sinn Féin's initial reaction to the UUP policy disappeared. Adams and McGuinness became increasingly irritated and frustrated by what they saw as the UUP's refusal to respect the electoral mandate Sinn Féin had received. McGuinness, in particular, made many aggrieved interventions on this point. And the other parties, seeing the effect which this tension was having on the chances of making progress, sided increasingly with Sinn Féin. The Irish and British Governments, needless to say, regarded the UUP's position as deeply unhelpful. Bertie Ahern and Tony Blair pressed the UUP leader constantly to reverse it – but to no avail.

On one occasion, with Taylor in the room, McGuinness ascribed internment and other tribulations to representatives of old-style unionism such as the UUP deputy leader. He went on to suggest that Taylor had had a personal involvement in selecting individuals for internment, including himself. In what was described later as 'almost direct engagement' with Sinn Féin, Taylor retorted that he had no executive responsibility for internment. The mood lightened subsequently when McGuinness told the meeting (to reactions of amused incredulity and loud guffaws) that he had not wished to cause any trouble with his remarks.

In the final phase of the talks, there was a slight thawing in the atmosphere between the two parties. After Sinn Féin's return to the talks on 23 March, the odd bantering reference would be made by John Taylor to 'Gerry' or 'Martin', the use of first names a mild departure from the frosty distance previously observed. Reg

Empey, we understood, had some casual corridor contact with Sinn Féin. David Trimble, rather than ruling it out altogether, would begin to attach conditions to direct engagement; it would happen, he suggested, whenever Sinn Féin decided to accept the principle of consent. The UUP appeared to be accepting that direct contact, though unpalatable in the short term, could not be postponed indefinitely. However, they managed to avoid it up to, and including, the moment of agreement on Good Friday itself.

Meanwhile, meeting in the Liaison Group on 20 March, Irish and British officials agreed that a final deal was unlikely to be reached until the last three days or so of the negotiations. Both teams felt that something was needed to provide structure and momentum over the coming period. Dermot Gallagher and I suggested that the two Governments might table over the next few days a short list of remaining key issues as the focus for intensive bilateral meetings. This was agreed.

Mitchell had told us earlier that, in his view, there would be no settlement unless the two Governments came forward with a single agreed draft of that settlement. While he himself could table the draft, it would have to come from the two Governments. We shared his view. The British team still resisted it, however, as they feared the impact this would have on the unionists. Dermot Gallagher pointed out that everyone knew that the two Governments would ultimately produce a text, however much we might try to disguise this. What came in via Mitchell would not have to break significant new ground; and there could be progressive refining of the draft in the light of intensive consultations with the parties. But a common draft from the two Governments would have to be put on the table as the basis for the final deal.

This of course is what ultimately transpired; this is how the Good Friday Agreement came into being. Within a few days, and under some pressure from Mitchell also, the British agreed that a single overall draft from the two Governments was the only way forward.

At a Plenary on 24 March which reviewed the state of the negotiations, Mitchell secured agreement to a timetable for the following week which allocated five days and evenings to the talks and 'as much time as would be required' in the subsequent week leading up to Thursday 9 April.

The UUP had sought this 'review Plenary' to air their concerns on decommissioning. The tone of the exchanges on this issue was becoming increasingly rancorous. We saw a risk, indeed, that it could poison the negotiating atmosphere over the remaining days, to the point of jeopardising progress in all other areas of the talks.

During the Plenary, Paul Murphy reiterated the standard British view of decommissioning as an 'indispensable part of the process' and noted that there would be a meeting the following day of the liaison sub-committee on this subject. When David Trimble asked Mo Mowlam whether she had anything to add to this presentation, she replied with a curt negative. Trimble responded by seeking an adjournment of the Plenary for the Secretary of State to reconsider her position. When the meeting resumed in the evening, Mowlam reiterated Murphy's presentation, emphasising her view that decommissioning should commence right away. Jeffrey Donaldson, professing to be troubled by her remarks, said that the UUP would not allow the decommissioning issue to be swept under the carpet any longer and sought a further Plenary in which to deliver a response. With some reluctance, Mitchell agreed to schedule a further such session for 30 March.

At a meeting afterwards with David Andrews, Liz O'Donnell and the chairmen, Mo Mowlam emphasised that neither she nor Tony Blair would be in a position to meet the UUP's concerns on this subject. Nor, of course, were we. There was no scope for the Governments to change, or advance on, the position we had long taken jointly on this issue.

We heard a suggestion from David Ervine that what the UUP were aiming for, specifically, was an agreement that parties linked to paramilitary organisations would be denied office in the Assembly unless their associates had begun to decommission weapons. This speculation later proved well founded.

On 25 March, Mitchell told David Cooney and a British colleague that the parties, with whom he had just completed a round of consultations, had urged him to bring forward a single comprehensive draft of the agreement. He wanted to do this by 1 April. He therefore needed the two Governments to give him an agreed draft by 30 March.

Unfortunately, the work under way between the two Governments in recent weeks was nowhere near completion. Agreement was eluding us in some of the most important and sensitive areas. While undertaking to relay his request back, Cooney and his colleague told the Senator it was highly unlikely that the two Governments would be able to reach agreement on each and every aspect of a draft settlement by 30 March. Mitchell said he was not too bothered as long as the number of points of continuing difference remained manageable. He would have no difficulty, in fact, if a joint draft were to contain alternative options on key points.

Cooney suggested that, even if we were able to meet his deadline of 30 March, the Governments would need to be able to come back subsequently with amendments arising from further discussion between them and contacts with the parties. He also mentioned a concern we had about the draft being tabled too soon. As it would inevitably be leaked as soon as it was tabled, and would be attacked immediately by enemies of the process, it would be better to keep to a minimum the interval between its appearance and the 9 April deadline. Mitchell was open to all of this and accepted that the arrangements would have to be fine-tuned with ministers in the following week.

The British colleague tried out again his Government's alternative approach, preferred by the unionists, under which the chairs of the three Strands would table individual papers on key issues. But Mitchell was having none of this. The parties had made it clear to him that they would not compromise on key issues in isolation. Agreement on such issues could be reached only on the basis of seeing the whole package and assessing its balances and trade-offs.

It emerged that Mitchell had not yet been able to consult the UUP leader on his plan to table a single draft agreement. When he did so a few days later, Trimble did not object but suggested that the draft might be discussed individually with the parties before it was formally tabled. Mitchell took this suggestion on board.

Generally, Mitchell was not optimistic from his contacts that agreement would in fact be achieved by 9 April. While the parties had all pledged their determination to reach agreement by then, they had also made it clear that there were still enormous differences between them on the key issues. Some British officials liked to think that an outline agreement might be achievable by Easter and that the details could be filled in afterwards. We were doubtful, however, that it would be possible to get an agreement without nailing down as part of this the detail on the key issues.

19

TEN DAYS TO GO

The week beginning Monday 30 March 1998 arrived. We were now into the final 10 days or so. The pressure on all delegations was mounting perceptibly and tension was rising. The two Governments had been working flat out behind the scenes on the joint draft sought by Mitchell. But there were still sizeable gaps between us on crucial aspects.

Mitchell was worried when we told him that our agreed draft would not be available before Thursday 2 April. He feared a negative reaction from the parties if, allowing time for himself to review the document, they were not to receive it until Friday. He was also worried about the public reaction to yet another week of low-key bilaterals, given the widespread assumption that there would be a marked change of gear in the negotiations as we entered the last 10 days.

To give focus and structure to the week, he circulated on 30 March a list of 'key issues' (a draft of which the two Governments had already prepared). He proposed that the parties engage in discussions on this list, bilaterally or multilaterally. Their discussions would help him as he finalised the draft agreement they had asked him to bring forward.

Mitchell told the parties that he planned to give them this draft by the end of the week. It would be based heavily on a joint paper which the two Governments hoped to give him by Thursday morning. His plan was to circulate the draft on Friday morning; to meet the parties on Saturday, following their own internal consultations; and to table the draft in final form on Monday 6 April. That would mean three days of intensive negotiations running up to 9 April.

This timetable was significantly disrupted, however. The key difficulty was that the two Governments needed a lot more time to reach agreement on the Strand Two section.

This was the most difficult and challenging part of the entire negotiations. It required sustained engagement at Head of Government level. While the British Government had no strong interests of their own here, they were zealous in their protection of unionist interests. The line which Blair took in his conversations with Ahern was that he would be broadly content with whatever we and the unionists managed to agree on the North/South arrangements. This professed neutrality, however, was less obvious in our negotiations with the British at official level.

For the Irish Government, the stakes were, of course, very high. We needed North/South arrangements which would be sufficiently meaningful and robust to ensure nationalist support for the agreement as a whole, in particular in a referendum context. The North/South Council and related implementation bodies would have to have a legal status which placed them beyond the control of the anticipated Assembly (and the all too predictable efforts by a unionist majority there to undermine the new structures). The post-Sunningdale experience had taught us that this time we would have to have the structures anchored in Westminster legislation. The British Government, however, were concerned first and foremost to ensure unionist support for the agreement. They were therefore susceptible to the UUP case that the Assembly would have to have some sort of role in relation to the establishment of these structures.

Various drafts on the North/South arrangements were exchanged between Irish and British officials in the last week of March. On 1 April, with the Taoiseach and the Prime Minister due to meet later that day on this issue, Paddy Teahon wrote to John Holmes to lay out our main concerns. We could not accept an approach involving a departure from the substance the two Governments had agreed in the Framework Document. That document had spelled out that there would have to be an explicit legislative basis for the North/South Council in both sovereign Parliaments. The functions for the Council and for the implementation bodies should be clearly set out in such legislation from the outset, as also agreed in the Framework Document. While we had no difficulty describing the institutional arrangements in the three Strands as all operating within the context of the 'totality of relationships' within these islands (a concept that we knew the unionists valued), we did not see any one of the three operating within the context of another. The Council, in other words, had to be independent and could not be subservient to the East/West arrangements.

To emphasise our expectation that the North/South structures would tackle issues of real substance, Teahon attached to his letter a list covering 17 areas in which we envisaged new implementation bodies performing an 'executive' function. There were three others in which existing implementation bodies could perform this function; and there were eight which would be appropriate for separate, though coordinated, implementation arrangments in each jurisdiction. A further list proposed some 40 areas for 'harmonisation' work under the Council.

It was against this background of increasingly difficult engagement over the detail of the North/South structures that Bertie Ahern travelled to London on 1 April.

He was to attend a two-day conference of European and Asian Heads of Government which Tony Blair was hosting. There was an original plan for a formal meeting that evening between the Taoiseach and the Prime Minister and speaking points were prepared for Ahern's use there. In the event, this did not take place because of the Prime Minister's commitments as summit host. However, in between Blair's schedule and a succession of lunches and dinners linked to the summit, the two leaders managed to have a series of exchanges on the Strand Two issues. A key 40-minute meeting took place after dinner at 10.30 p.m. on 2 April. In total, the two leaders met for three to four hours over the couple of days. They also passed notes to each other on developments in between.

Interviewed in Dublin en route to London, the Taoiseach did not disguise the importance he attached to a good Strand Two outcome. As matters stood, he said, there were large disagreements between the two Governments which could not be cloaked. What was in the Framework Document would have to stand. He did not know if the differences between the two Governments could be overcome.

Ahern was alerting Blair to an issue that was of critical importance for us. We had to have Strand Two structures on the basis set out in the Framework Document. David Andrews was warning Mo Mowlam at the same time in Belfast that, if the two Governments resiled in any way from what they had agreed in the Framework Document, they would lose both the SDLP and Sinn Féin. Ahern knew this to be the case, having talked to the leaders of both parties ahead of his visit to London.

There was also, however, a tactical consideration. The Taoiseach wanted to set the bar high on Strand Two so that, if concessions had to be made eventually in the interests of an emerging agreement, we could do so from a position in which our key requirements had been met and we had some room for manoeuvre. We needed to establish a base from which, when the time came, we could row back slightly.

Supplementing Ahern's various conversations with Blair, the accompanying Irish officials, led by Paddy Teahon and Dermot Gallagher, followed up with a British Government team led by John Holmes and Bill Jeffrey (who would be taking over shortly from Quentin Thomas at the NIO). The work went on throughout Thursday and Friday. The officials met more or less continuously in Downing Street, working through successive drafts of the Strand Two section.

The British team proposed various dilutions of the Framework Document language to make the section more palatable for unionists. Provided the core substance remained intact, we were willing to look at some minor presentational adjustments. We were ready, for example, to substitute softer formulations for the 'executive', 'harmonising' and 'consultative' functions planned for the North/South Council (language which had been drawn from the Sunningdale Agreement).

Both sides envisaged that annexes to the agreement now in prospect would list policy areas in which the Council would exercise functions. We expected, therefore, that such annexes would be attached to the overall draft which Mitchell would shortly circulate.

Overall, we wanted, on the one hand, to give nationalists clear-cut messages about how the new North/South structures would operate and what kind of policy areas they would address. But, on the other, we recognised that a shift away from Sunningdale terminology might make it easier to get unionist buy-in. Much would hinge on getting the balance right between these competing demands over the coming days.

20

THE JIGSAW GETS ASSEMBLED

I n parallel with the work being done in London, the Strand Two issues were also at the top of the talks agenda in Belfast that week. Meeting the UUP on Thursday 2 April, David Andrews and Liz O'Donnell explained in detail our thinking as to how the North/ South Council would operate. David Trimble and Reg Empey were concerned that we might be envisaging a formal transfer of powers from the Oireachtas to the Council. Andrews made it clear that this was not the plan; rather, we envisaged the Northern and Southern representatives bringing with them the functions conferred on them by their respective legislatures. Our representatives would be authorised by the Oireachtas to exercise their current functions on the Council, just as they did, for example, in the EU context. The UUP reacted positively to this.

David Ervine told our ministers that, while the PUP recognised the practical value of implementation bodies and could agree to the establishment of a number of them, they questioned the need for any advance designation of functions. Like the UUP, they sought reassurances that, in the event of the Assembly being prorogued, the implementation bodies would cease to operate. Gary McMichael and his UDP colleagues, for their part, wanted these bodies to be accountable directly to the Assembly and the Oireachtas.

During the week, work was continuing at official level between the two Governments, both in Belfast and London, on the remaining sections of the draft overall agreement. These were, in particular, the sections dealing with constitutional issues, rights and equality, the British–Irish Council, policing, security, prisoners, the Irish language, and validation, implementation and review of the agreement. On most issues, the Irish side deliberately offered more extensive texts, which meant that in practice the two sides negotiated off the Irish draft. We were also, not surprisingly, the more ambitious of the two sides, pressing for language that would commit to deep policy reforms and go far beyond mere reiteration of the status quo.

On policing reform, regularly described by Seamus Mallon as central to the prospects for reaching any agreement, both Governments envisaged that an independent commission would be set up to make recommendations and report by the summer of 1999. There were, however, differences over the exact nature of this commission, how ambitious its remit should be and whether the future Assembly would have a role in relation to the implementation of its recommendations.

With unionist anxiety to protect the RUC growing, the British and the UUP favoured a Royal Commission with low-key terms of reference which would not explicitly flag the prospect of fundamental change.

We, the SDLP and Sinn Féin preferred a more clearly independent body, with an international dimension, which would bring forward proposals for a new policing service and serious reform of policing and not merely review current arrangements.

At the end of the day, our vision largely prevailed. Agreed terms of reference for what would eventually become the Patten

Commission were attached to the Good Friday Agreement. Securing agreement on these was one of the more arduous battlegrounds in the final days.

On criminal justice in Northern Ireland, the British Government would initially agree only to a review and not to the establishment of a commission on this subject. We brought SDLP concerns more squarely into this debate, however, and in due course the two Governments agreed that there would be an independent review of criminal justice that would report by the autumn of 1999. It would have agreed terms of reference, which would be attached to the agreement.

Another piece of text looked forward to the 'normalisation' of security arrangements in a peaceful context based on the new agreement. It spelled out a reduction in the security presence in Northern Ireland to peacetime levels, the removal of security installations, the removal of emergency powers and 'other measures appropriate to, and compatible with, a normal peaceful society'.

A further section dealt with rights, safeguards and equality of opportunity (a theme we had managed to re-insert). The British Government would complete its incorporation of the European Convention on Human Rights into Northern Ireland law. A new Human Rights Commission would be established in Northern Ireland. To give statutory force to principles such as 'parity of esteem', this Commission would be asked to advise on the scope for a Bill of Rights for Northern Ireland which would add to the ECHR in recognition of Northern Ireland's particular circumstances.

The Irish Government, for its part, would establish a Human Rights Commission with a remit equivalent to the Northern one and would take various steps to strengthen human rights protection in its jurisdiction. (While the case for incorporation of the ECHR was much weaker in our case, in the finalised agreement we said we would be willing to examine this question further.) There would also be a joint North/South committee which would bring together representatives of the two Commissions to consider human rights issues on the island as a whole, including a possible charter for the protection of fundamental rights of everyone living on the island. (This responded to calls from various parties for an all-Ireland human rights body and an all-Ireland charter of this kind, as proposed in the Framework Document.)

There would also be a statutory obligation on all public authorities in Northern Ireland to promote equality of opportunity and a new Equality Commission for Northern Ireland. (Sinn Féin had pressed for a dedicated Department of Equality and in the finalised agreement this would be flagged as a possibility.) In addition, support was pledged for organisations working on reconciliation (and, in the final agreement, for victims of violence as well).

A draft on economic, social and cultural issues emphasised issues such as social inclusion, employment equality, support for the Irish language and the need to use symbols and emblems in ways which promoted mutual respect rather than division.

There was to be a short introductory Declaration. (Rory Montgomery, who was asked to produce a draft, did so within half an hour and agreement was reached by both sides on this, with slight changes, quite quickly.) A further section would set out the arrangements for validation, implementation and review of the agreement (the planned referendums, follow-up legislation and the various arrangements for remedial action if any problems arose in the operation of the agreement).

As all of this drafting work proceeded, we had intensive contact with the SDLP and Sinn Féin while the British stayed close to the UUP. The Irish Government team in Belfast also touched base continually with the NIWC, the PUP, the UDP, NI Labour and Alliance. Gradually, agreement was reached on most of these issues (though policing remained difficult).

The Strand Two text, however, was missing from the jigsaw. And it was recognised that Strands One and Three could not be completed until a deal was reached on Strand Two.

In London, broad agreement began to emerge between the two Government teams over Thursday and Friday on how the North/ South structures would operate. Receiving proposals for new language from their officials, Ahern and Blair were able to sign off on most of the Strand Two section during Friday. However, a number of points remained unresolved.

The two leaders recognised that they were not going to be able to get a completed Strand Two text to George Mitchell, as the latter had hoped, by that evening. They were also influenced by a comment Mitchell had made to them earlier: knowing in broad terms the direction of the conversations in London, he had suggested that, if issued in those terms, the text would face UUP rejection. Foreseeing a weekend of possible unionist denunciation of the entire draft when they saw the Strand Two section, Ahern and Blair preferred to take a little longer to finalise that section.

The Senator had originally hoped to have the entire draft from the Governments by the morning of Thursday 2 April. We stayed in continuous contact with him and his staff as that deadline was missed and anxiety levels rose. At 1 p.m. on Thursday the two Government teams passed to him four sections which had been agreed up to then. More followed later.

The Senator told us that, when presenting the overall draft to the parties (on Friday morning as he still hoped), he would be drawing attention to any areas of continuing disagreement between the Governments. This caused dismay on the British side, where there had been a fond – if somewhat naïve – hope that the two Governments' authorship of the draft would remain hidden. We took a more realistic view: the parties already knew that the text to be presented by George Mitchell would only nominally be his and would in fact have been negotiated word for word between the two Governments. The Senator might, of course, add some editorial refinements to the draft. That would be a matter for his own discretion. In the event, he did not amend it.

I remember much impatience and unease on Mitchell's part throughout Friday as he waited for good news from London but saw his schedule coming under significant threat. He was determined to circulate the draft before the day was out. My sense was of a slight disconnect between his view of Friday evening as an absolute deadline for circulation, with the talks in serious jeopardy if this were not respected, and the views of the Taoiseach and the Prime Minister, who felt they had to get Strand Two right, no matter how long this took, and did not consider the Friday timing to be crucial.

In Belfast, we found ourselves dealing not only with a frustrated Mitchell but also with parties who were becoming increasingly edgy, all by now aware of a serious delay in London and unsure what this might mean for the process.

Around 6.30 p.m., the Taoiseach and the Prime Minister phoned Mitchell. They reported that good progress had been made on the Strand Two text, but that work had not yet concluded. They were close to agreement but needed more time; the weekend should suffice. They asked, therefore, that the overall draft should be issued that evening but without a Strand Two section.

Mitchell was, by his own account, stunned at this development. He consulted with his fellow chairmen and then with the two Government teams in Belfast and some of the parties. He was initially sympathetic to SDLP representations that, if there was to be no Strand Two section in the draft he circulated, there should be no Strand One section either. We in turn suggested, and he agreed, that material on Strand Three variants which was to be included should also be held back. However, when the UDP asked that no paper of any description be issued that evening (on the basis that a holistic approach was required across the full agenda of the negotiations), Mitchell decided to go with that suggestion. The other parties also agreed with this approach.

We suggested to Mitchell that it would be in the ultimate interests of the negotiations if, in presenting his decision to the parties, he could avoid blaming the Governments directly for the delay. He agreed readily to this. In a meeting which finally took place at 9.30 that evening, he told the parties that he was unable to give them a complete paper, as scheduled. Emphasising the complexity of the issues under discussion, he took personal responsibility for the failure to proceed as planned. He suggested, however, that, with a little more time to prepare the draft, it might be possible to get closer to a final document. The chairmen would work hard over the weekend to advance matters and he asked the parties to remain on stand-by in this connection.

Mitchell then rang Ahern and Blair to say he had decided to delay the overall draft. They accepted his decision. He asked for the Strand Two section to be provided to him by Sunday evening, so that he could circulate the complete draft on Monday morning, and this was agreed. Mitchell also briefed the media on developments, playing down the significance of 'our' failure to meet this deadline, hoping to produce the full draft within days and insisting that the talks remained very much on target for a potential agreement by the following Thursday (9 April). That he was ready to present himself as responsible for the delay, in the interests of achieving that agreement, spoke to Mitchell's innate statesmanship and sense of obligation to the process.

Whether we would in fact reach agreement by Thursday, however, remained very much in the balance.

THE MITCHELL DRAFT

21

The Taoiseach flew back from London to Dublin on Saturday afternoon. He told the media on his arrival that there were 'potentially irreconcilable difficulties' with the British on North/South structures. He added that he had no intention of accepting mere 'chat shows' (Strand Two arrangements without executive powers).

He talked on the phone that evening to John Hume and Seamus Mallon. On the following day, the two SDLP leaders came to Dublin for a meeting with him in the Sycamore Room at Government Buildings. They urged him not to disappoint them on Strand Two. The Taoiseach promised them that he would not conclude his negotiations with Tony Blair on that subject without ensuring that the SDLP was happy with the outcome.

While his SDLP visitors were there, Ahern received news that his 87-year-old mother, Julia, had been taken ill with a heart attack. She was rushed to the Mater Hospital but did not regain consciousness. Her death around six o'clock on Monday morning was a devastating personal blow for the Taoiseach. Still reeling from the shock, he had to continue with preparations for what was likely to be the most momentous week of his political life.

Over that weekend, Irish and British officials worked to resolve the points still at issue in the Strand Two text. The main one was how to describe the relationship between the implementation bodies and the Council. This work was mainly done by phone between Paddy Teahon and John Holmes, though I also had some exchanges with my British colleague in the Secretariat.

By Sunday afternoon, an agreed text was ready for forwarding to Mitchell. The British view, Teahon sensed from Holmes, was that difficulties with the unionists would be inevitable. They recognised, however, that Strand Two was very important for the Irish Government and nationalists, that the detailed functions would have to be negotiated anyway between ourselves and the unionists, and that the British Government ultimately could not stand in the way of the language we needed.

We felt our key requirements had been satisfied in the work done over the previous few days. The British had moved from the fairly minimalist approach they had taken in their early drafts and there was now better consistency with the Framework Document.

During the London negotiations, little detailed attention had been paid to the question of how many, and which, policy areas would be designated from the outset for assignment to implementation bodies. This was a matter which in any event required extensive consultation and technical examination within each Government system. The teams in London did, however, look briefly at possible presentational improvements from a unionist perspective.

In Dublin and Belfast, work on defining the areas was under way between other sets of officials. Wally Kirwan of the Department of the Taoiseach was leading for us and David Lavery of the NIO was his main British Government interlocutor.

In the Framework Document, the Irish and British Governments had agreed to put proposals to the Northern Ireland parties for areas which might be designated from the outset. 'By way of illustration', these proposals would include, at the executive level, well-defined functions from within four broad categories. These were (1) sectors involving 'a natural or physical all-Ireland framework'; (2) European Community programmes and initiatives; (3) marketing and promotion activities abroad; and (4) culture and heritage.

Again illustratively, the Governments would make proposals, at the harmonising level, for functions from within 10 categories. These covered aspects of agriculture and fisheries, industrial development, transport, energy and so on. The document went on to give examples of these specific aspects and added that the Governments also expected a wide range of functions to be designated at the consultative level.

Building on this, the Heads of Agreement paper in January – which unionists had enthusiastically embraced – had accepted that implementation bodies would be required in relation to policies agreed by the North/South Council 'in meaningful areas and at an all-island level'. There was clearly a need, therefore, to identify what such areas might be and to draw up lists of options in the different categories.

The Irish Government had taken decisions accordingly and Wally Kirwan had led a process of interdepartmental consultation, in conjunction with the Department of Foreign Affairs. This culminated in a broad and ambitious set of proposals for policy areas across the full spectrum of Government responsibility which would merit either 'executive' or 'harmonising' treatment. Similar preparatory work was done by the six Northern Ireland departments.

While the London negotiations were in progress, Kirwan was in contact with Lavery to talk through the options and to see what kind of joint proposals might be contemplated. Their discussions continued throughout the weekend. We had already, of course, signalled our thinking in the lists attached to Paddy Teahon's letter. We also flagged to the British that we would be looking for 10 implementation bodies, operating in significant areas.

Irish officials went on Sunday to Belfast to meet the SDLP, Sinn Féin and other delegations in Castle Buildings. We briefed them on the latest developments and discussed tactics for the coming week.

Strand One would clearly be a major priority. The SDLP and Alliance told us that, from their most recent contacts with the UUP, they saw signs of the gap narrowing in that Strand and potential for eventual agreement there. The big issues remaining were the SDLP's insistence on a 'sufficient consensus' provision for decision-taking and on the future Executive operating on the basis of collective responsibility.

Sinn Féin, however, retained fundamental reservations about the legitimacy of any Assembly in Northern Ireland and had accordingly not moved from the sidelines of the Strand One debate.

On Friday evening, David Andrews, Liz O'Donnell and their officials had had a trilateral meeting in Castle Buildings with Sinn Féin and the SDLP. We went through Sinn Féin's concerns on each draft in detail. Gerry Adams indicated his party's broad satisfaction with the way in which the constitutional and North/South parts of the agreement were coming along. However, he hoped for more ambitious and detailed language on policing, prisoners, rights, equality and the Irish language.

As for the other parties, much would clearly depend on the attitude of the UUP over the coming days. Our sense, from our encounters with them during the week, was that the UUP were now fully engaged and seeking to do a deal. It remained to be seen, however, whether they would be up to the compromises needed to make this happen.

The first moment of truth would come with the appearance of the draft overall agreement, which Senator Mitchell had promised for Monday morning.

That Sunday evening, Irish and British officials met Mitchell in Belfast to hand over the completed Strand Two text. The Senator has described elsewhere his dismay on seeing this text. As he read through it, he judged that Trimble would object to the independence envisaged for the implementation bodies and to the planned listing of specific areas for North/South cooperation.

The officials asked him not to make any changes to this text, which had been agreed by the Taoiseach and the Prime Minister with great care and after several days of intensive negotiation. This was a key point for us, and Mitchell agreed. Secondly – and this was a point of greater importance to the British side than to us – we wanted him once again to take public ownership of the text, presenting it as the chairmen's own rather than as the work of the Taoiseach and the Prime Minister. Mitchell, though a little uneasy because all at the talks knew of the two Heads of Governments' intensive involvement in recent days, also agreed to this.

Early on the following morning (Monday 6 April), the British copied the text to Trimble. This had a predictable consequence: the UUP leader demanded changes of various kinds and the British came back to us looking for these. This meant that Mitchell's hopes of tabling the overall draft early in the day were dashed.

Having heard Trimble's initial reaction, Blair was sufficiently uneasy that he contemplated going over to Belfast straight away. He felt he would need to be physically present in Belfast to calm down the UUP leader and rescue the prospects for an agreement in which he and Ahern had already invested so much.

At his request, John Holmes asked Paddy Teahon, who was in Castle Buildings, to talk to Trimble about this. Teahon did so, conveying also a message of goodwill from the Taoiseach. In reply, Trimble on the one hand expressed appreciation for the Taoiseach's message (particularly in difficult personal circumstances) but, on the other, warned Teahon in the plainest terms about the damage he felt our ambitions in relation to the North/South bodies would do.

In the event, the Prime Minister decided against going to Belfast that day. The Taoiseach, for his part, was briefing the Opposition parties in Dublin that day and also bringing President Clinton up to speed on the latest developments.

Our British colleagues sought to reopen the agreement reached by the two leaders on Sunday and to get a role of some kind for the Assembly in relation to the establishment of the implementation bodies. We resisted this initially. A very careful balancing of unionist and nationalist interests had been achieved in the text, notably in the paragraphs on how the implementation bodies would be set up, and we were not prepared to see this disrupted.

All of this meant that the tabling of the draft had to be postponed. Another delaying factor was the work required on the annexes. The two Governments had to finalise their content, agreeing this with the parties. There was to be much back-and-forth with key delegations, in particular the UUP. A complication was that, with these discussions now in their final stages, there were more interlocutors on the Northern Ireland side: David Lavery was joined by wider and more senior representation from the Northern Ireland departments. On our side, Wally Kirwan was accompanied at different times by Tim O'Connor, Rory Montgomery and Ray Bassett, with Paddy Teahon and Dermot Gallagher also following these negotiations closely.

We had agreed that there would be three annexes. The first of these, Annex A, would list areas in which the Council would endeavour to reach agreement on the adoption of common policies. Annex B would list areas in which it would take decisions on action for implementation separately in each jurisdiction. And Annex C would list areas in which new bodies would be established to implement Council decisions on an all-island and cross-border basis.

Annex C was clearly going to be the most sensitive and significant of these. Nationalists would want to see implementation bodies in substantial and meaningful areas which combined practical logic with political resonance. The SDLP and Sinn Féin were not disguising their hopes, indeed expectations, that we would table a broadly based and ambitious set of proposals. We, for our part, were conscious that we would not achieve everything we wanted in the negotiations but that, for tactical reasons, it would be important to set the bar high from the outset.

The Irish Government team therefore proposed a set of 10 implementation bodies in the following areas: (1) trade promotion and indigenous company development; (2) tourism promotion, marketing and product development; (3) the management of EU programmes such as the INTERREG programme; (4) transport planning; (5) animal and plant health and food safety; (6) environmental protection; (7) promotion of the Irish language; (8) promotion of the arts; (9) science and technology; and (10) support for the voluntary and community sector. On a reserve list we had waterways management, marine research, forestry, inland fisheries, youth affairs and information policy.

These proposals were a distillation of the work process within the Irish Government system, which had begun provisionally the previous autumn and had come to a head with Government decisions in early March.

Our discussions with the Northern Ireland and British

colleagues on the annexes lasted for the entire day on Monday and were at times quite fractious. This was where the rubber was hitting the road. After a period of general and essentially non-committal exchanges between the two sides on what might be viable, the moment had arrived when the hard detail of the functions, and of what would be placed in one or other category, had to be settled. And, with Mitchell's deadline now only three days away, this had to be done under considerable time pressure.

We agreed eventually to reduce our Annex C list from ten to eight, though on the understanding that further options remained open between us. We agreed to transfer three areas into Annex B (animal and plant health, science and technology and voluntary/ community policy) and one into Annex A (food safety). However, waterways would be elevated from our reserve list into Annex C.

In most cases, the rationale for these changes was technical, some consideration coming to light which suggested that the area in question might be better handled in another way. There were, however, two areas that the unionists viewed warily: first, trade promotion and support for indigenous companies; and second, promotion of the Irish language. The UUP evidently feared that Northern business interests, on the one hand, and the unionist cultural identity, on the other, could suffer from closer North/ South cooperation under these headings. While we insisted on the retention of both areas in Annex C, it was clear that we could expect significant unionist resistance on these two fronts over the coming days.

In sum, the two Governments settled in the course of Monday what would appear in Annex C. And we also agreed on 25 areas to be listed in Annex A and 16 areas for Annex B.

Senator Mitchell agreed that these three annexes should be attached to the overall draft. The assumption made by both

Governments was that, if the lists were held back, there would be immediate demands from the parties to see them. A strategy of keeping them in reserve and releasing them at a later stage would have provoked suspicions and would probably not have worked.

During the day, unionist pressure was intensifying for the Assembly to be involved in some way in the establishment of the implementation bodies. From the beginning we had recognised that, while Westminster and the Oireachtas would give these bodies their broad legislative foundation, the granular technical detail required to get each of them up and running would have to be settled between the relevant departments in Ireland, Northern Ireland and the UK. We knew that a transitional period was likely before the new institutions were established and that some consultation of the Executive-in-waiting and the parties would be necessary during this period. So we recognised that there could be a practical case for giving the 'shadow' Assembly a carefully circumscribed role in preparing the detail of each body's remit. This was the starting point for what was to become a key compromise with unionist concerns which paved the way for eventual agreement in Strand Two.

There were deep divisions also over the potential for one institution to block another. Unionists feared a scenario in which the Assembly might be unable to function (through, for example, a nationalist boycott) but the implementation bodies would continue regardless. They were also worried at the possibility that the implementation bodies might come into existence before the Assembly was constituted. Conversely, nationalists needed an assurance that the Assembly would not be in a position to obstruct or delay the Council or the implementation bodies.

We addressed these dilemmas by inserting into the agreement's introductory Declaration a general indication that all the institutions covered under the agreement would be interlocking and interdependent. In practical terms, the Assembly and the Council would have to be interlocking, each tied to the other in order to promote maximum participation and to deter abstentionist tactics. We used the term 'mutual assured destruction' from nuclear warfare doctrine to describe an assumption that Sinn Féin would not block the Assembly if they knew that to do so would jeopardise the linked North/South arrangements; and that the unionists, vice versa, would not block the North/South Ministerial Council or implementation bodies lest that bring down the Assembly.

Throughout Monday we had been consulting closely with the British Government and the chairmen and their staff. We agreed together on a number of amendments to individual sections of the overall draft and also to the terms of a covering statement which the chairmen would issue with the draft. The Strand One section would necessarily be presented as a series of options (given how little progress the parties had made there pending a Strand Two agreement).

At last, late on Monday evening, the overall draft, annexes and chairmen's covering statement were ready and were circulated.

Mitchell called the parties to a brief Plenary at 12.30 a.m. He introduced what he presented as the chairmen's own draft agreement, while recognising that many parts of it were based on work done by the two Governments. It was, he maintained, primarily a synthesis of positions put forward by the participants themselves.

The Senator pressed delegations not to leak the draft to the media. Remarkably, for a process bedevilled by leaks for partisan advantage at every juncture, this was taken to heart by everyone. Over the next few days, there was plenty of comment on all sides about how the talks were going but the actual text we were negotiating was not leaked. There was a rumour, whether well founded or not, that the chairmen's staff had given the parties copies of the draft with telltale variants to help them to identify leakers.

It was at this meeting, as I recall, that George Mitchell put us on notice about why we had to take seriously the Holy Thursday deadline. He mentioned that he had a newly born son whom he had barely seen over the past few months because of the demands of these negotiations. He would be going back to New York for Easter to see his wife, Heather, and his son Andrew. And, he added in a polite but firm tone, he would not be coming back. He had made a significant personal sacrifice since the birth of his son; he owed it to his family to be with them from then on. I sensed that this warning, whether intended seriously or just as a tactic, struck home with delegates that night. Without the universally respected Mitchell in the chair, it would be extremely difficult to bring this process to a successful conclusion. It was, in a very real sense, now or never: agreement by midnight on Holy Thursday or not at all.

22

THE END GAME

I n the short term, however, we had a crisis on our hands.

As the morning of Tuesday 7 April dawned, the unionist reaction to the draft that Senator Mitchell had circulated was swift and unambiguous.

John Taylor said in an early-morning interview that he 'would not touch it with a forty-foot pole'. An irate David Trimble denounced the draft to the chairmen and the two Governments. Elements had slipped in, he maintained, which we would have known the UUP could not accept. In addition, various Strand Two points he had discussed with the Prime Minister over the weekend were missing. Attached to the draft, furthermore, were lengthy lists of areas for cross-border cooperation, over 60 in all.

Trimble told Tony Blair that he could not recommend the draft to the people he represented. He asked whether the two Governments would be prepared to consider radically different measures. Claiming (erroneously) that our Government had been unwilling to meet his party the previous day, he wanted an early assurance from Blair that we would be prepared to negotiate in good faith.

None of this came as a particular surprise. With the appearance of the Mitchell draft, as I will term it, we had reached the end game. There would, of course, be pain for each of the main players as they faced up to the difficult political compromises required of them in individual areas. In the interest of achieving an overall settlement, everyone would have to be willing to adjust their ambitions, trading compromise outcomes in one area against advances in others.

It was natural that some players would make last-minute efforts to deflect this pressure onto the Governments. In truth, the Mitchell draft contained nothing particularly new about the way in which the North/South Council and implementation bodies would be constituted or would operate. What it said on these issues had been well signposted both in the Heads of Agreement and in our Government's numerous bilateral meetings with the UUP ever since. While Trimble may have hoped to see clearer results from his intensive lobbying of the Prime Minister, the Strand Two content could not have come as any real surprise to him or his party.

The Achilles heel was, however, the presentational impact on unionism of the long lists of potential areas for North/South cooperation. The sudden appearance of these lists, spanning over 60 policy areas, had a deeply unsettling effect. A hasty perusal of them by unionist readers might have missed the distinctions between the three categories and created undue alarm. There would have been fears about the use to which the DUP and other opponents of the process, including internal UUP sceptics, could put these lists. I sensed that this, perhaps even more than concerns about the legal basis for North/South cooperation, lay behind the vehemence of Trimble's reaction. He seemed unnerved more by the scale of the annexes than by their actual substance.

In retrospect, this is an aspect to which both Governments should have paid more attention when finalising the document. These two issues, the legal basis for the North/South structures and the definition of functions, were being negotiated in isolation from each other. They were closely interrelated in terms of their likely impact on unionism and therefore on the prospects for a successful outcome to the talks. It would perhaps have been better if the two Governments had looked at both issues together holistically, as a single exercise, then assessed what the overall unionist reaction was likely to be and decided on a strategy for responding to this.

Publishing just Annex C on its own (the eight proposed implementation bodies) would have been easier to manage. While it was logical and coherent to provide the full picture (particularly as we envisaged potential additions to the list of implementation bodies, by agreement and over time), the problem was that the vast range of areas covered by all three annexes could be exploited by the DUP to claim that the new North/South arrangements would control virtually every aspect of life in Northern Ireland. It was, at heart, an issue of presentation rather than of substance; the small print would reveal that the 60 areas involved three quite different approaches, with only a handful earmarked for special implementation bodies. But the visual impression created by the appearance of three lengthy annexes together was unfortunate.

Trimble's complaints were echoed by John Alderdice, the Alliance leader, who wanted Annexes A and B to be deleted. Alderdice had asked the Prime Minister in a weekend phone call to come to Belfast with the Taoiseach for the final stages of the negotiations. He now called publicly on Blair to 'get here fast' if the process was to be saved. Trimble also favoured the Prime Minister coming.

Mitchell, who met Trimble on Tuesday morning, told us that he felt the UUP's reaction to the draft was partly tactical but largely serious. The party would not accept the Strand Two content in its present form, he believed. At lunchtime this was confirmed in a UUP press release.

In the afternoon, we had a meeting with a UUP delegation led by Jeffrey Donaldson. The tone of this meeting, somewhat against our expectations, was low-key and businesslike. The UUP press release had accused the Irish Government of bad faith; and afterwards Donaldson renewed these accusations at a media briefing. But, as was frequently the case with Donaldson, the meeting itself was entirely constructive.

We began with an exchange about efforts to arrange a meeting the previous day between the UUP and the Taoiseach. David Andrews explained that, because of Bertie Ahern's bereavement, it had not been possible to schedule a meeting. We had offered a morning meeting but that had not suited the UUP leader. Our delegation in Belfast remained, of course, continuously available to Trimble and his colleagues. (This was indeed the case; while I personally suffered from the disadvantage of association with the hated Maryfield Secretariat, all my colleagues on the Irish Government team had developed easy working relations with the UUP, above all Dermot Gallagher, who had been building up excellent personal contacts since the mid-seventies.)

Donaldson went through his party's difficulties with the Strand Two proposals. In particular, they could not accept an arrangement under which a North/South Ministerial Council would be established by legislation at Westminster and in the Oireachtas and would have a separate legal personality by virtue of this. They needed the Assembly to have a role in relation to the Council and to any implementation bodies. While they could contemplate common policies being adopted, decisions being taken and implementation bodies being established, those sitting on the Council would have to be accountable to the respective legislatures North and South. The Assembly, he added, must also be free to establish its own budgetary priorities; and in that context it might decide that it did not wish to prioritise some or all of the eight areas stipulated in Annex C.

Liz O'Donnell mentioned our political requirement for a number of implementation bodies to be specified up front in the agreement and in legislation. Donaldson replied that it all came down to trust; if unionists gave their word to do something, they would stand by that. We pointed to the risk that, even if the UUP abided by their word, an agreement they had entered into could be blocked in the Assembly by the DUP.

Donaldson proposed instead the idea of a work programme for the Council and was ready to explore this in detail. However, when we asked if this would be underpinned by a unionist commitment to establish a number of implementation bodies, he remained non-committal.

Consistent with the approach they had taken to Strand Two from the outset, the UUP team also wanted to see a connection made between the North/South Council and the British–Irish Council as well as reinforcement of the latter in a number of respects. As regards the proposed British–Irish Intergovernmental Conference, they objected to the Irish Government having a role in relation to non-devolved matters in Northern Ireland (as this would give us an involvement in areas such as rights and justice issues). And they were predictably unhappy, of course, with the proposal to give the Conference responsibility for reviewing the operation of the new agreement.

Another issue raised by Donaldson and his colleagues was the future of the Maryfield Secretariat. While accepting that there would be a practical need for a secretariat to support the new Conference, they saw no reason why a Northern Ireland location would be required for this if the new Conference was not going to be dealing exclusively with Northern Ireland issues. (Ken Maginnis commented, tongue in cheek, that it would not be desirable to give, say, the Irish community in Liverpool an impression of being second-class citizens by locating this secretariat in Northern Ireland.) Donaldson suggested that the new secretariat be located in London or Dublin. He went on to reiterate a long-standing UUP proposal for an Irish Consulate in Belfast (an idea which might commend itself from a unionist perspective but would be completely unacceptable to nationalists).

The Maryfield Secretariat had come up in a different context the previous week when John Alderdice warned our ministers that a North/South secretariat in a single permanent location – 'another Maryfield' – would be unacceptable to unionists. David Andrews and Liz O'Donnell underlined the practical arguments for a fixed-location North/South secretariat. (Later on, agreement was reached on Armagh as the location for this institution.)

In general terms, the UUP savaged the Mitchell draft, complaining that it went well beyond what the two Governments had agreed in the Heads of Agreement document. We pointed out that the draft addressed many issues of concern to unionists: amendment of Articles 2 and 3, incorporation of the consent principle, a British–Irish Council (reflecting the unionist proposal for a 'Council of the Isles') and, above all, replacement of the Anglo-Irish Agreement. We sensed, however, that Donaldson would remain an implacable opponent of what was proposed on Strand Two and would keep his leader under pressure on this subject.

We also had contact with the two loyalist parties. Although they closed ranks with the UUP in publicly criticising the Mitchell draft, our impression was that they were more willing to negotiate on it and were generally more relaxed about it.

John Alderdice told us that he considered the document to be fatally biased in Sinn Féin's direction. While he had no difficulty with implementation bodies per se, he feared that the detailed annexes would be exploited by Ian Paisley. Objecting to many other points in the draft, he said it had simply no hope of being saleable to the UUP.

In sharp contrast, the SDLP were entirely content with the draft, as were the NIWC and NI Labour. In a radio interview, Seamus Mallon said it should come as no surprise to David Trimble that the Strand Two elements had been written as they had been. The UUP leader had had constant meetings with Tony Blair over the past two years in which they had essentially been talking about the North/South relationship. Trimble had seen 'draft after draft', from both Governments, of the kind of proposals which had now been made in the Mitchell draft. So the professed surprise and shock were, he suggested, aimed primarily at getting leverage inside or outside the talks.

Sinn Féin's public response, for tactical reasons of their own, highlighted a range of shortcomings in the draft. They sent the chairmen and the two Governments a list of points of concern. This covered most sections of the draft: the constitutional provisions (repeal of the Act of Union was missing, the proposed changes to the Irish Constitution were problematic), Strand One institutions (they now favoured a Cabinet-style administration in Northern Ireland), Strand Two institutions (the functions envisaged for the implementation bodies were limited and inadequate), Strand Three institutions (the British–Irish Council was unnecessary, the two Governments' oversight role through the Intergovernmental Conference was very vague) and so on. They also criticised the language on rights, equality and justice, the Irish language, prisoners, decommissioning and other issues.

We had a long meeting with them on Tuesday evening to hear

their concerns. While recognising privately that the draft was a valuable achievement, they wished to see various provisions strengthened. They needed this, they told us, in order to mitigate the impact on the republican community of an agreement involving changes to Articles 2 and 3, an Assembly in the North and the continuation of partition. On prisoners, they had told our ministers the previous day of their dissatisfaction with the number and pace of releases envisaged by the British Government.

In short, in the course of Tuesday we came under sustained pressure from both ends of the political spectrum to revisit the Mitchell draft and make fundamental changes. The changes sought by both would, of course, cancel each other out to a significant extent. We knew that, if the two Governments were to achieve a comprehensive settlement capable of attracting popular endorsement North and South, this would depend on keeping the balance which had been struck across the various sets of interests.

We did, however, see some scope for presentational adjustment that, without disturbing basic substance or balance, would improve the chances of a deal. With our British colleagues, we began to explore formulations which might give the Assembly-in-waiting, and the Executive-in-waiting, a role in preparing the ground for the implementation bodies. We also considered ways in which the presentation of the annexed lists could be improved.

Meanwhile, with alarm signals reaching him from various quarters, Tony Blair was getting ready to fly to Belfast. The plan had been all along for him and Bertie Ahern to come to Castle Buildings for the finale of the talks, essentially to endorse an agreement already reached or to be there on the final day or so with an agreement clearly on the horizon. All going well, there would have been a more promising reaction to the draft agreement, and the main purpose of their visit would have been to lend moral support and nudge the participants across the finishing line. In the event, with the Mitchell draft generating a deep crisis (though one which was probably inevitable and ultimately salutary), the role of the two Heads of Government in coming to Belfast was to save the talks altogether.

They were to spend the best part of three days locked in intensive negotiations with the key players, with very little sleep, fresh air or sustenance (and, in Bertie Ahern's case, with the added strains of bereavement). Each, of course, was incurring significant political risk throughout this period. The longer they remained closeted in Castle Buildings, spending days there rather than hours and with little to show for their efforts, the greater would be the loss of political face and capital if they ultimately failed. It was a significant gamble.

Blair, who had been chairing a summit of European socialist leaders on Tuesday morning, decided by lunchtime that he should travel to Belfast. He was motivated in particular by his phone conversations with David Trimble. He could see that the talks were in crisis and required intervention by the two Heads of Government. He spoke to Mitchell, who agreed that they should come. He spoke several times to the Taoiseach, the original intention having been that both would arrive there together. However, given his bereavement and the impending funeral, there were question marks over when the Taoiseach would be available to travel. The initial plan was that he would travel up only after his mother's funeral on Wednesday.

Blair told Ahern that he sensed that the UUP leader wanted to do a deal but was apprehensive. Trimble had raised with him a series of points about the Mitchell draft: the problems created by the annexed lists, the need for the Assembly to have some degree of control over the North/South Council, queries about some of the Strand One provisions and his need to dilute the reference to support for the Irish language as well as to add some language to the decommissioning and policing sections which would be helpful from a unionist perspective. Blair felt the points raised were essentially presentational, though he recognised that some still had the capacity to be 'showstoppers'. Ahern said he was willing to look at the points to see whether we were 'in do-able territory or not'.

Blair indicated that he saw a need to stay close to Trimble over the coming days. The Taoiseach, in turn, knew the importance of his own presence in Belfast with the Prime Minister in order to demonstrate the unity of approach between the two Governments at this critical juncture.

23

THE TWO LEADERS ARRIVE

That afternoon, Tony Blair arrived in Belfast. Coming over on the plane, as Alastair Campbell, Blair's press secretary, has recorded, the Prime Minister went over the annexes in detail. He was a little irritated that the UUP were up in arms over lists which he and the Taoiseach had not themselves negotiated. Blair felt that Trimble had a point, however, in relation to the scale of the areas being proposed for cooperation.

On arrival, Blair went straight to Hillsborough Castle. Seamus Mallon would remark years later that the image of Blair's helicopter landing gave him the sense that, whatever might have happened in the talks hitherto, the end game had most definitely arrived.

Speaking to the media, Blair delivered what would become his infamous sound bite: 'A day like today is not a day for sound bites, we can leave those at home – but I feel the hand of history upon our shoulder with respect to this, I really do.'

David Trimble arrived to see him shortly afterwards. Blair took him for a stroll in the grounds. The UUP leader reiterated that his party could not do a deal on the basis of the Mitchell draft. The British Government team then spent a couple of hours going through the draft with Trimble to see what amendments might make it acceptable to the unionists.

Blair also rang the Taoiseach. Apologising for intruding on Ahern's bereavement, he asked him to come to Belfast the following morning as he saw a real risk of the talks collapsing. He also rang John Hume, who acknowledged the UUP's political difficulties but urged the Prime Minister not to let the unionists veto the agreement. Blair also had a visit from John Alderdice, who repeated the points he had made to us earlier. David Ervine gave the Prime Minister similar views.

Later on, Blair had a meeting with Senator Mitchell, who had had his own contacts with the UUP during the day and echoed what the Prime Minister's other visitors had said. Mitchell hoped that the two Governments would be ready to consider amendments to the Strand Two part of the draft. At our earlier meeting with him, he had thought of ringing the Taoiseach to make this point. Blair suggested that it would be good for the Taoiseach to hear directly on this from Mitchell.

That evening, Bertie Ahern was attending the removal of the remains of his mother, Julia, in Drumcondra. Afterwards, he went for a long walk on his own. His thoughts were divided between grieving for his mother and deciding on how to respond to the immediate challenges facing the negotiations in Belfast. Planning strategy for the next few days was in some ways therapeutic, he reflected later – a useful distraction from his personal loss.

The Taoiseach took a call from Paddy Teahon in Belfast, who told him of the UUP's unhappiness with the Mitchell draft, their demand for renegotiation of it and the risk that they might otherwise withdraw from the talks.

He then rang George Mitchell and they had a long phone conversation. (Mitchell would joke subsequently about the length of the street Ahern was walking up and down, given that he never seemed to leave it throughout their lengthy conversation; Griffith

Avenue in Drumcondra is in fact one of the longest avenues in Dublin and Ahern walked up and down both sides of it before their phone call ended.) They went through the entire draft circulated by Mitchell but particularly the Strand Two section. Mitchell asked the Taoiseach what was absolutely non-negotiable and what might be open to adjustment. He suggested finally that, if (despite the pressures of bereavement and the funeral) the Taoiseach were able to travel up to Belfast early the following morning and to show his readiness to negotiate with the UUP, 'we can settle this'.

Ahern had already decided that he would do this. He recognised that this was a make-or-break moment for the talks. He would travel up for breakfast with Blair and a meeting with the UUP and would then return to Dublin for his mother's funeral at noon. Mitchell has often spoken of his admiration for the political courage displayed by Ahern in challenging personal circumstances.

The Taoiseach was gambling that he would be able to modify what he had agreed with the Prime Minister in Strand Two without losing in the process the SDLP and Sinn Féin. He knew ultimately that 'everyone has to be a winner', a phrase he would use several times that week. We would get nowhere unless all key players had ownership of the agreement and felt that their core needs had been accommodated. (A telling phrase used once by Mark Durkan was that the agreement would be 'like a hologram where hopefully everyone will see their own image when they look at it'.) Everyone had to feel that they had made significant gains in the agreement and that these outweighed the concessions made. It is arguable, from this perspective, that the unionist furore over the Mitchell draft actually brought us closer to the Good Friday Agreement: the changes we made subsequently to the Strand Two section could be represented as UUP victories which made it easier to accept an agreement that in several other respects was problematic for unionists.

Early on Wednesday morning, the Taoiseach arrived at City Airport. I collected him with his accompanying officials and we transferred by helicopter to Hillsborough Castle for an hour-long breakfast with Blair beginning at 7 a.m.

The Prime Minister, who had already been talking to Trimble that morning, said at the outset that he saw no prospect of the UUP, the Alliance Party or the loyalist parties agreeing to the Mitchell draft in its present form. What Blair found maddening was that there did not seem to be fundamental disagreement on substance. The two Governments had to decide whether the situation was salvageable. It seemed that publication of the annexed lists had taken the UUP over the brink. The previous night, Trimble had given the British Government team a range of changes he was seeking. He had been calm and matter-of-fact in his presentation and the Prime Minister did not think he was bluffing. He was about to walk, Blair believed. And, if the talks were going to break down on these issues, Trimble, in Blair's view, would not be blamed. Alderdice, for one, would say that the UUP leader was not being unreasonable. We would have to look at how we might alter the presentation in Strand Two without any fundamental change of substance.

Blair went on to suggest that we withdraw Annexes A and B and present their substance in a different fashion. (He observed in passing that the present lists were, if anything, limiting: the North/ South Ministerial Council should be able to adopt common actions, and so on, on anything it wanted.) It would also be desirable to explain more clearly what we were saying about implementation bodies. There were a host of other problems, he continued, but they were probably negotiable. Without movement on these two points, the two Governments would probably have to begin to work out an exit strategy.

The Taoiseach acknowledged the intensive work being done to try to keep things together. A lot of problems had been signalled by the UUP, Alliance and others. If the two Governments were to look at these, we would need to consider them in their totality and see whether solutions could be found which would attract Trimble's support without jeopardising the support of others. A balanced approach to all suggestions for amendments was essential. Pre-empting any possible British suggestion to this effect, he went on to reject any notion of Senator Mitchell tabling a new draft. (Reg Empey of the UUP, though not David Trimble, would later ask for this.)

Recalling the history of unionist efforts to thwart cross-border bodies over 75 years, from the twenties to the Sunningdale Agreement and its aftermath, Ahern said it seemed that the unionists were once again trying to frustrate these bodies. The reason we were insisting on a North/South Council with implementation bodies was that throughout that period Northern nationalists had had their rights systematically trampled on by unionists – to the point where Westminster had had to take power back from the latter. If the UUP was not prepared to contemplate arrangements of substance in Strand Two, it would indeed be best to start working out an exit strategy. We were, after all, proposing to do something historic in relation to Articles 2 and 3. We could only do this in return for substantial North/South cooperation.

Blair said he honestly believed that Trimble *was* prepared to agree to substantial North/South bodies. If that was the case, Ahern replied, we could look at all the proposed amendments – doing so collectively, not piecemeal – and see whether we could work out meaningful solutions. He warned, however, that this would not be easy; he would look at presentational issues but could not move on core substance.

Teahon emphasised the need to boil things down to a handful of key points covering both nationalist and unionist concerns. We would hope, furthermore, for a firm guarantee from the UUP leader that he would support the agreement in exchange for any amendments made in the UUP's direction.

The conversation then turned to the idea of a preparatory role for the shadow Assembly in relation to the implementation bodies. The Taoiseach said he could contemplate an approach of this kind but only on the basis that there would be no Assembly vote to trigger the establishment of the bodies.

Blair suggested that the two Governments could agree that the bodies would be established, that they could come into existence without being subject to an Assembly veto but that the remit and constitution for each of them would be the subject of advance agreement with the shadow Assembly. Expecting that Trimble would ultimately have to be pushed into a deal in Strand One, he felt that this might be easier if some change were on offer in the Strand Two section of the Mitchell draft (even if this was more of presentation than of substance).

On constitutional issues, Blair mentioned Trimble's concerns in relation to Articles 2 and 3 and the terms of the amendments we might have in mind. David Byrne, who had accompanied the Taoiseach to Belfast that morning, reported his own sense from his recent meeting with UUP lawyers Peter King and Austin Morgan that, if the UUP were to get satisfaction on other matters, the precise terms of the constitutional amendments in our jurisdiction would not be an obstacle to agreement.

Evidently reflecting a point raised with him by Trimble, Blair asked if a reference to 'Northern Ireland' could be inserted in our proposed constitutional amendments. Did we have a fundamental problem with mentioning Northern Ireland in our Constitution? Ahern replied that there was no such reference at present and that we would indeed have a fundamental problem. He went on to re-emphasise the emotive significance of Articles 2 and 3, saying that nationalists would need something substantial by way of compensation if these were to be amended.

The Taoiseach and the Prime Minister also considered what might be done on prisoner releases. Blair indicated he was open to doing something imaginative. He would respond to the inevitable criticism from right-wing British tabloids by emphasising the historic deal now available and the need for a special approach in this context. However, while knowing that a special approach was needed to keep Sinn Féin on board, he would also have to have Trimble's support for it. Taking everything into account, he would prefer to hold back on this issue for the time being. A situation in which unionist support for the overall agreement was uncertain and at the same time an announcement was being made that there would be early release for paramilitary prisoners – say, after one year's imprisonment – would be politically unsustainable.

Ahern agreed broadly with Blair's reasoning. He recalled that, at a meeting he had had with Trimble in London recently, the UUP leader had accepted that an agreement on prisoners would have to be part of a comprehensive settlement. Blair feared, however, that the unionists might try to link prisoner releases to decommissioning. Gerry Adams had told him this week that 'if that's there, I'm out'. Blair thought that efforts to make such a linkage could be headed off if there were a strengthening of the agreement's language on decommissioning.

Noting DUP claims that the Irish language would be made compulsory in Northern Ireland in the future, the Prime Minister suggested that a qualification such as 'where appropriate' might be needed in the section of the agreement which promised that use of the language would be facilitated. Teahon suggested something on the lines of 'where they so wish'.

Blair wrapped up by saying that, if we could agree to withdraw Annexes A and B in their present form, he would push Trimble to be more positive generally in media interviews about the prospects for agreement. Ahern hoped that, in exchange for adjustment of the two annexes, Trimble would also move towards a Strand One deal.

With the breakfast discussion drawing to a close, it was agreed that Irish and British officials would stay on at Hillsborough Castle to work on possible modification of the Strand Two language.

The Taoiseach then travelled to Stormont House to meet the rest of the Irish Government delegation, led by David Andrews and Liz O'Donnell. From there, he went on to Castle Buildings, where he had a meeting with the UUP. This was a positive and constructive encounter. The UUP delegation, headed by John Taylor, told him they were making good progress with the SDLP on Strand One. Ahern told them in turn that we would be flexible in Strand Two provided we got a significant North/ South dimension, which was vital to retaining SDLP and Sinn Féin support. After the meeting, he was touched by Taylor's private condolences to him and recognition of the huge personal effort he was making in these circumstances. Overall, he felt that this meeting had an important calming effect and put relations between the Irish Government and the UUP on a better footing for the final phase of the negotiations.

Ahern went on to have brief meetings with Sinn Féin and the SDLP. He then returned to Dublin for his mother's Requiem Mass and funeral at noon.

Meanwhile, Tony Blair and his team transferred from Hillsborough to Castle Buildings, moving into offices on the floor above ours.

Sinn Féin came into us with a 26-page document seeking multiple amendments to the Mitchell draft. These included restoring the Framework Document terminology for the powers of the North/South Ministerial Council ('executive', 'harmonising' and 'consultative'); dropping the British–Irish Council; and adding an all-Ireland Human Rights Commission, an Irish Language Act and other measures in support of the Irish language and the release of all paramilitary prisoners by the end of 1998. They also signalled their support for an Assembly, a Cabinet with ministers, a Department of Equality, key decisions to be taken by 70 per cent weighted majority and so on. On constitutional issues, they sought, inter alia, repeal of the Act of Union as well as the Government of Ireland Act (Section 75) and the Northern Ireland Constitution Act of 1973. They also proposed Dail representation for Northern nationalists. On the envisaged provision for a border poll, to be held by the Secretary of State for Northern Ireland, they wanted this governed by the imperative 'shall' (rather than 'may'). They envisaged such polls being held at five-yearly intervals, beginning in 2000, and wanted a 'majority' to be explicitly defined as 50 per cent plus one.

We advised Sinn Féin to pursue a small number of key priorities from this paper. They did so, concentrating essentially on policing, prisoner releases and the Irish language. Throughout the day, we stayed in intensive contact with them, keeping them up to speed on our discussions with the British Government.

We also had continual interaction with the SDLP. In mid-afternoon, they gave us a paper with their detailed proposals for Strand One (on which we had been giving them some assistance). They were particularly anxious to secure acceptance of the principle of 'parallel consent' as the basis for key Assembly decisions. By requiring the support of a majority of both unionists and nationalists for a given legislative proposal, they wanted to make explicit – for the first time in Northern Ireland's history – the need for nationalist consent. They also wanted to ensure that no combination of unionist parties could defeat key reforms.

During the afternoon a row blew up when British officials, acting at the behest of the UUP, attempted to introduce a linkage between decommissioning and participation in the Assembly and other institutions. A meeting Blair had had with the UUP in the morning had led to a difficult exchange with Ken Maginnis over the policing, decommissioning and other security-related parts of the Mitchell draft. Jonathan Powell, Blair's adviser on Northern Ireland, had met Maginnis separately to look at possible amendments. George Mitchell got wind of this and suggested that the drafting exercise be widened to include Irish Government officials and himself and his staff. Having already made clear that we were not ready to negotiate proposed amendments on a piecemeal basis, our officials declined.

The British officials went on to forward to Mitchell draft language which would make participation in the Assembly dependent on decommissioning. This involved the participants expressing their 'conviction that those who participate in democratic bodies should be using only democratic means' and agreeing that the process of decommissioning would begin as soon as this agreement came into force. They also forwarded language which bowed to UUP concerns on a range of security, policing and judicial issues.

The fact that we received the proposed amendments not directly from our British colleagues, as we might have expected, but only indirectly from Mitchell did not improve our mood. We were disgruntled over this initiative, which was contrary to the spirit of cooperation between the two Governments throughout this process. Ahern had words with Blair about it on his arrival back from Dublin in the late afternoon and Blair and Powell were apologetic. Within a couple of hours, however, the air was cleared and we were back on track, moving on together to the next challenges.

Taking our cue from the breakfast discussion at Hillsborough, the Irish and British teams fleshed out further the idea of a preparatory role for the Assembly in relation to the implementation bodies.

This came into focus as follows. While basic legislative authority for the implementation bodies would come from Westminster and the Oireachtas, and their broad scope and potential would be indicated in the agreement, the detailed functional remits for each of them would be elaborated at a later stage by representatives of the shadow Assembly and the Irish Government. This would happen during the transitional period between the Assembly election, expected in June, and the formal transfer of power to the Assembly a few months later. The reality was that, as existing legislative workloads at Westminster and in the Oireachtas would mean a delay of several months before the new institutions could be formally established, there would have to be a transitional, or 'shadow', period for these institutions in the meantime. We would, in effect, be making creative use of this inevitability. A work programme – an idea contributed by the UUP – could be undertaken over that period by what would be the shadow North/ South Ministerial Council.

From the Irish Government's perspective, the key thing was that a set of implementation bodies, covering broadly the areas identified in Annex C of the Mitchell draft, would be guaranteed to come into existence from the outset of a new agreement and would not be dependent on an Assembly vote.

As a general reflection, the degree of unionist concern that week over the Strand Two issues surprised some in both Governments. We had expected that, in its initial response to the Mitchell draft, the UUP would concentrate its fire on other aspects such as prisoners, policing, decommissioning, the constitutional amendments or perceived Sinn Féin ambivalence about the consent principle. In the event, the middle of the week was dominated by Strand Two, almost to the exclusion of everything else. It was only after an acceptable outcome was reached there that the UUP directed sustained attention towards the other issues.

It could be argued that the very concentration on Strand Two for a good part of the week served a useful purpose. It reduced the scope for major confrontation over the other issues (as the negotiations were likely to end on Thursday or Friday) and arguably, therefore, facilitated the agreement at the end of the day.

24

THE BEGINNINGS OF ENGAGEMENT

In Dublin, Bertie Ahern barely had time to attend his mother's funeral at Glasnevin Cemetery at noon that Wednesday (8 April) before an official appeared to collect him for the return flight on the Government jet to Belfast. He remembers managing to get to the Skylon Hotel, where a family reception was to take place; all he had time for there was to thank all who had come and then to leave for the airport.

Back at Castle Buildings around 6 p.m., he told the media on his arrival that he believed the Mitchell draft offered the basis for an agreement. The parties should outline what they needed and what they could live with. Everyone would have to move a little bit, he emphasised.

Privately, the Taoiseach was prepared to show some flexibility in Strand Two – and indeed had kept this in reserve all along, knowing that this might be necessary to win unionist support for the agreement as a whole. However, certain issues were non-negotiable. And there would be political limits to what he could do anyway, bearing in mind the major gains unionists would be making in other parts of the agreement (notably acceptance of the consent principle, the establishment of an Assembly in Northern Ireland and the amendment of Articles 2 and 3).

At a meeting in our delegation offices after he had seen the Prime Minister, the Taoiseach was quietly determined on all of these points. A British official, he told us, had just put a proposal to him which he would not have liked even at better times. Having come straight from his mother's funeral, Ahern had turned down the idea with a curt response: 'Wrong week.' In the midst of his bereavement (and perhaps, in some ways, because of it), he was calm, clear-sighted and focused on what he had to do. One Irish official described him as being in an 'almost Zen-like' mood on his return from the funeral.

At a tripartite meeting that evening with Blair and the UUP, Ahern told Trimble and Taylor that he was willing to look at a number of points of concern to the unionists in Strand Two. In exchange, however, the UUP would have to engage seriously in Strand One.

Taylor responded in a cautiously positive way: on the basis of what the Taoiseach had told them, he saw some room for manoeuvre. He felt business could be done. And he emphasised his party's desire to do a deal. Taylor had moved on from the truculence of his 'forty-foot pole' dismissal of the Mitchell draft the previous day and now seemed to be in more pragmatic mode. David Trimble also indicated that he had been reassured by what he had heard from the Taoiseach. There was also a tripartite meeting that evening between the Taoiseach, the UUP and the SDLP. My British colleagues told me that they were heartened by what seemed to be an improving unionist mood. And our own assessment was favourable: the unionists seemed at that point to be serious about doing a deal broadly on the lines we needed.

It did not stay like this, however. At a further meeting which the Taoiseach and his officials had with the UUP just before midnight, the UUP proposed a revision which sought to remove an explicit commitment to the establishment of implementation bodies, replacing this with mere 'feasibility studies' in that direction during the transitional period.

There had been some indications earlier in the day that the UUP might refuse to grasp the nettle on the implementation bodies. The SDLP and Sinn Féin picked up hints about 'feasibility studies' and were very concerned.

The Taoiseach made clear our strong reservations about the UUP proposal. Meeting Blair and Mitchell after this meeting, he compared notes on this disappointing development. The UUP were now trying to dilute what was already a compromise reformulation in the paragraph in question. Our willingness to look at any modifications to Strand Two, he pointed out, was on the strict understanding that this would facilitate UUP movement on all other issues – which we were not yet seeing.

Meanwhile, work was continuing between the two Governments on potential revisions to various other parts of the Mitchell draft. On Tuesday and Wednesday, the parties had come up with a wide range of amendments they wished to see. To an extent, of course, they were simply responding to the options flagged in a number of areas. Meeting in continuous session throughout Wednesday evening, the two Government teams worked to agree a set of amendments which could be taken on board as part of a balanced package of changes.

Many of the parties' requests related to Strand One. There was a significant gap between the minimalist approach being taken by the UUP and the desire of most other parties to see a Cabinet-style power-sharing Executive in Northern Ireland. The Mitchell draft had left many questions deliberately open in this respect and the SDLP and others wanted to answer them.

On the definition of 'cross-community support' (required for particular votes), the SDLP wanted to make explicit that, at the first meeting of the Assembly, members would designate themselves as nationalist, unionist or 'other' as the basis for establishing this. Key decisions, the party held, should pass only if they were supported by either (a) 'parallel consent' (i.e., a majority of members present and voting, including a majority of those designating themselves as unionist or nationalist) or (b) a weighted majority comprising two-thirds of members present and voting, including at least one-third of the unionist and nationalist designations.

The SDLP wanted it spelled out that executive authority would be discharged by a First Secretary/Minister and Deputy First Secretary/Minister, who would be jointly elected by the Assembly voting on a cross-community basis. They also wanted the posts of up to 10 Secretaries with departmental responsibilities (later called ministers) to be allocated to parties in the Assembly on the basis of the d'Hondt principle.

The notion of joint election of the two top office-holders was important to the SDLP. They envisaged in effect a twin-headed leadership, one post inseparable from the other and all functions being exercised jointly. The idea had originated with Mark Durkan after he saw Seamus Mallon and David Trimble walking up the hill together at Poyntzpass a month earlier (in a poignant visit to the family of one of two young friends who had been killed by the LVF). The party had developed the concept subsequently and had put it to the UUP at a meeting on 3 April. Since then, they had proposed joint election on the basis of 'parallel consent'. (Late on Thursday evening, they would agree this model with the UUP and would also agree that the two office-holders would be called, respectively, the First Minister and Deputy First Minister.)

Beyond the Strands, a succession of other issues was claiming urgent attention. Of enormous importance for Sinn Féin, and also for the two loyalist parties, was the question of prisoner releases. Securing Sinn Féin and loyalist support for an agreement would in large measure depend on the arrangements on offer for the early release of paramilitary prisoners.

The arrangements which would apply within Northern Ireland fell within the responsibilities of Mo Mowlam as Secretary of State. On our side, they were the responsibility of the Minister for Justice. The key official representing the latter at the negotiations was Tim Dalton, with assistance from Mick Mellett and Paul Hickey, who did much of the detailed work with NIO officials.

We found the initial British proposal on prisoners, which focused on increasing remission rates for good behaviour rather than on early release as such, underwhelming. Pressing Mo Mowlam and her officials to take a more generous approach, we argued for early releases based on a sentence review when one year of a sentence had been served. Mowlam responded by floating 18 months as a possible compromise. She also hoped for an agreement that decommissioning would be completed within the same time frame.

In the Mitchell draft, general reference had been made to 'an accelerated programme' for prisoner releases but no time frame or other details were given. This was the approach we had agreed with British officials. On the one hand, we wanted to give an early signal that the two Governments envisaged early prisoner releases as part of the agreement. The Irish Government saw merit in demonstrating this clearly to Sinn Féin, to keep them in the game, and the British Government agreed with us. But on the other, the detail of what we each envisaged – the same regime would, of course, apply in both jurisdictions – was something we felt should be left to later in the negotiations.

Partly there was a concern that providing this detail too soon could jeopardise unionist support for the agreement. Partly also, the nature of the detail – including the fact that prisoners would not be given absolute releases but would be let out on licences which could be revoked – might not suit the undifferentiated messaging prefered by Sinn Féin. (Because of the technical complexity of the issue, the two Governments had envisaged setting out the detailed arrangements in a parallel document to the agreement.) However, even if there were good political reasons to hold back on the detail for now, we knew that we were rapidly approaching the final stage when it would have to be settled.

Unsurprisingly, Sinn Féin began to step up their pressure on the two Governments in relation to both prisoners and policing (where they wanted clearer commitment to radical reform). These issues were at the top of their agenda. Adams and McGuinness saw Blair and Ahern several times about them during Wednesday evening. Unsettled by the protracted exchanges with the UUP in Strand Two, they saw tactical advantage in repeated reminders to the Governments of their own needs, already articulated in their 26-page document. They signalled clearly that, while they wanted to sign up to a deal, it would have to be the right kind of deal.

There was, of course, converse pressure from the British Government and the UUP to strengthen the agreement's provisions on decommissioning.

Some minor amendments to the decommissioning text were agreed on Wednesday and Thursday. The Mitchell draft had, for example, referred back to the procedural motion of the previous September and its description of a resolution of the decommissioning issue as 'an indispensable part of the process of negotiation'. It had gone on to declare that 'it is, therefore, an indispensable part of this agreement'. Sinn Féin complained that this was a false conclusion. We resolved this point by dropping the contested sentence but adding instead a cross reference to a paragraph in the Strand One section which said that office-holders who did not use exclusively non-violent means should be excluded or removed from office. (The latter was added in response to UUP complaints, now growing louder, that Sinn Féin could be in Government, and republican prisoners out, before any decommissioning had begun.)

Other amendments achieved similar balance between Sinn Féin and unionist concerns in this area. From the perspective of both Governments, we brought out more clearly our expectation that there would be constructive engagement with the Independent Commission with a view to the achievement of full decommissioning within two years of the agreement being endorsed and 'in the context of the implementation of the overall settlement'.

Late on Wednesday evening, with his deadline of midnight on the following evening looming, Senator Mitchell asked the Taoiseach and the Prime Minister to commit themselves absolutely to this deadline. They did so. Mitchell wanted the delegates to understand that, when they returned on Thursday morning, they would be working right through the day up to midnight. There would be no breaks or adjournments, Mitchell decided. The participants would be kept under maximum pressure to reach a deal; and, by implication, we would go on beyond midnight for as long as it took.

The mood in our camp at the end of the evening was, frankly, not good. While some progress was being made in Strand Two and we could see the basis for a possible deal there, we were still nowhere near reaching that deal. The UUP proposal about 'feasibility studies', furthermore, had sent a worrying signal. Without a Strand Two deal, the stalemate in Strand One could not be overcome and the arrangements envisaged in Strand Three could not be finalised.

Both Governments were despondent at the way things were going. We felt that, unless there was a marked improvement on Thursday morning, we would need to begin planning an exit strategy. Mitchell was privately in agreement. Nobody saw any merit in allowing the talks to continue indefinitely if there was no clear prospect of agreement. The contingency plan, accordingly, was for the two Governments to take stock around lunchtime on Thursday and, if necessary, to advise the chairmen formally at that point to set a deadline in the late afternoon for the conclusion of the talks.

Around 1.30 a.m., after an exceptionally strenuous and draining day, the Taoiseach headed to City Airport and flew back to Dublin. Tony Blair, meanwhile, retired to Hillsborough Castle. The Irish ministers overnighted in Stormont House; our officials were mostly accommodated either there or with me in Maryfield. The following night would see us all overnighting, without the benefit of beds, in Castle Buildings.

25

THE FINAL DEAL TAKES SHAPE

O nly a few hours later, Bertie Ahern was back in the air, arriving at City Airport around 8.30 a.m. I met him and took him and his officials to breakfast with Tony Blair and his team at Hillsborough Castle.

The mood was a little more fractious than at the previous day's breakfast. Blair had been hoping that more tangible progress would have been made in the interim on Strand Two between the UUP and ourselves. This had not proved possible, however. While some of the unionist suggestions offered a basis for a workable compromise, others did not. And the proposal for mere 'feasibility studies' had undermined our confidence in the UUP's willingness to commit to the North/South structures we required if an agreement was to be approved by our electorate.

Opening the discussion, Blair said he had spoken to David Trimble earlier and had emphasised a number of points about the implementation bodies. First, any work programme in relation to these must list specific policy areas. Second, there must be a minimum number of bodies (there were indications that Trimble might be open to five). And third, there must be specific language placing beyond any doubt that these bodies would happen. Trimble had told Blair that, if asked whether there would definitely be implementation bodies, he would reply in the affirmative.

The Taoiseach reiterated our need for Westminster legislation to set up an initial set of implementation bodies. It seemed that the UUP wanted to be able to block these bodies through the Assembly. That was why we had been unable to make more progress with them. He was not sure he could trust them. It was clear to us that, unless the implementation bodies were anchored in Westminster legislation, they were not going to happen.

Blair believed that Trimble *was* committed to implementation bodies. He recognised the Westminster legislation issue as important but pointed to the protection afforded by the 'mutual assured destruction' concept. Ahern was uneasy about this argument, as it would dilute the case to be made for North/South bodies in their own right. He told Blair that it would be politically impossible for him to rely on it in an emotive referendum campaign focused on the removal of Articles 2 and 3.

Another concern we had was that the Assembly should not be in a position to thwart the implementation bodies by deciding that they would not be among its budgetary priorities. Dermot Gallagher suggested that, in order to allow all the new institutions to come into existence at the same time (as intended by the two Governments), funding should be provided to cover the first year of operation for the initial set of implementation bodies. He hoped that the Prime Minister could provide reassurances on this point. Blair indicated that he could say this, though not in legislation.

On the constitutional front, Blair said that the UUP seemed to think that they would be offered some further changes in the Irish Constitution beyond what had previously been signalled to them. The Taoiseach made it clear that there was no basis for this belief. He drew Blair's attention to the political pressure his Government was under in relation to Articles 2 and 3.

Martin Mansergh added that we had gone to the outer limit of what could be done in this area. The Attorney General reiterated that the UUP representatives whom he had met recently had indicated that, if all other issues were OK, this area would not be an insuperable obstacle. He and the Taoiseach both emphasised the extent of contact with the UUP's legal advisers in recent weeks. The Taoiseach had discussed the proposed constitutional amendments with Opposition leaders, and also with his own party, and there was no scope for even the tiniest change. Blair said finally that he would make it clear to Trimble that this was a matter for the two sovereign Governments and could not be negotiated further.

On policing, Blair noted some work that had been done on this section of the Mitchell draft. Anticipating that there could be morale problems in the RUC with the prospect of an independent commission and of disbandment, he wanted to include some recognition of the RUC officers who had died during the Troubles. We had already encountered this idea in exchanges with the UUP and had mentioned it to Sinn Féin, who had been predictably hostile. We made it clear to Blair, however, that we could go along with the proposal. He said that the unionists had also sought language about the involvement of local communities with policing arrangements. Again, we indicated we could agree to that.

In turn, Ahern wanted to see reference made to a new 'policing service' (a concept to which Sinn Féin attached importance). Blair said he could refer broadly to a new approach involving fundamental structural and cultural change but could not promise a 'new service'. Ahern hoped nevertheless that we could find language which would be as strong as possible in this regard. (In the final version of the agreement, we did indeed secure references to a new 'policing service', both in the agreement proper and in the annexed terms of reference for the envisaged Commission on policing.)

On prisoners, Blair felt he had got Trimble to agree to the approach he planned to take, along with us, on early release arrangements. As for defending these arrangements in public, Blair would be 'broad-shouldered', making it clear that he considered them vital to ensuring peace.

On equality issues, Blair was willing to look at stronger formulations for Sinn Féin's benefit. Teahon and Gallagher pressed him for a further element on the Irish language which would require public bodies to provide services to people wishing to conduct their business in Irish.

Blair asked what could be done to ease unionist fears about symbols and emblems. I noted the balanced and non-threatening terms of the current text. Blair wondered whether some language could be devised to help deal with unionist claims about increased flying of the Tricolour. Noting nationalist objections to the flying of the Union Jack at police stations, for example in West Belfast (unlike anywhere in Britain), Gallagher suggested that this could be dealt with through police regulations.

On decommissioning, Blair wanted to be able to say that a process would get under way as soon as the agreement was reached. The unionists were pressing the British Government to rule out Assembly office for members of parties linked to paramilitary organisations which were not decommissioning. Against this background, he wondered whether Sinn Féin might be able to live with a reference merely to a 'process' getting under way after the agreement was concluded. It could be argued that this was, in a sense, already in existence (the Independent Commission). He wanted some form of words which would not be a 'showstopper' for Sinn Féin.

Tim Dalton mentioned that we had suggested a formulation involving decommissioning being achieved by a given date and this date coinciding with a release date for prisoners. The standard qualifications would, of course, apply: the former would happen only in the context of implementation of the agreement and the latter would be subject, as usual, to circumstances on the ground. (Ultimately, the agreement would commit all to working with the Independent Commission, and using 'any influence they may have', to achieve decommissioning within two years of the referendums 'and in the context of the implementation of the overall settlement'.)

The two leaders reflected generally on how secure Trimble's position was within the UUP and on the posturing for internal advantage by some of his colleagues which was then apparent. Ahern urged Blair to highlight to the UUP the various gains they would be making in the revisions to the draft agreement which were now being considered.

The Taoiseach and the Prime Minister and their teams then departed by helicopter for the Stormont estate. The clock was ticking. Within a few hours, the two Governments would need to make a call on whether a deal was achievable or not.

Ahern went first to Stormont House, where most of the Irish Government team were gathered over breakfast. He told them that, while he would dearly like a deal, he would not be prepared to accept one at any cost. If we had to call it now, the odds were probably against an agreement being reached. But we had a responsibility to try to get one. We would go forward today on the basis of the Mitchell draft. If the negotiations were to break down, we would want that to happen on the basis of the Mitchell draft and not some diluted version of it. We would look at individual components such as Strand Two, work on these (revising them as appropriate) and then put them back into the framework set out in the Mitchell draft.

This was, in fact, what would happen over the next one-and-a-half days. The Mitchell draft was very largely preserved as the basis for the agreement reached on the afternoon of Good Friday.

The most urgent task for the two Governments on Thursday was to try to resolve the Strand Two issues with the UUP – in the hope that a deal there would unlock positive movement elsewhere in the negotiations. Ahern and Blair were also bracing themselves, however, for a host of other issues from the UUP even after a Strand Two deal was reached. In addition, there would be a long list of issues from Sinn Féin, who were already unhappy about the degree of attention the two leaders had been paying to the unionists' political needs. And, in all of this, the SDLP could not be taken for granted. Nor could the other parties involved in the talks. All had entirely legitimate interests and claims on the two leaders' time.

Bertie Ahern and Tony Blair set out, accordingly, to meet all of the parties in the course of the day. These encounters were not always easy: lengthy wish lists were presented, and with rising levels of anxiety and vehemence now that the end game had arrived. In between, the two leaders had frequent sessions, either alone or with officials present, to assess how things were going. Blair stayed largely in the British Government offices on the third floor, while Ahern moved around the building more, chatting to delegates in the corridors. At one point, Blair urged Ahern not to go too far on his tour, joking that 'we're the only sensible people in this building, you know'.

David Andrews and Liz O'Donnell, for their part, also had contacts with the parties and stayed in close touch with Mo Mowlam and Paul Murphy.

Mo liked to have regular chats on developments with our two ministers. We sensed that she was feeling somewhat isolated within the British Government team. She was often excluded from key meetings the Prime Minister was having and did not disguise her annoyance and frustration at this. In one conversation, she described herself rather plaintively as 'Her Majesty's tea lady'. She had, as I observed earlier, difficult relations with the UUP. David Trimble did not disguise his low regard both for her and for the NIO more generally (whom he believed to be too open to persuasion by the Irish Government). He would claim later that the agreement was reached that week only because Mo Mowlam and the NIO officials were excluded from the negotiations.

Some of us noticed that, if Blair needed a political errand to be done with the UUP, he would ignore Mo and ask Jonathan Powell to handle it instead. Blair and his team had to carry most of the burden of the day-to-day dealings with the unionists that week and this may have rankled with them as the pressures from that quarter increased.

From Thursday morning onwards, more or less continuously until late on Friday afternoon, my colleagues and I were involved in intensive consultations with the British Government team on all aspects of the draft agreement. We also stayed in continual contact with the parties.

In addition, David Cooney and I liaised regularly with the chairmen and their teams. The final couple of days of the negotiations were not a particularly easy time for them. They were used to being in control of things and now found, with the arrival of the two leaders and their teams and an exclusive emphasis on deal-making in small groups, that they no longer had an obvious role. Ahern did make a point, however, of calling on Mitchell regularly and the Senator appreciated this.

Mitchell had originally hoped that, if all went well and progress was made rapidly during Thursday, he would be in a position to put a revised version of his draft to a Plenary in the evening for approval ahead of his midnight deadline. That was not to be, unfortunately. The political and technical work still needed on key parts of the agreement, in particular Strands One and Two and prisoners, plus the potentially constraining factor of a UUP Executive meeting scheduled for six o'clock that evening, all conspired against this optimistic timetable. (In the event, that Executive meeting passed off well from Trimble's perspective: the party leader received a standing ovation for his conduct of the negotiations to date and came back to Castle Buildings a couple of hours later clearly buoyed by the support he had received.)

For several hours on Thursday, our engagement with the UUP was at one remove. While there was plenty of informal contact with UUP delegates in the corridors, the main channel for negotiation involved the British Government acting as intermediary between the UUP and ourselves, with drafts going back and forth over several hours. Tim O'Connor and Rory Montgomery were asked to prepare some ideas on our side, building on elements that had been agreed the previous evening.

Bit by it, and sentence by sentence, we fleshed out the detail of the compromise in Strand Two. The plan was to have a short Bill at Westminster which would establish the Assembly in shadow form. At the same time, the North/South Ministerial Council and the British–Irish Council would also come into existence in shadow form. These institutions would meet initially in this transitional capacity in order to establish their working procedures and so on. The two Governments would table Westminster and Oireachtas legislation, respectively, to ensure, 'as an absolute commitment', that the implementation bodies would start functioning when a new British–Irish Agreement formally transferred powers to the Assembly and the other new institutions entered into force.

In other words, the implementation bodies would be guaranteed to come into existence. David Trimble inched gradually towards acceptance of the Council and the bodies being established on the basis of enabling provisions in Westminster legislation. The Assembly, meeting in its shadow form, would have an input to the process of agreeing the exact number of bodies and the detailed areas each would cover. This, however, would be on the basis of parameters already set in a list annexed to the agreement. And there would be scope to add to the number of bodies, by agreement, over time.

Furthermore, if for any reason the Council or the implementation bodies were not set up when the transition period expired, the Assembly would be closed down. And, to ensure that ministers in the Executive took up their places on the Council, there would be a stipulation that participation would be mandatory for the holders of all relevant posts in the administrations North and South. We also accepted that the Council would operate in accordance with normal rules for accountability in the Assembly and the Oireachtas respectively.

We were edging, therefore, towards a compromise deal which would carry forward the essential content of the Framework Document and the Sunningdale Agreement, even if we were willing to show flexibility in relation to some of the language and concepts used in those documents. What we had to do was to strike a careful but workable balance between two deeply diverging sets of political requirements in this area. And we felt that we were getting close to that now.

The references we would be making in the agreement to the number of implementation bodies and their broad functions also needed to be settled. We worked intensively on these issues with British Government officials, who in turn were in close contact with the UUP. A draft arrived from the UUP around midday on Thursday which agreed to six implementation bodies and, more generally, envisaged a sample list of areas for North/South cooperation being annexed to the agreement.

On the number of bodies, we had always intended to be flexible. Six was probably as much as was achievable with the unionists for the moment. However, by qualifying this with 'at least', we could signal the possibility of the list being added to by agreement, either over the coming months or further into the future. Paddy Teahon had suggested internally several months earlier that, while tactically it would be useful to come up with a longer list of options, an outcome involving 'six good implementation bodies' at the end of the day would give the Government what it needed politically. However, the policy areas in question would have to be credible and significant.

In the context of the emerging understanding about a work programme which the shadow North/South Ministerial Council would undertake, it was agreed that the Council would identify and agree by 31 October 1998 – we needed an early and fixed deadline for completion of the work – 'at least twelve subject areas' in which cooperation and implementation for mutual benefit would take place. The three lists of areas attached to the Mitchell draft – Annexes A, B and C – would be boiled down to a single list suggesting 12 areas and indicating that others would be considered by the shadow Council. (This reflected the reality that an individual policy area might be relevant under more than one heading.)

This single list would span the areas covered in Annexes B and C. It would create two new categories, in each of which the shadow

Council would identify and agree 'at least six' matters. One of the categories would be new implementation bodies, acting at a cross-border or all-island level, while the other would be cooperation through existing mechanisms in each jurisdiction. It was accepted that there would be six implementation bodies to begin with and that more could be added, by agreement, over time. The phrase 'identify and agree' was deliberately chosen to balance the unionist desire to avoid specific commitments against the nationalist need for precisely such commitment.

We then had to nail down what the broad policy areas would be for the initial six bodies (with the more detailed remits to be settled during the shadow period). In effect, we would be jettisoning much of the detail which had been set out in Annexes A and B to the Mitchell draft – and which had caused the unionists such anxiety. The agreement itself would now contain only broad policy headings.

What would these broad policy areas be? We already had the eight areas listed in Annex C. Five of these had been agreed between the two Governments on Monday. These were tourism, environmental protection, the implementation of EU programmes, transport planning and inland waterways. (Annex C also gave a short elaboration of what would be covered within each area.)

Three areas on which we had not yet reached agreement – essentially because of British Government fears about a unionist backlash – were promotion of the Irish language, promotion of trade and indigenous company development and promotion of the arts.

Our British colleagues, unsettled by the adverse UUP reaction to the annexes, were now arguing more strongly that the areas chosen should involve clearly demonstrable added value and should also steer clear of any political or cultural sensitivity. We, on the other hand, needed the implementation bodies to be in areas which were credible and meaningful and which would combine practical benefit with political significance.

I was personally wedded to the proposed trade promotion body, considering that it would meet these criteria admirably. It foundered ultimately, however, on the unionist fear that a joint promotional effort in overseas markets by Southern and Northern agencies, particularly with an inward investment focus, could end up to the detriment of Northern Ireland and its companies.

The most sensitive proposal, pushed by Sinn Féin but firmly resisted by the unionists, was for a body which would promote use of the Irish language. During the negotiations, the UUP had tried to maintain that Ullans, the Ulster-Scots dialect, was comparable to Irish in terms of usage and cultural importance and that any special arrangements made for Irish should extend to Ullans also. Though both Governments were extremely sceptical about the claims made for Ullans (with, for example, a derisory figure being provided for the number of Ullans speakers when Bertie Ahern sought details), we were willing nevertheless to contemplate a remit for an implementation body which would cover both. However, the UUP would not countenance this, maintaining that Ullans was not a Celtic language and had to be treated apart.

Late on Thursday evening, an Irish official who had been asked by the Taoiseach to sound out the unionists on the Irish language body had informal contact with two UUP representatives. This conversation suggested that the UUP would agree to our proposals for bodies dealing with the Irish language and trade promotion. On this basis, the colleague arranged with the chairmen's staff to have the Irish language added to a list of agreed implementation bodies which the staff were keeping. However, his understanding proved later in the night to be incorrect; the conversation had been misunderstood. Trimble made it clear, when contacted later by the Taoiseach, that the UUP had not agreed to these bodies. He also resisted efforts made by the Prime Minister on this issue.

On promotion of the arts, we had had an insight into UUP concerns when Trimble told Paddy Teahon on Monday night of his opposition to the proposal for an implementation body in this area. He saw, it seemed, a risk of adverse unionist reaction to such a body taking over the functions of the Arts Councils North and South.

The Taoiseach and the Prime Minister eventually had a meeting with Trimble to try to settle the list of implementation bodies. Ahern repeated our proposals in relation to the Irish language and trade promotion and business development; and he added training and employment services and science and technology (R&D). But Trimble remained adamantly opposed to these. It was decided eventually, however, to add a body on health cooperation. And, even if there was to be no implementation body on the Irish language, there would be strengthened language in the agreement to spell out measures of support which were planned for Irish, with a side reference also to Ulster-Scots.

In the hectic shuttle diplomacy during Thursday and into a very long evening, the two leaders played the central role, involving themselves directly in the search for compromise concepts and formulations and playing an effective duet as they pushed key protagonists towards agreement. Blair surprised several on the Irish side with his zeal for drafting; though partly perhaps a reflection of his legal training, his enthusiasm to engage in detail with drafts of all kinds was unusual in a Head of Government. Strand Two was his top priority for most of Thursday. We had a sense that, with the midnight deadline rapidly approaching, Blair was telling his team to wrap up the negotiations as quickly as possible on everything else so as to keep a clear focus on Strand Two and maximise the chances of getting a deal there.

Not surprisingly, the SDLP and Sinn Féin were uneasy about many aspects of the Strand Two package. In particular, they feared that the role envisaged for the shadow Assembly could be exploited somehow by the unionists to undermine the scope, impact and effectiveness of the implementation bodies. Hume met Blair on Thursday evening to express concern about the unionists' potential ability to drag their feet on, and frustrate, the establishment of these bodies. The SDLP also had misgivings about some of the topics agreed for the bodies, fearing that they might appear inconsequential.

More generally, Sinn Féin were worried that the changes the two Governments seemed willing to make in Strand Two to get the unionists on board encroached on substance and could no longer be described as purely presentational.

In bilateral meetings, we reassured both parties repeatedly about our Government's bottom line in this area. The Taoiseach had a long meeting with the SDLP in the early afternoon and also had frequent contact with Sinn Féin. We went back to the British several times and secured a couple of changes to address the SDLP and Sinn Féin concerns.

We pressed also in this context for additions to the list of potential implementation bodies. However, the British feared that this would threaten unionist support. The Taoiseach and his officials went through a number of suggestions in detail with the Prime Minister, Mo Mowlam and the British team. In the middle of a tense negotiating session, there was a moment of light relief when Wally Kirwan suggested we remove food safety from the list 'because the Irish Government is not ready for it' and Ahern quipped: 'We're going to poison everyone instead.'

Agreement was finally reached around midnight between the two leaders on the text of Strand Two. With the work on the implementation bodies continuing well into the night, however, this list would not finally be agreed until mid-morning on Friday.

The final outcome was that an annex to the agreement would list areas for North/South 'cooperation and implementation'. These would include 12 subjects spanning the two headings (and with 'others to be considered' by the shadow North/South Council). The list would not be expressly subdivided into six for implementation bodies and six for handling through existing bodies in each jurisdiction. This was because the detailed technical work during the shadow period would determine finally how each subject would be handled. It was clearly understood, however, that there would be at least six implementation bodies and that these would be in the areas of tourism, environmental protection, EU programmes, inland waterways, transport planning and health.

26

THE PENDULUM SWINGS BACK

During Holy Thursday (9 April), a general sense had begun to spread among the delegaions that the Strand Two impasse was easing and that a solution of sorts was in sight. UUP representatives became more relaxed in their corridor comments and a little more upbeat in their remarks to the media than they had previously been.

The pendulum then, inevitably, began to swing in the opposite direction. The happier the UUP appeared to be, the more suspicious Sinn Féin and the SDLP became.

Sinn Féin complained to us about the major concessions which the unionists appeared to have extracted on an Assembly and implementation bodies, against a background where they would also be securing the removal of Articles 2 and 3. In the evening, they presented the two Governments with a document setting out 67 questions across the whole agreement.

Irish officials reacted privately with exasperation when they saw this document. The questions covered well-trodden ground and they had already been answered in one form or another in the Governments' multiple exchanges with Sinn Féin. Apart from the fact that preparation of the replies would be very time-consuming, the purpose of the exercise was not entirely clear. There were suspicions that Sinn Féin might be getting ready to walk out, over prisoners or some other issue, and needed to be able to claim as an alibi that the Governments had given inadequate responses when Sinn Féin raised a series of concerns with them. A more positive interpretation was that they needed answers they could show to questions being asked within the wider republican movement.

Bertie Ahern decided that it would be safest if comprehensive replies were prepared, however tedious this would be. At his request, Paddy Teahon went to Tony Blair and asked if Mo Mowlam could join us for this work. (Many of the questions asked bore on her responsibilities, of course.) The Prime Minister agreed. Mo was not best pleased and responded in colourful terms, evidently fearing that she would be left with responsibility for making some very difficult policy calls on behalf of the British Government. Later on, she vented her fury on Sinn Féin also. But she gamely got down to the work.

Liz O'Donnell was also involved, along with officials from both Government teams. It was the Irish team, in fact, who prepared most of the draft responses. The questions were divided up among them, with Tim Dalton in a coordinating role. Tim O'Connor, Rory Montgomery, Ray Bassett, Eamonn McKee, Wally Kirwan and others were closely involved. Sometimes all that was required was a simple 'yes' or 'no'. Over a period of a couple of hours, from about 11 p.m. until nearly 2 a.m., the two sides went through each of the questions and agreed on brief joint replies to them. When the exercise was completed, Blair asked Teahon if he thought it would prevent a walkout by Sinn Féin. Teahon replied that Ahern's instinct, as a veteran negotiator, was that the preparation of these replies was essential.

In parallel, Gerry Adams and Martin McGuinness had meetings first with the Taoiseach and then with the Prime Minister to lay out their concerns. They did so in fairly trenchant terms.

Blair noted the prospective wins for Sinn Féin in the emerging agreement (significant movement on policing, prisoners and equality, the implementation bodies plus the protection afforded by the concept of 'mutual agreed destruction', UK constitutional change). But Sinn Féin were not persuaded. By some British accounts, Blair was despondent after this meeting, fearing that a Sinn Féin walkout was now a real possibility. Speaking to the media afterwards, McGuinness made clear his party's unhappiness at the way things were going and at the UUP's efforts to change key parts of the Mitchell draft. He complained also that, although we were only hours away from the end of the negotiations, no unionist had yet said hello to him.

Later in the evening, Sinn Féin took much persuasion to accept the compromise in Strand Two. Ahern and Blair had to work on them long after they had signed off together on that compromise. Sitting down with Adams and McGuinness and going through the replies which had been prepared to the list of questions – with which Sinn Féin were broadly happy – was part of this process. Effectively, it took multiple trade-offs – with new language which the party had sought on policing, prisoners, equality and many other issues – before Sinn Féin were ready to accept the Strand Two arrangements.

This process took the whole night and continued, indeed, for much of Friday. Lengthy exchanges on the prisoner release arrangements ran in parallel. Ahern and Blair knew they were getting somewhere with Sinn Féin, however, when Mitchel McLaughlin, a senior party representative, gave a positive message to the media around 7.30 on the morning of Good Friday.

As we had all hoped, the resolution of Strand Two around midnight on Thursday unlocked Strand One and the potential for a deal there.

While there had been desultory Strand One discussions throughout Thursday, the UUP were still not represented at senior level there. There was still a fairly wide gap between that party's view of what the Strand One institutions should involve and the preferences expressed by virtually everyone else.

Within minutes of the Governments reaching agreement on Strand Two, however, contact was established between the parties, and the party leaders sat down together to engage seriously in Strand One.

In other rooms, intense work was under way at the same time on prisoner releases, policing, equality issues and a series of other components of the agreement. And, slightly to our surprise, the UUP chose this moment to revisit the constitutional issues with us.

Shortly before midnight, a UUP delegation consisting of Jeffrey Donaldson, Peter Weir, Peter King and Austin Morgan paid an unexpected visit to the Irish Government offices. They were met by the Attorney General, Jim Hamilton and me. They were seeking, even at this very late stage, revisions both to the proposed amendments to the Irish Constitution and to Article 1 of the envisaged British–Irish Agreement. Their request for a meeting was presented as a follow-up to the Attorney General's meeting with King and Morgan in Dublin 10 days previously.

Morgan demanded action in relation to alternative formulations which he said he had discussed at a meeting a few days earlier with Deputy Brian Lenihan. (The late Brian Lenihan was at that time the chair of the Oireachtas Constitutional Review Group.) Among the changes he sought were a reference in the agreement to the 'peoples' of the island of Ireland and the explicit naming of Northern Ireland in the new Article 3 of our Constitution.

The Attorney General dealt politely but expeditiously with these points, expressing surprise at the efforts to reopen matters which had been substantially settled at the Dublin meeting. King acknowledged that this was so. Donaldson, Byrne recalled later, seemed surprised by this and brought the meeting to a close. He hoped that our Government would make it clear in its public comments that the proposed amendments to the Constitution involved a removal of the 'territorial claim' and of the 'constitutional imperative'.

My impression was that Donaldson, who had not been involved in the earlier contacts on constitutional matters, was largely unsighted on these issues. It was not clear whether the request for a meeting was a personal initiative on his part or something that had Trimble's active support. The unionists' main aim, it seemed, was to get a reference to Northern Ireland into the new Art. 3 of the Irish Constitution. On Wednesday and Thursday, as we have seen, Tony Blair had already raised this point on their behalf with Bertie Ahern and David Byrne and had been told in clear terms that it would not be possible. With renewed confirmation of this from the Attorney General, Donaldson accepted the outcome gracefully and returned from our offices to the Strand One talks, which were in progress elsewhere in the building.

A little earlier, Ian Paisley had led a group of DUP supporters in bleak wintry conditions up to Castle Buildings to protest at the emerging agreement and the part played in it by the UUP and the loyalist parties. The DUP had already held a barnstorming press conference outside the venue on Wednesday afternoon. The protest now was meant to be a follow-up, based on the assumption that by late Thursday evening, as midnight approached, the sell-out would have been complete.

In the event, the demonstration was something of a damp squib. A couple of hundred DUP supporters entered the gates of the Stormont estate, marched up the 'Stormont mile' (the long road leading up to Parliament Buildings) and tried to get access to the Castle Buildings venue. Paisley sought admission so as to hold a press conference inside. Following consultation between the two Governments and the chairmen, this was refused but he was given permission to hold one outside instead. This ended up as a chaotic event in a Portakabin, in rainswept conditions, with Paisley's remarks largely drowned out by the sustained heckling of PUP supporters. It was an ignominious affair which did Paisley no favours. What had been intended as a stunt to intimidate the UUP and undermine the emerging agreement ended up drawing attention instead to the DUP's isolation within the broader unionist community.

27

A NIGHT TO REMEMBER

We were now in the middle of a long and agonising night of negotiations on many fronts simultaneously. It was a night which none of us will ever forget. The delegates were at this stage exhausted after several days of round-the-clock exertion, unrelenting pressure and a succession of emotional highs and lows. We had had very little sleep. We had to put up with stuffy, overheated conditions in the building and had rarely been able to venture out into the fresh air. Outside for a brief walk at one point, Tony Blair told Alastair Campbell that this felt 'like prison exercise'; many of us would have been able to relate to that.

Castle Buildings had never seemed more cramped or claustrophobic. And all the more so as delegations became noticeably larger. With an agreement now tantalisingly close, the parties were turning out in full strength. In the case of Sinn Féin and the two loyalist parties, this meant the arrival of a number of individuals who had not been sighted previously at the talks but whose presence now was considered significant. Shadowy figures who were judged to be closer to the 'military' side of republicanism than to its political wing were spotted in the building. Their imprimatur for what was hopefully about to happen would be critical. The same pattern was observed in the loyalist camp.

Bríd Rodgers of the SDLP has recalled her alarm when she saw a man wearing a balaclava close to her in the corridor, only to relax when he told her that it was just to keep his head warm while cycling to Castle Buildings in cold conditions to deliver pizzas a few minutes previously.

The creature comforts of Castle Buildings, such as they were, began to disappear. Although it might have been anticipated that this could turn into a very long night, the modest bar, lounge and canteen offering light refreshments closed up, as I recall, around 9 p.m. The traybakes usually on offer, which were very popular with the delegates (as they were during the 1996 talks when Ian Paisley, then in attendance, was a keen customer), were no longer available. No further sustenance of any kind was to be had. There were no coffee machines or vending machines in operation.

I survived for the entire night on successive slices of a sticky cake which the cook at the Maryfield Secretariat had thoughtfully baked and sent up to mark the birthday of one of my colleagues, Gerard Keown. I still have the taste of that elixir in my mouth; it gave me vital energy at a time when I needed everything to stay awake and concentrated. I heard accounts afterwards which suggested that Tony Blair and his officials had survived variously on Mars bars, bananas and tea. Some of the more enterprising delegations were able to send out for bacon sandwiches and other snacks from nearby stores. Mo Mowlam supposedly kept the British delegation fortified with tea and sandwiches.

There were some lighter moments in the midst of all the stress. Rory Montgomery recalls Gerry Adams arriving at one point for a meeting with the Taoiseach and the Prime Minister. While Adams was waiting to go into the office, someone in a small group assembled outside asked what everyone else was looking forward to over the coming days (apart from a break at Easter). When

Montgomery mentioned that he was looking forward to seeing a new puppy that his wife and son had recently acquired, Adams gave him detailed advice on canine matters. It emerged that the Sinn Féin leader was a dog lover. We had long known that Martin McGuinness was an enthusiastic fly fisherman, but this was a new angle on the more inscrutable Gerry Adams.

During the night, we in the Irish Government delegation tried to grab a few minutes' rest whenever and wherever we could. This might mean lying across, or under, a table or finding a perch stretched across two armchairs in one of the delegation rooms. For the most part, however, we were working at fever pitch, alternating between tense drafting sessions in small groups and constant meetings with other delegations. Bertie Ahern, on the go the whole night, never slept. Tony Blair reportedly used two seats put together to grab a few winks. I remember people pale with fatigue and in huddles everywhere along the building's narrow, overcrowded and freezing corridors. The place was abuzz with speculation, rumours and false leads.

The first major breakthrough of the night was the Strand Two deal, reached around midnight. The second followed some two hours later: an agreement in Strand One, involving the SDLP and the unionists in particular.

This agreement drew heavily on the SDLP's model and gave the party a significant victory. There would be a Cabinet-style Executive Committee with ministers, not the system of committee chairmanships which the UUP had pushed for so long. The Executive would be led by a First Minister and Deputy First Minister. There would be 'up to ten' ministers with departmental responsibilities; the exact number was left open for now but in due course the UUP, who had earlier preferred a smaller number, accepted 10. (A flaw in the arrangements, as Mallon observed privately years later, was that a commitment to collective Cabinet responsibility, long resisted by the UUP, was not explicitly nailed down; while the First Minister and Deputy First Minister would be required to act jointly, there was no explicit requirement for the full Executive to approve decisions.)

It was agreed that there would be a new Assembly for Northern Ireland, with committees corresponding to the functions being discharged by the Executive. Ministerial posts and committee chairmanships would be allocated on the d'Hondt principle. A special committee could be appointed to check conformity between proposed Assembly legislation and the European Convention on Human Rights. Key Assembly and Executive decisions would be taken on a cross-community basis involving either 'parallel consent' or a weighted majority (60 per cent) of members present and voting, including at least 40 per cent of each of the unionist and nationalist designations.

The two-hour negotiations that achieved the Strand One breakthrough had involved the SDLP, the UUP, Alliance, the NIWC, NI Labour, the PUP and the UDP. The dominant figures, however, were Seamus Mallon and David Trimble. In a final session between the SDLP and the UUP, as Mallon has recalled, the two men reached broad agreement on Strand One and shook hands on it. A key point conceded by the UUP at the end was that the First and Deputy First Ministers would have joint and equal powers.

Looking at the relative speed with which the parties came to terms, we sensed that the UUP had perhaps decided some time previously that they would broadly accept the model promoted by the SDLP if satisfactory arrangements were agreed in Strand Two. Trimble, who had already gone along with this in principle in the Heads of Agreement paper, agreed finally to an Assembly with both legislative and executive powers and to an Executive which would operate on a cross-community basis.

Minutes after the SDLP secured their dramatic victory, Hume and Mallon came in to see the Taoiseach. They entered our delegation room in celebratory mood, punching the air exuberantly. Their delight and excitement were palpable: the vision they had had for decades of a power-sharing Executive, with crucial safeguards to ensure it could function effectively, was at last going to be realised. They sat down at our conference table where the Taoiseach, flanked by his ministers, the Attorney General and officials, warmly congratulated them. It was a memorable meeting, with Hume and Mallon quite emotional at the enormity of what they had achieved.

At one point, I noticed the door to our room opening and Mo Mowlam padding in (she was characteristically without her shoes, having absent-mindedly kicked them off somewhere else in the building). She seemed to be half-sleepwalking (not unusual given the hour and the extreme fatigue affecting most of us). There was a slightly surreal, Lady Macbeth-like quality to her sudden, silent appearance. She came over to the table without a word, slipped in beside Mallon, lay her head on his shoulder and snoozed away for a moment or two. Mallon, unfazed, continued with his excited commentary on the Strand One victory until Mo, jerked awake by his gesticulations, abruptly said: 'That's f---ing brill, Seamus!' and then fell back prone onto his shoulder. A moment later, she abruptly got up and left the room.

Unscheduled visits by Mo to our offices were nothing unusual. She was not someone to stand on ceremony and, with characteristic informality, joined us for this moment of special celebration.

The SDLP did not rush to bring Sinn Féin in on the Strand One agreement they had achieved. Mallon had always complained about Sinn Féin's detachment from the Strand One discussions. This was, of course, a deliberate policy choice. Of greater concern to Sinn Féin than the internal arrangements for Northern Ireland were the nature, scope and potential of the Strand Two structures as well as the need to keep the latter immune from any Assembly veto. And higher still on their agenda were the changes they hoped for on policing, criminal justice, 'demilitarisation', equality and identity issues and, perhaps most important of all, prisoner release arrangements. However, when word of the Strand One deal emerged, Sinn Féin asked the SDLP for a meeting about it. The request was brusquely dismissed by Mallon, who observed that they had never sought discussions previously with the SDLP on Strand One and it was a bit late to be starting now.

Negotiations on the electoral system and the size of the Assembly continued for some time after the basic Strand One deal was finalised. The UUP, the SDLP and the loyalist parties came to see Tony Blair at different times on this subject. Ahern also had a meeting with Blair about this. Agreement was reached eventually on a 108-member Assembly involving 18 constituencies with six members each.

The Northern Ireland Women's Coalition and the UDP had pushed for a 'top-up' mechanism to maximise the representation of smaller parties in the Assembly. They had support from the SDLP and Sinn Féin, and Mo Mowlam and Liz O'Donnell were personally sympathetic. Mo suggested the addition of a provision which would in effect guarantee an Assembly seat to any party which secured 1 per cent of the vote. Ultimately, however, nothing came of this proposal due to opposition from the UUP and Alliance.

It was no accident that the NIWC had been the champion of this idea. Their presence at the talks in the first place was due to a top-up provision which had secured them two seats in the 1996 Forum elections; without this, they were going to find it very hard to secure election to the new Assembly.

One consolation for the smaller parties, perhaps, was an agreement that the North/South Ministerial Council would consider establishing a consultative civic forum covering social, economic and cultural issues. The NIWC had been pushing for this for some time, maintaining that a 'second chamber' of this kind, appointed by the administrations North and South and reflecting a cross section of sectoral interests, would be an important complement for the Assembly in Northern Ireland's special circumstances. Part of the NIWC's argument was that mainstream politics in Northern Ireland gave insufficient outlets to social, economic and political activism at the grassroots level in both communities. Both Governments had supported the idea. (In the event, it would founder on resistance from the larger parties.)

It was also agreed that the Assembly and the Oireachtas would 'consider' establishing a joint Parliamentary Forum. We and several of the parties backed this. However, the UUP were opposed and nothing came of this finally.

The Strand One breakthrough in turn led to convergence on Strand Three. (That section of the agreement was finalised on the basis of an Irish draft as amended by the UUP.) Other sections were finalised in short order; the agreement was at last coming together.

Late on Thursday night, and into Friday morning, Trimble and the UUP brought up with Blair and the No. 10 officials a matter which had not featured prominently in the talks but was one of the UUP's priorities. Trimble wanted to see the Maryfield Secretariat closed and asked Blair for a written assurance on this point. By various accounts, it was not immediately clear to the British team what the issue was here; on hearing the name pronounced in rich Ulster tones, Blair and others imagined that for some reason the closure of Edinburgh's rugby stadium (Murrayfield) was being sought.

The Prime Minister confirmed to the UUP leader in writing that the Maryfield Secretariat would be closed by the end of the year. This pledge was made unilaterally; in the hectic circumstances of late-night negotiations across multiple issues, there was no formal consultation on this between the two Governments. The British knew, however, that the Taoiseach would not have had a difficulty with the idea. Given that the new agreement would replace the Anglo-Irish Agreement, dismantling the Secretariat which had been established 13 years earlier to service that Agreement would be a natural consequence. A new British–Irish Secretariat would come into existence to support the new Intergovernmental Conference.

It was clear, however, that Trimble needed the trophy value of a public announcement that the Maryfield premises would be closed. He may also have wanted to forestall any idea the two Governments might have had of locating the new Secretariat, or the North/South Secretariat, in the same premises.

Sinn Féin, for their part, were in disgruntled mood during the night, having seen both the UUP and the SDLP emerge with spoils from the negotiations. While answers had been prepared to their 67 questions, they still felt that their own concerns and requirements were not receiving adequate attention.

They began to signal, both in private and in public, deep unhappiness at the way things were going. Mitchel McLaughlin gave a downbeat assessment to the media around midnight which, in the febrile atmosphere of that long night, got translated into a rumour that the party was considering pulling out of the negotiations. Personally, I never believed this. The Sinn Féin leadership had invested too much in the peace process and, however challenging the issues facing them, they were never likely to abandon the talks at that stage. But, for a few hours that night, there was considerable unease about Sinn Féin's intentions.

Ahern and Blair made it a priority, therefore, to engage with Sinn Féin. Over a period of two to three hours, from 5 a.m. until close to 8 a.m., they remained closeted with Adams and McGuinness. They were not accompanied by officials. (Mo Mowlam made moves to join them, as prisoners were to be the main topic, but was unsuccessful.)

The key issue for Sinn Féin throughout the night was the detail of the arrangements to be made for early release of paramilitary prisoners. Both Governments would have to agree to these. (The bulk of the prisoners concerned were in Northern Ireland or in Britain; we had a relatively small number in our own jurisdiction.) Blair had originally hoped to hold over this issue until the last minute, calculating that a scheme which he would present as generous might be the crucial sweetener needed to get Sinn Féin over the line and secure republican support for the agreement as a whole. But in the event, after unintentionally revealing his hand on prisoners at a meeting with John Hume during Thursday evening, Blair decided that Sinn Féin would have to be given a full briefing at that stage on his intentions. (Sinn Féin in fact already knew broadly what was planned but were missing the details.)

The British plan was to release prisoners after they had served two years. They would be released on licence, i.e., their release could be revoked if there was any return to violence. (This was an important point from the unionist perspective but, not surprisingly, was resisted by Sinn Féin.) Sinn Féin pressed hard for release after only one year. They reportedly tried to get the loyalist parties to row in behind this also, but the loyalists refused. The

UUP originally favoured five years, we heard, then came down to three; the SDLP, we understood, also favoured three.

At some point, Mo Mowlam gave an indication to Adams and McGuinness that release after one year might indeed be possible. This caused consternation, by several accounts, in the British camp. Sinn Féin naturally tried to bank this concession, and further difficult conversations with British ministers and officials ensued. As Secretary of State, Mo had policy responsibility for this area and was also under constant pressure from the UUP, who feared that undue leniency might be shown. With rumour and counter-rumour flowing all night about what was planned, there was abundant scope for misunderstanding.

In the middle of the night, Mo had words briefly with Tim Dalton, believing that she had been kept in the dark about some development. This was not the case. Mo had worked very closely with Dalton over the previous few days on these issues and they had an excellent relationship. They quickly resolved the misunderstanding, walking amiably up and down the corridor arm in arm, Mo in her stockinged feet.

There was an amusing sequel the next morning when, at a meeting convened by George Mitchell with the two Governments, Mo asked for the floor at the outset. She told the gathering that she wanted to apologise to Dalton for her remarks during the night, as she had not had an opportunity to do so privately before now. She proceeded to repeat, as part of her apology, the colourful terms in which she had berated our colleague. While Dalton took this with good grace, and the rest of us enjoyed this moment of light relief, the look on Mitchell's face as he listened to Mo's intervention was memorable.

At their three-hour meeting with Adams and McGuinness earlier, Blair and Ahern had made it clear that a two-year mark for prisoner releases was what they envisaged and that the prisoners would be released on licence. These arrangements would be conditional, they emphasised, on Sinn Féin signing up to the overall agreement. Sinn Féin, however, took the opposite position: they would sign up to the wider agreement only if they got satisfaction on prisoners.

By the time the meeting ended, however, Ahern was satisfied that a meeting of minds had been achieved on prisoner releases and that this would not be an issue in terms of Sinn Féin acceptance of the overall agreement. McGuinness confirmed this subsequently to him.

A final agreement on the prisoner release arrangements was always likely to be reached only at the very end of the negotiations. This issue was perhaps the most difficult of all for Sinn Féin. The IRA leadership were keenly interested in the fate of republican prisoners, ahead of virtually all other aspects of the agreement. They also wanted promises of immunity for what were called 'on the runs': people wanted in Northern Ireland or Britain for questioning in connection with paramilitary crimes committed during the Troubles. Whatever about early release for people who had been convicted and were serving sentences, it would be a much more difficult proposition for either Government to extend an amnesty to those who had not even gone through due process.

The Governments knew that what they were offering on prisoners would not satisfy all of the republican movement's hopes. They were calculating, however, that if this issue could be left until all the other building blocks were in place, it would be more difficult for Sinn Féin to exploit it tactically. It would also be harder for Sinn Féin to hold the entire agreement hostage to the outcome on prisoners. Adams and McGuinness, in turn, would have been better placed by the end of the process to demonstrate the full measure of republican achievements in the negotiations. This would help them to sell the agreement to their constituency, even with arrangements on prisoners which fell a little below their ambitions.

If there was one issue on which Sinn Féin might have walked in the final stages of the talks, it would in my view have been the prisoner release arrangements. But they achieved an outcome that most observers would have characterised as a fair compromise in all the circumstances. And the intensive personal engagement of the Taoiseach and the Prime Minister with them on this issue, with assurances that this close interest would continue, was no doubt also a factor in building republican confidence.

Ahern and Blair were determined to show their readiness to go through each of Sinn Féin's concerns and to ensure that there were no credible grounds for a walkout. However long it took, they wanted to do everything possible to keep the party on board. The Sinn Féin negotiating style required them to dig deep into their reserves of patience and stamina. Adams and McGuinness, who frequently played a kind of 'nice cop/tough cop' routine to extract maximum advantage, would habitually pocket whatever concessions they could squeeze out of the Governments and then come back looking for more.

These were standard Sinn Féin tactics. Even when the supposedly final version of the Mitchell draft appeared at midday on Good Friday, the party was still seeking a raft of amendments to it. The relentlessness of this approach may have been exasperating and may indeed have been counterproductive at times. But it still drew expressions of grudging respect from the Governments. Blair has described how, after receiving yet another list of demands at a very late stage, he laughingly told Adams that 'you're a compulsive negotiator'. The package was balanced, Blair insisted to the Sinn

Féin leader, 'and you know it'. Adams would himself say later that the best thing he ever achieved by haggling was the Good Friday Agreement.

The marathon session from 5 a.m. onwards was, as Ahern recalls, the first occasion on which Blair had a sustained and in-depth discussion with Adams and McGuinness. The direct and frank exchanges between the four men, without officials present, gave Blair a better understanding of republican thinking and laid an important foundation for the many interactions with Sinn Féin which would follow over the coming years.

By the end of those discussions, it seemed to Ahern that Sinn Féin were now on board for the agreement as a whole. While Adams and McGuinness were saying they would have to refer it to a special party Ard Fheis, it was clear they saw no fundamental obstacle to republican endorsement of the agreement.

A pivotal factor during Thursday night was a series of phone calls made by President Bill Clinton to all the key players. The importance of the US President reassuring all involved of his personal support and dedication to their interests as this agreement was implemented could not be overestimated. It helped that these were all people whom he had met previously and who knew of his deep commitment. This was a card which the two Governments had intended all along to deploy; the only issue was when, and how, it could be used to maximum effect. Clinton was standing by as the talks entered the crucial final phase, ready to do whatever Ahern and Blair felt would be helpful to encourage the parties towards agreement.

The two leaders had a direct line to Clinton. They and their teams also worked through key US officials such as Tony Lake, Sandy Berger, Jim Steinberg and Nancy Soderberg. In addition, Sean O hUiginn and his colleagues at the Irish Embassy in

Washington were keeping Clinton and his staff up to speed on all developments.

The first call was made to Clinton by Blair about 3.10 a.m. (Belfast time). Ahern, who would have a total of three calls with Clinton that night, followed half an hour later. They each briefed Clinton on the key issues which had arisen, including the long list of questions presented earlier by Sinn Féin and the responses given.

From about 4 a.m. onwards, and over a period of several hours, Clinton made a series of calls to Trimble, Adams and Hume, looping back to Ahern and Blair in tripartite calls and to George Mitchell. (Mitchell recalls a call at 3 a.m. Washington time, when Clinton told him he couldn't sleep and had to stay involved.) Clinton heard from Adams about Sinn Féin's concerns on various fronts, in particular prisoners and the equality agenda, and from Trimble about unionist unhappiness over decommissioning. There was, of course, a slightly surreal dimension to these calls, Clinton speaking from 3,000 miles away to two protagonists who were only yards away from each other but were not in direct dialogue with each other. Clinton's general pitch to Trimble and Adams, it seems, was to seek extra movement from each of them on one or other issue, on the basis that the other was now willing, he understood directly, to 'go the extra mile'.

Clinton's interventions with the protagonists began to bear fruit. While levels of mutual suspicion between the UUP and Sinn Féin remained high, the personal assurances given to each by a benevolent US President who was close to the process and its detail undoubtedly had a stabilising effect. The Taoiseach supplemented some of the calls, contacting Adams, for example, to add his voice to the reassurances about the prisoner release scheme. Clinton's calls were to continue well into Friday and concluded only minutes before the final Plenary. This level of sustained personal engagement on the part of a US President was extraordinary and without precedent. By nudging the protagonists towards each other and towards a comprehensive settlement, Clinton made a decisive contribution to the success we achieved on Good Friday.

28

GOOD FRIDAY DAWNS

By 7.30 a.m., Sinn Féin's mood was noticeably improving. Mitchel McLaughlin went out to the media and hailed this 'beautiful day', in sharp contrast to his gloom earlier in the night. As the two Governments had been worried for several hours about Sinn Féin's intentions, this was a welcome contrast.

And more generally, delegations began to sense that the agreement was at last coming together. News of the Strand One breakthrough had been given to the media by the UUP and the SDLP at 2 a.m. John Taylor had told journalists that he now rated the chances of a deal at 75 per cent. Rumours were trickling through of progress on various fronts during the night. People gathered together in the corridors, bleary-eyed and exhausted, a little apprehensive but quietly hopeful that success might at last be at hand.

I woke up, or at least emerged from my final disturbed 10-minute nap, under a table in our delegation room. A short while later, I encountered an equally exhausted Seamus Mallon and asked him how he was feeling. He told me, quite simply, that 'this is the happiest day of my life'. I will never forget that remark.

There was a real sense of waking up, literally and metaphorically, to a new day for Ireland. This was enhanced by weather conditions which were strange and a little surreal for that time of year. The rainswept night had given way to sharp, brilliant sunshine with very cold temperatures and light snowflakes swirling around.

I went outside to say hello to some journalist friends who had also had to put up with a very uncomfortable night. For all of us, there was a sense that something historic was about to happen.

Overcoming the strain and fatigue of a sleepless night, and of the preceding weeks of intensive negotiation, delegates from various parties were announcing to the media, and to the world outside, that the talks were approaching a successful conclusion.

David Andrews told journalists about 8.30 a.m. that the prospects for a deal today were very positive and that 'we are at this moment making history'. David Ervine said he had never thought that he would see something like this in his lifetime. A local broadcaster said on an early-morning programme: 'Think of all the bad days we've known here. Bloody Sunday. Bloody Friday. Bloody Monday. This really will be Good Friday.'

In the Irish delegation rooms, bottles of champagne which had been brought in the night before were opened. Irish officials wandered out tentatively into the early-morning sunshine, the April snowflakes adding to the strangeness of the moment. We had been cooped up in our rooms all night, like everyone else, and now had the chance to mingle freely with others. Wally Kirwan had emotional memories of the civil rights activism of his Northern-born wife in the late sixties and of everything that had happened in Northern Ireland since. David Cooney remarked to Rory Montgomery that, whatever else they might do in their later careers, it would probably not match the importance of this moment.

But our hopes were tinged also with scepticism: after so many bitter disappointments and failures over the years, would this prove to be another false dawn?

The two Government teams met the chairmen around 9 a.m. to review where we stood. The mood was positive but cautious;

much could still go wrong. On the strength of the optimistic noises he had heard, Mitchell wanted initially to convene a Plenary for about 9.30 a.m., in the hope of adopting a finished text at that point.

The first sign of trouble came shortly afterwards. We heard that all was not well in the UUP camp and that decommissioning was the main issue. John Holmes warned Paddy Teahon that the deal was not yet done, as Trimble was running into difficulties.

The Strand One agreement had created the prospect of Sinn Féin ministers not only being in the Assembly but becoming ministers in the Executive before any decommissioning of IRA arms had begun. This was unacceptable to Jeffrey Donaldson and some other members of the party's delegation. The UUP's ranks had been swollen by the arrival of hardliners such as Roy Beggs and Willie Ross, who were sceptical about the emerging agreement. (Several of the party's MPs were at best lukewarm in their support of David Trimble and had not been included in the UUP's talks delegation.) There was also unhappiness at the idea that there could be a scheme for early prisoner releases without prior decommissioning. More generally, a number of UUP representatives were focusing only for the first time on the prisoner release arrangements, it seemed, and this added to the tensions.

A heated debate broke out on these various issues when the UUP delegates, reassembling on Friday morning, heard the detail of what had been agreed overnight. SDLP jubilation at their Strand One achievement would not have helped, of course. Nor would the positive public signalling from Mitchel McLaughlin. The remorseless logic of the 'zero sum game' was imposing itself; the pendulum was swinging back once more.

In light of this discontent, David Trimble went to Tony Blair to seek an explicit provision to prevent Sinn Féin taking up ministerial posts in the Executive unless the decommissioning of IRA weapons had begun before the formation of the Executive. This was an unsettling development. We had concluded from Trimble's confident demeanour after the UUP Executive meeting the previous evening, and also from the lengthy subsequent negotiations with him on many issues, that the UUP were comfortable with the emerging agreement and all that it entailed. Furthermore, the Strand One agreement which the UUP had concluded with the SDLP and the other parties had not stipulated decommissioning as a condition for holding office in the Executive.

The rebellion we were now hearing of suggested a last-minute fit of nerves as some unionists confronted the prospect – now more real than at any previous time – of sharing power with Sinn Féin. Such unionists may have been banking on Sinn Féin walking away from the agreement at the last moment, unwilling, for example, to accept the principle of consent. But now this calculation was proving unsound: Sinn Féin were, it seemed, ready to accept the agreement. There was, therefore, the very real likelihood of Sinn Féin becoming ministers. So a decommissioning obstacle had to be rapidly erected.

Meanwhile, Sinn Féin had gone to see Blair about 9.45 a.m. in a last-minute effort to improve the prisoners deal. (It stayed at two years.) They also sought further movement on policing and criminal justice, as well as a commitment to an implementation body on the Irish language. So two key participants were trying at the last moment to stretch the fabric of the agreement – in opposite directions.

Tim Dalton talked to Sinn Féin later in the morning, when the final version of the agreement was out, to emphasise in plain terms that this was a good deal which should be accepted.

Bertie Ahern met David Trimble several times during Friday to provide reassurance on a number of issues. The UUP leader was in volatile form, on one occasion flaring up over the list of implementation bodies but then calming down and apologising. Trimble tested the patience of the usually imperturbable Ahern a couple of times over these few days. However, there was a fundamentally good working relationship between the two men which brought them through this period of exceptional strain.

Ahern had, for example, put in writing to Trimble the proposal he had made around midnight on Thursday for four additional implementation bodies. On Friday morning, he received a reply, polite and conciliatory in one, in which Trimble pointed to the possibility for additional areas to be proposed by the shadow North/South Council and suggested that, as time went by, those on the Council would 'have other and better thoughts than those we have today'. Ahern, for his part, gave the UUP a note confirming the six areas that had been agreed for implementation bodies – but again on the basis that these could be added to.

The Taoiseach also had good relations with the two loyalist parties, in particular Gary McMichael of the UDP, and kept in touch with them during the day.

With uncertainties mounting, estimates for the timing of the Plenary to adopt the agreement were put back. First, it was to take place at 1 p.m.; then we heard that it would be 3 p.m. Rumours circulated that Jeffrey Donaldson was on the point of walking out of the talks, or had already done so. Doubts were being expressed widely about Trimble's ability to commit the UUP to the agreement. There was a sense of imminent crisis and breakdown. I remember going for a walk with Martin Mansergh around the perimeter of Castle Buildings at lunchtime. We both feared that the talks were about to collapse. Mitchell would return to the US and it could be five years before the Governments were able to reassemble a talks process of this kind and get it to the point where we were now.

To maintain a positive dynamic, however, and to have everything ready should this last-minute crisis be overcome, the chairmen and their staff prepared the final version of the agreement for circulation to delegations. They had worked closely with the two Governments on this from earlier that day; Rory Montgomery and I had been proofreading the agreement shortly after dawn.

The finalised text was circulated about 12.30 p.m. It brought together all the revisions which had been agreed over the past couple of days. These included the big changes in Strands One and Two as well as relatively minor technical corrections and adjustments which the two Government teams had agreed in the course of Thursday and overnight. The text was ready for presentation and adoption if – and this was a big if – the final hurdles could be cleared.

Circulation of the finalised agreement, however, produced fresh problems. As no updated versions had been issued since the Mitchell draft had first appeared on Monday evening, many delegates were seeing for the first time the key changes made in the interim and were not entirely prepared for these. Studying the agreement closely, UUP delegates objected not merely to the prospect of Sinn Féin joining the Executive in the absence of decommissioning but also to the prisoner release scheme, the plans for police reform, the requirement for cross-community consent in key Assembly votes and several other aspects. And Sinn Féin's delegates were poring over the text, gathering points for improvement from their perspective. The other parties, for their part, were broadly content with what they were reading and ready to accept it as it stood.

Trimble, Taylor, Donaldson and other UUP representatives went to Blair to seek a decommissioning precondition for the holding of ministerial office. They also sought it, I heard, in relation to early prisoner releases. Donaldson indicated that, without something of this kind, he could not support the agreement.

The two Governments knew, of course, that there could be no change to the agreement on the lines sought by the UUP. There would be no consensus to reopen the language which had been painstakingly agreed on decommissioning. However, with the UUP demanding a link between holding ministerial office and decommissioning, the idea grew on the British side of the Prime Minister sending Trimble a side letter which would address the party's concerns on this subject.

Side letters or 'letters of comfort' had no legal standing. They were only unilateral statements of position, personal communications from one participant to another. Those not in receipt of them generally denounced them as betrayals of the collective basis of the talks. One from the Prime Minister would, however, carry a certain political charge and would keep Sinn Féin under continuing pressure on this issue.

We on the Irish Government side were uneasy at anything which might enable Trimble to claim that there had been a volte-face by the British Government on decommissioning. The two Governments had achieved a shared analysis which they had reflected in many common positions during the talks. What we had not done, however, was to attach a decommissioning precondition to the holding of ministerial office in the Executive. We had no difficulty as such with the idea of a side letter going to Trimble, a possibility which Blair had himself mentioned to Ahern the previous day and which we had also heard about from British officials. However, we had to be sure that its contents would not stray into unacceptable territory. The two Government teams therefore stayed in close contact on this, and Ahern had several meetings with Blair.

The assurance eventually given by Blair was, in fact, something we could live with. The Prime Minister said that, if in the course of the first six months of the shadow Assembly the agreement's provisions on decommissioning were shown to have been ineffective, his Government would 'support changes' to enable these provisions to be made 'properly effective' in preventing persons connected with paramilitary organisations which still held weapons from holding office. (No detail was provided as to what these changes might be or how they would be taken forward.) Blair went on to say that, in the British Government's view, the effect of the agreement's language on decommissioning, with schemes coming into effect in June, was that 'the process of decommissioning should begin straight away'. (We had no difficulty with this view.)

However, even if its terms were in themselves unproblematic, and even though it helped the UUP leader to manage the immediate crisis in his party, this side letter was to fuel unionist discontent over decommissioning. It created the impression that, if decommissioning did not get under way, there would be Prime Ministerial action at some stage to drive Sinn Féin ministers from office or to deny them office in the first place. No such action ever happened, of course, during the period between 1998 and the beginning of IRA decommissioning. Unionist discontent over decommissioning would lead to successive crises in the implementation of the agreement and to Trimble's eventual resignation as First Minister.

In the final days of the negotiations, I remember thinking that, on the one hand, we had no alternative to the agreement's deliberately non-committal language on decommissioning. Given the deep divisions over this issue and its relevance to a political settlement, no agreement would be possible if efforts were made to include in it a prescriptive approach to decommissioning. But, on the other hand, short of a fundamental change of mindset among unionists, it would be only a matter of time before a crisis developed due to the agreement's unavoidable ambiguities on decommissioning.

The finale of the side-letter episode on the afternoon of Good Friday has been well documented, notably by Jonathan Powell. Blair asked Powell to type it up as he dictated it to him. Powell did so on his laptop. He then rushed downstairs to the UUP offices to pass this to Trimble, found that he could not get access initially because of the number of people inside in intensive consultation and eventually managed to pass it in under the door. When Trimble got hold of it, he read it with Taylor looking over his shoulder and they both agreed that this would do the trick.

We heard that, after further internal UUP consultation, Trimble took another phone call from President Clinton, which evidently strengthened his resolve, and that shortly after that he told his delegation: 'I'm going for the agreement.' He then went to Senator Mitchell, shortly before 5 p.m., to say that he was 'ready to do the business'.

This was a pivotal moment for the entire process. While admittedly Blair had given him something to help quell the UUP's internal revolt, Trimble was nevertheless still on very shaky ground with his party. Donaldson and others were threatening to walk, side letter or not. Trimble was gambling, partly because he had Taylor at his side, that he could deal with the dissidents and that a bold move forward to embrace the agreement was the best course for the UUP at this stage. Another consideration may have been the solid support of the two loyalist parties for the agreement (illustrated also in the PUP's loud heckling at Paisley's late-night rally), which gave Trimble valuable political cover within the wider unionist community. While Trimble had tested the patience of the two Governments on many occasions, we recognised this as one of a handful of moments during the peace process when he showed undoubted political courage and leadership.

As it transpired, Blair's side letter was not enough to prevent Jeffrey Donaldson leaving the talks. He did so in the afternoon shortly before the Plenary began. Though he disguised his departure with reference to his young family and Easter holidays, the political reasons for his departure at that stage were clear.

Immediately after Trimble came to see him, Mitchell rang us to say: 'You won't believe this but I've just had David Trimble in my room and he's prepared to sign up straight away to the agreement.' Without further ado, the Senator convened the much-postponed Plenary for about 15 minutes later. We all gathered hastily in the Plenary room, barely able to believe the turn of events.

29

AGREEMENT AT LAST

The room was packed to the rafters. The excitement was palpable. People had rushed in from all the delegation offices; speed was of the essence, some calculated, lest David Trimble change his mind.

For the first time, TV cameras were admitted to cover part of the proceedings, in recognition of the historic nature of what was about to unfold. The room was hastily reconfigured to allow much greater numbers of delegates and support staff to squeeze in for the finale. People stood massed behind the leaders and senior delegation members seated at the table.

George Mitchell, ever the master of correct procedure, opened by giving participants an opportunity to propose amendments to the agreement before them. Mercifully, all declined this opportunity; Sinn Féin asked merely that the party's 26-page document of proposed amendments from Wednesday be placed on record. The NIWC had been contemplating an amendment in relation to the electoral system but also opted to have their concern noted on the record.

Mitchell then invited statements. Gerry Adams said Sinn Féin's negotiating team would be reporting back to the party's Ard Chomhairle, who would assess the proposed agreement in a 'positive and constructive way'. Trimble referred to his own party's consultations (the previous day's Executive meeting and a meeting of the Ulster Unionist Council planned for 18 April) and showed an interest in getting to a vote quickly.

The Senator then asked each delegation leader to say whether or not they supported the agreement. In turn, each of them – beginning with the Prime Minister and the Taoiseach – gave their assent in the simplest terms, responding either 'For the agreement' or 'Agree'. Trimble paused for a moment and said simply: 'Yes.'

It had come down to this: after all the years of negotiation, of entrenched opposition and distrust, we had ended up with the clarity and succinctness of a simple affirmative. Ulster was saying Yes.

Adams, it is true, qualified his 'Agree' with reference to a special Sinn Féin Ard Fheis which would have to endorse the agreement. This came as no surprise, as we had been alerted in advance. Most of us knew, furthermore, what lay behind the caveat. And, as Adams gave renewed hints about a positive outcome, there were good reasons to be optimistic about the consultation in question. His carefully chosen words gave the chairman enough of a basis to conclude that Sinn Féin were in favour of the agreement.

At 5.36 p.m., therefore, Mitchell declared the agreement approved, saying he was 'pleased to announce that the two Governments and the political parties in Northern Ireland have reached agreement'.

It was a moment to savour. Tony Blair warmly thanked Senator Mitchell (who received a standing ovation from all present) and Bertie Ahern. He followed with thanks to the other chairmen and to all delegations. Gifts were presented by Mo Mowlam to the three chairmen. Senator Mitchell, remarking on a 'bittersweet feeling of dying to leave but hating to go', paid fulsome tribute to his colleagues and to the people of Northern Ireland. In his own account of this meeting, he has described it as one of the most emotional moments of his life, though he tried to stay calm during it.

There followed a round of tributes from party leaders to the chairmen and the two Heads of Government (with the Taoiseach receiving particular praise for his unflinching commitment at a time of bereavement). Responding with accolades for the Taoiseach, the Prime Minister and officials of both Governments and their predecessors, Senator Mitchell declared the Plenary was now adjourned *sine die*. This, in Mitchell's best Senate legalese, was an important phrase: it meant the negotiations were now formally over.

The proceedings concluded with a statement from the Senator describing the merits of the agreement just reached. Mitchell said that he looked forward to a day, a few years hence, when he would come back to Northern Ireland with his young son, born during these negotiations. They would travel on a rainy day to Stormont, sit in the visitors' gallery of the Assembly and look down at the Assembly members, who would be debating practical issues such as health, trade and education. There would be no talk of war (it would be long over) or of peace (by now taken for granted). Not for the first time, the Senator succeeded in capturing in a single potent image the hopes we all had for this agreement. (Years later, the BBC would bring him back, with his by then teenage son Andrew, for a special TV programme which in effect realised his inspiring vision; and yes, there was a minister there delivering a speech which, Mitchell said, was 'dry as dust'.)

There followed a series of statements from delegations. For the Irish Government, David Andrews described this as a day which many had thought would never come. The success of these negotiations would, he believed, come to be seen as a turning point in the affairs of this island. Nothing in his own life in politics had come near to the satisfaction of being involved with all the people in this room in seeking to overcome the legacy of history and to create a new society free from conflict. He paid warm tribute to the 'unending support' provided during the negotiations by Liz O'Donnell and the team of Irish Government officials.

A signing ceremony was never envisaged for the new agreement, primarily because some parties would not have been able to sign it immediately (with internal consultations still pending). The closest we came to signature was the informal circulation of a small number of copies of the agreement to which the most senior participants appended their autographs.

The mood in the Plenary chamber, once the agreement had been declared adopted, was euphoric. Despite the physical exhaustion from which we were all suffering by then, feelings of utter relief and exhilaration swept the room. Mixed, it must be said, with a degree of disbelief that we had got that far and that the agreement, which had seemed to be slipping away earlier in the day, was done at last. Many of those present were emotional, a consequence not only of the nervous strain and sleeplessness of the past few days but also of contemplating of the long road we had all travelled. Even some hardened NIO officials near me were misty-eyed. People hugged each other, tears flowed. There were also, of course, many – including myself – who were simply numb with fatigue and could only stand there trying to take it all in.

I remember, in one slightly incongruous moment, noticing both Martha Pope and Gerry Kelly (of Sinn Féin) beside me. I introduced one to the other, taking advantage of the relaxed and celebratory mood in the room. Gerry told Martha that he was delighted to meet her – 'for the first time', as he added pointedly.

Then, in the middle of all the cheering and celebrations, I heard something that stopped me in my tracks. I was approached by a senior representative of a well-placed delegation with information he had just picked up about an LVF plot to kill me. While this was not the first time I had been given such information, the new element on this occasion was that the attack would supposedly involve a contract killing and would be carried out in the South. Similar intentions were also mentioned in relation to another senior member of the Irish Government team.

Thanking my interlocutor for this information, I made a phone call to my wife. 'First the good news,' I began, telling her about the agreement that had just been reached. I went on to explain that, because of information I had received, she and I and our 18-year-old son would have to leave Dublin, when I returned later that evening, and go elsewhere for a while. Though perhaps in itself not a surprise (the LVF were not on ceasefire and saw threats of this kind as a way of signalling their protest against the agreement), the news I had received was nevertheless an unsettling codicil to an already extraordinary day.

The Taoiseach and the Prime Minister, meanwhile, had gone straight out to the media following the approval of the agreement and George Mitchell's formal adjournment of the proceedings. With rain and then hailstones pelting them, they stood pale and exhausted in front of Castle Buildings and presented the agreement together. Recalling his remark about the 'hand of history' from three days earlier, Blair hoped that 'the burden of history can at long last start to be lifted from our shoulders'. Today was only the beginning, he went on. 'Today we have just the sense of the prize that is before us. The work to win that prize goes on.'

Ahern saluted the agreement as 'a new beginning for all of us'. We could all be proud of what we had achieved. (Wearing his black tie, he allowed himself a passing reference to his late mother and what she would have thought of the day.) There was no room for triumphalism, he warned. None of us had achieved all that we had set out to achieve. But each could point to real gains in areas of particular concern. Many had doubted whether we would ever see this day. Others had actively sought to make the talks fail. Several factions were still trying to destroy the prospects for peace and agreement. But this agreement showed that this and future generations need not be condemned to an endless cycle of violence and loss.

Ahern went on to applaud the contributions made by George Mitchell, President Clinton, Tony Blair, Mo Mowlam, David Andrews, Liz O'Donnell and people previously involved such as John Major, Albert Reynolds, John Bruton and Hugh Coveney. At the press conference, John Taylor reached across to Ahern and warmly shook his hand, thanking him for all he had done to make this happen.

In the meantime, the new British–Irish Agreement was waiting to be signed. The Taoiseach and the Prime Minister finished their press conference and went back inside to a small room which had been set aside for this purpose. The text of the agreement had been prepared in bound copies and officials were on hand, including Rory Montgomery on our side, to guide the principals. One of our colleagues had been despatched down to Dublin to bring up supplies of special Treaty paper, not usually required in Castle Buildings.

The setting was a little modest and there had been no time to remove used paper cups and make the room presentable. The main consideration, however, was to ensure signature of the agreement without delay. In particular, with Tony Blair rushing off to join his family on holiday in Madrid, there was a concern that logistical difficulties could cause an uncomfortable delay of several days unless the two Heads of Government were brought in to sign it before they left the building. Accordingly, with a single photographer present, they signed it.

The agreement we had all reached had had until then no name. The text circulated by the chairmen at lunchtime had merely been entitled 'Agreement reached in the multi-party negotiations'. They were keeping things studiously neutral in the absence of any consensus at that point on what the agreement should be called. The British wanted to call it the 'Belfast Agreement' (which had, of course, a pleasing resonance for unionists). However, Bertie Ahern did not favour that. While he could have lived with something like 'the Agreement concluded in Belfast', he disliked the term 'Belfast Agreement' (which failed to respect the broad scope of the agreement) and made it clear that he had not authorised this.

The Taoiseach did an interview before leaving Belfast in which he described the agreement as the 'Good Friday agreement'. While he recognises that he might simply have been echoing what someone else had said to him a moment before, this lodged in his mind as a name for the agreement. Before our delegation left for home, he issued instructions that it was to be called the Good Friday Agreement. On his arrival back in Dublin, he took a call from US Senator Ted Kennedy, who congratulated him on his achievement that Good Friday; this cemented the name further. Naming the agreement after Good Friday, with its Easter associations, would resonate with nationalists and republicans. Tony Blair was also sympathetic, seeing the appeal it should have for all Christian faiths. It was christened the Good Friday Agreement in much of the euphoric media coverage over that Easter weekend.

Neither the Belfast Agreement nor the Good Friday Agreement is an official title, however. Both were, in effect, working titles. The

British Government and Unionists have always preferred to call it the Belfast Agreement. A compromise aimed at balancing unionist and nationalist sensitivities crept in at some stage: the 'Belfast Agreement signed on Good Friday'. Some prefer the combination 'Belfast/Good Friday Agreement'. It is probably fair to say, however, that the name by which it has been best known over the past 25 years, in Ireland and around the world, is the Good Friday Agreement.

Other protagonists followed the Taoiseach and Prime Minister in presenting the agreement to the media.

While en route to his press briefing, David Trimble had an encounter with one of my colleagues in which he held that, due to excessive ambition on the part of Irish Government officials in relation to the original Strand Two annexes, the agreement had nearly not been achieved at all. He had earlier made trenchant comments to another colleague about the prisoner release arrangements. We made allowances for the strains of that week and, in particular, for the turmoil the UUP leader had had to face all day within his party.

Trimble went out to the media, to whom he claimed that he and his party would rise from the table with the Union stronger than it had been when they had started. The principle of consent was now accepted by all but one party, he went on, and would, he trusted, shortly be enshrined in the Irish Constitution. The delay in reaching agreement that day had been due to concerns about the prospect of parties getting into the new Northern Ireland administration without decommissioning. However, the UUP had been greatly relieved by assurances received from the Prime Minister on this subject. Trimble then read out the terms of the letter (which the UUP later published). He referred also to the decision made to close the Maryfield Secretariat.

John Hume heralded the new beginning represented by the Agreement and the equal partnership which it offered within Northern Ireland and between North and South. Outside, with his hands raised gently skywards as if saluting a miracle, he remarked: 'Only once in a generation does an opportunity like this come along, an opportunity to resolve our deep and tragic conflict.'

Gerry Adams welcomed the intensive engagement of the Taoiseach and the Prime Minister over the past few days. The days of unionist supremacy were over forever, he declared; republicans looked into the future 'confident and determined'.

In a gesture of 'demob' happiness to which we could all relate, Monica McWilliams of the NIWC threw a handful of press releases into the air, having promised herself that she would do this if the deal was ever done.

After a marathon of some 32 hours locked in continuous negotiations, the Taoiseach departed for Dublin, while the Prime Minister left to join his family on holiday in Madrid. (Before boarding his plane, Blair recalled later, he was told that someone was on the phone for him – 'she says she's the Queen'.) The Irish Government team flew back to Dublin later in the evening, exhausted but in ebullient form.

On arrival home, Bertie Ahern had to cope with the emotionally draining experience of taking calls, on the one hand, from well-wishers around the world about the Agreement and, on the other, from family and friends about the loss of his mother a few days earlier.

I had mixed emotions myself as I travelled home that night. On the one hand, I wanted to join my colleagues in celebrating our achievement. But on the other, I had to process the more unpleasant news I had received. Happily, I was able to have a belated celebratory drink a month later when the LVF announced a ceasefire.

On Easter Saturday, George Mitchell flew back to New York after a job well done. On the same day, the UUP's Executive had a four-hour meeting in Belfast to assess the Agreement. Despite fears that the party's dissidents would prevail there (with four or five of its MPs rumoured to be opposed) and that Trimble's leadership could be in danger, the UUP leader secured a comfortable two-to-one majority. A week later, Sinn Féin's Ard Chomhairle met and decided to recommend the Agreement to a special Ard Fheis which would be held in May.

It had been a very Good Friday, as John Hume remarked. Ireland would never be the same again.

30

LOOKING BACK

My own journey reached its destination that Good Friday. In various roles, and for almost a quarter of a century, I had been working towards what we collectively achieved on that strange, unseasonably cold day. Everything afterwards had a touch of anti-climax about it.

I stayed on for another year in Belfast, helping with the implementation of the Agreement and the creation of a new Secretariat. Then I went abroad on a new assignment, as the Irish Ambassador to Russia. I never worked on Northern Ireland issues again.

The real work, of course, was only just starting with Good Friday. Earlier in Easter Week, George Mitchell had told of how, when he first climbed a mountain in Maine, he thought he had reached the summit, only to find that it was merely a ridge and that the actual summit was still far away. That image sums up well where we found ourselves. We had scaled an important height. Indeed, we had never been up at that elevation before, and the view was very promising. But there would still be several ridges, and obstacles and reverses, before we reached the summit.

There is a single cryptic entry in my diary for 10 April 1998: '5.36 p.m. – Nirvana?' The doubt in that question mark was not surprising. None of us could quite believe what had happened; the summit, I felt in my bones, was still some distance away. George Mitchell remarked that afternoon to several of the participants that the easy bit had been negotiating this Agreement; the hardest part, implementing it, lay in front of us.

What Good Friday delivered was, in a sense, the end of the beginning. Almost a decade of frustration, and only occasional success, lay ahead for the two Governments as they struggled to get the Agreement implemented. For Bertie Ahern and Tony Blair, it would be a long and painful journey to 2007, when they would finally manage to get all of the Agreement's institutions up and running.

In the first instance, the referendum campaigns were launched, North and South. These culminated in an overwhelming endorsement of the Agreement by both electorates on 22 May 1998. The approval rate was 94 per cent in the South and 71 per cent in the North. We had expected an emphatic endorsement in the South; less predictable was what would happen in the North, but in the event a respectable majority was secured there. The combined result of the two referendums amounted to a national act of self-determination by the people of Ireland, the first since 1918. This gave effect to a key provision of the Downing Street Declaration, the document which had laid the basis for the IRA's 1994 ceasefire decision.

The Sinn Féin leadership had worked hard for a 'yes' vote in both jurisdictions. Securing broad support for the Agreement from the republican constituency was never going to be easy. There were hardline sceptics who remained deeply unhappy at any proposal to amend Articles 2 and 3. At the special Ard Fheis in May which had been convened to endorse the Agreement, the Balcombe Street Four made a surprise appearance and were given a warm welcome with triumphalist overtones. Newly transferred back to Ireland, they had been granted temporary release by our Government to enable them to attend. Though their appearance offended the British Government and unionists, this was probably a price that had to be paid in order to achieve broad republican endorsement both of the Agreement and of the constitutional changes which would go with it.

On 25 June the elections to the new Assembly took place. The UUP and the SDLP were returned as the largest parties. However, while pro-Agreement parties won all the seats on the nationalist side, the UUP were joined in the Assembly by the DUP and the UKUP, who had won seats on an anti-Agreement platform.

A week later, the Assembly had its first meeting in shadow form. David Trimble and Seamus Mallon were elected as First Minister and Deputy First Minister, respectively. Hume asked Mallon at the last moment to take on this responsibility. It was the wise and correct choice, even if it surprised some that the party leader did not seek the post for himself. We knew that Mallon would be better suited to the daily negotiating grind and the challenges of forging joint positions with Trimble across the multiple policy challenges presented by the Agreement. Hume's strengths lay in the vision and tenacity which had got us this far; the detailed management of implementation would be for others.

One horrific event in August 1998, the Omagh bombing, underscored the fragility of peace in Northern Ireland. The single worst atrocity in the history of the Troubles, this attack by a dissident republican group claimed the lives of 29 people and injured many more. All parties to the Good Friday Agreement, including Sinn Féin, condemned it in the strongest terms. There was a profound sense that the only way to eradicate such horrendous violence from the island was by working the new Agreement to the full.

In September 1998, the UUP and Sinn Féin had formal talks for the first time. In the following month, David Trimble and John Hume received the Nobel Peace Prize.

Discussions got under way between the Irish Government, the Northern Ireland departments, the UUP and the SDLP on the detailed remits for the implementation bodies. With the architecture for the North/South arrangements resolved to unionist satisfaction in the Agreement, these negotiations proved generally less contentious than the equivalent exchanges during Easter Week. The 31 October deadline was missed but this did not arouse particular comment.

Agreement was eventually reached at 4.30 a.m. on 18 December on a final list of six implementation bodies. A body dealing with the Irish language came in after all (with its remit also to include Ullans). In addition, there would be one handling trade and business development (though a combination of unionist opposition and unease on the part of our Industrial Development Authority ruled out an inward investment dimension). And there would be another for special European Union programmes. The UUP proposed three further bodies relating to inland waterways, food safety and aquaculture/marine issues. In addition, a company to market the whole island for tourism purposes was agreed. Six further areas for cooperation were also agreed.

An argument which the UUP used with their supporters, once the legal framework for the new bodies had been settled, was that North/South coordination had already been taking place anyway in the EU context in many of these areas. The deal reached on 18 December was a pragmatic compromise: three bodies proposed by nationalists and three by unionists, with an additional company handling tourism marketing. Sinn Féin were primarily interested in getting an Irish language body. The SDLP, for their part, were content with the EU programmes body and the one on trade and business development. Overall, it was a good outcome to a difficult chapter in the negotiations.

After all the heat generated in Easter Week over their legal status and functions, the implementation bodies came into existence with remarkably little controversy. Over the past 23 years, furthermore, they have operated with quiet efficiency and a generally low profile. They also managed to stay operational despite the recurrent suspensions of the institutions set up under the Agreement.

Late in 1999, after a lengthy hiatus over decommissioning, the power-sharing Executive finally took office. Ten ministers were appointed (from four parties, including Sinn Féin). The devolution of powers took place. Articles 2 and 3 of our Constitution were formally amended. The new British–Irish Agreement entered into force. The North/South Ministerial Council, the British–Irish Council and the British–Irish Intergovernmental Conference all met for the first time. At last the Agreement seemed to be coming to life. I remember quietly toasting what had been achieved when news of these developments reached me in Moscow.

However, the Assembly and the Executive would function for only limited periods over the subsequent years. The biggest challenge was how to manage the decommissioning issue, which had not gone away, in such a way that wider implementation of the Agreement would not fall victim to it. Unfortunately, differing interpretations of what the Agreement had said on this subject led to prolonged periods of paralysis. The UUP would not agree to the formation of the Executive unless there was a start to decommissioning. We, the SDLP and Sinn Féin pointed out that this was not a prerequisite under the Agreement.

In March 1999, there had been a round of negotiations at

Hillsborough Castle to try to overcome this impasse. On each such occasion there would be a fresh declaration on the subject but the underlying differences were never resolved. In the summer of 2000, the row led finally to the suspension of the Executive. It was restored in 2001 but it collapsed, along with the Assembly as a whole, in 2002.

The decommissioning issue was to prove David Trimble's undoing. In an Assembly election in 2003, the DUP and Sinn Féin replaced the UUP and the SDLP, respectively, as the largest parties. Trimble paid a political price for his inability to deliver a start to decommissioning. But, as this required a voluntary move by others and had not been expressly stipulated under the Good Friday Agreement (which, indeed, would never have been achieved if there *had* been an express requirement), this was ultimately not a deliverable objective.

For the best part of a decade, the decommissioning stand-off would frustrate implementation of the Agreement. Bertie Ahern and Tony Blair would remain heavily engaged, making an enormous personal investment over the years in the efforts to resolve it. George Mitchell was brought back in the autumn of 1999 to preside over a review of implementation, in particular decommissioning. For a period two distinguished international figures, Martti Ahtisaari and Cyril Ramaphosa, were used to inspect paramilitary arms dumps for confidence-building purposes.

Some other thorny issues had been deliberately parked under the Agreement and left for gradual implementation over time. We had not attempted, for example, to solve Northern Ireland's policing problems in the context of the negotiations. Nor could we have hoped to resolve deep-seated human rights or criminal justice issues there. These were left to independent Commissions which would take several years to report. The issues involved did not go away, however, and would remain intractable for years to come.

The decommissioning issue was finally resolved through acts of decommissioning, by the IRA and loyalist paramilitary organisations, respectively, which were supervised by the Independent Commission. The first IRA act took place in 2001. This was followed by more in 2002 and 2003 and by a final act in 2005, after which the IRA formally announced an end to their armed campaign.

This cleared the way for intensified efforts to implement the rest of the Agreement. In October 2006, Bertie Ahern and Tony Blair hosted talks with the parties in Scotland which led to the 'St Andrews Agreement'. This achieved a breakthrough on policing and criminal justice issues. A number of minor modifications made as a consequence of the St Andrews Agreement enabled the DUP to claim credit and to present the latter as justification for entering government with Sinn Féin. A month later, the DUP and Sinn Féin indicated their acceptance of power-sharing in the context of implementing the St Andrews Agreement.

In fresh Assembly elections in March 2007, the DUP and Sinn Féin surged ahead of the SDLP and UUP once again. Finally, in May 2007, an Executive was formed with the unlikely pairing of Ian Paisley and Martin McGuinness as First Minister and Deputy First Minister, replacing the Trimble/Mallon combination. This ushered in a period of relative tranquillity, assisted by an unexpected bonhomie between the two principals. This was carried forward by McGuinness and Peter Robinson when the latter succeeded Paisley a year later.

The 2016 Brexit vote, however, had a cataclysmic effect. It drove a wedge between the DUP and the nationalist parties, bringing to an end much of the cooperative spirit which had been achieved under the Agreement. It eroded much of the political will required on the unionist side for North/South cooperation under the Agreement. And it created deep tensions between the Irish and British Governments. The close partnership which had carried the two Governments through the negotiation and implementation of the Good Friday Agreement could no longer be taken for granted. More broadly, Brexit has polarised the political debate in Northern Ireland and beyond, prompting republican demands for an early border poll and in the process deepening unionist anxieties about the future. In the past couple of years, British Government and DUP manoeuvring over the Northern Ireland protocol have exacerbated these tensions.

How well has the Good Friday Agreement served us over the past quarter of a century? And can it provide a path through the many uncertainties, constitutional and otherwise, which Brexit has generated?

The Good Friday Agreement is not perfect. Some believe that Sunningdale, had it been implemented, would have been a better deal for nationalists. Some complain, from a different perspective, about the rigidity of the Strand One safeguards, which were intended to protect a nationalist minority from abuses by a unionist majority. They argue that changing demographics and political tastes, including a steady growth in the number of people identifying as neither nationalist nor unionist, may make such protections obsolete eventually. Others regret the absence of detail and clarity under individual headings.

The Agreement is still a work in progress. Its implementation has been slow and patchy and much of its potential has yet to be realised. Some aspects on which there had never been a firm consensus to begin with were thwarted. It has not succeeded in ending sectarianism in Northern Ireland (far from it). It has not delivered all the hoped-for economic and social benefits; working-class loyalism has felt particularly left behind. There have been long periods of atrophy when the institutions were suspended. There have been frequent rows over many aspects of the Agreement's implementation, including policing, criminal justice, a Bill of Rights and treatment of the Irish language.

There is no doubt, however, that the Good Friday Agreement is a better guarantor of lasting stability on the island than anything which preceded it. The principles and institutions which it created give nationalism and unionism equal legitimacy and standing. The Agreement gives balanced reassurances to each of these traditions and grounds the possibility of constitutional change firmly in the principle of consent.

All along we had expected the negotiations to end up broadly in the vicinity of the Downing Street Declaration and the Framework Document. This is, indeed, what happened. While there was some variation of language, the Good Friday Agreement shows a high degree of continuity with the concepts set out in the Framework Document and the careful balancing achieved there between nationalist and unionist concerns.

The Agreement's unique strength lies in the fact that it was negotiated, and agreed to, in an inclusive round-table process involving all key players. And that it was then resoundingly endorsed by the people of Ireland, North and South. No other agreement ever enjoyed this degree of legitimacy and authority.

In itself, what we achieved at Easter 1998 cannot guarantee lasting peace. But, as George Mitchell has often remarked, the Good Friday Agreement made peace possible. It brought together all political parties in Northern Ireland on the basis of an absolute commitment to peaceful politics and the achievement of constitutional change by peaceful means only.

While no two conflicts in the world are identical, it is possible nevertheless to distil from this Agreement some elements and principles which are of near-universal value. These include the importance of an inclusive talks process (which gives the outcome legitimacy and stability); the benefits of independent chairmanship; the value of building an agreement incrementally ('nothing is agreed until everything is agreed'); and the usefulness of a deadline (even if this is not necessarily adhered to).

The two Governments' role as the motor of the process was a vital ingredient for our success. A willingness to take political risks in the interests of an overall settlement was required of all participants – and, in one way or another, was demonstrated. Endless reserves of patience and perseverance were also required on all sides. And implementation, as we found out, can be as challenging as reaching the Agreement in the first place – and often more so.

In later years, I would find myself applying some of these insights in other contexts. When in 2015, as Ireland's Ambassador to the United Nations, I co-chaired the UN negotiations which delivered new global Sustainable Development Goals, what I had learned during those long days and nights in Castle Buildings almost 20 years earlier proved surprisingly instructive. Even if we had been working within a much smaller space in Northern Ireland, the challenges faced in both contexts were broadly similar: how to reconcile conflicting rights and perspectives, how to redress historic grievances and how to ensure that all participants emerged as equals at the end of the day.

With the Good Friday Agreement, we were all winners ultimately. While attempts were made at the time to identify victors and losers, the truth was that there could only ever have been an agreement which was based on an equal partnership, and a 'parity of gain and pain', between nationalism and unionism.

The Good Friday Agreement was achieved against all the odds. Many described it at the time as near-miraculous. Bill Clinton hailed it as a 'work of genius'. While it may not quite merit that description, it has stood the test of time. It has survived Brexit and other challenges. The principles it enshrined are as useful and relevant today as they were in 1998. The institutions it set up, when they have been allowed to operate, have not been called into question. One, indeed, is potentially more useful than ever: the British–Irish Intergovernmental Conference, which facilitates continuing cooperation between both Governments in the post-Brexit context.

The Agreement undoubtedly has weaknesses. Some may become more apparent as demographic changes in Northern Ireland soften, or supersede, the traditional polarities. The Agreement's relevance may come to be questioned in a context in which Northern Ireland politics is no longer dominated by issues of identity. In the Brexit debate, furthermore, it risks becoming collateral damage as Brexiteers in Northern Ireland and in Britain misrepresent it for short-term political purposes. The normal functioning of the Agreement has often been a casualty in the same context.

But, for all of these threats to it, the Good Friday Agreement has been responsible for delivering peace, stability and prosperity, on an unprecedented scale, over the past quarter of a century. A generation has grown up and come of age under it. It has saved many lives and transformed the prospects for all of Ireland's young people, North and South. It provides a framework to manage the burdens of the past. And at the same time it commits nationalists and unionists alike to reconciliation and a shared future.

David Trimble once said: 'Just because you have a past doesn't mean you can't have a future.' That, in essence, is what the Good Friday Agreement is all about.

EPILOGUE

My father, with whom I began this narrative, died last year. For almost 40 years, Northern Ireland had been the dominant topic in our conversations. Despite (or perhaps because of) his ambivalence about the place in which he had grown up, he would seize on every piece of news and ask me in detail about its implications. He would interrogate me on all developments, even if his conclusions were invariably the same: Northern Ireland was irredeemable and all efforts to heal its divisions were futile.

Thus the Anglo-Irish Agreement was dismissed because it involved a degree of legitimisation of Northern Ireland that he could not accept. It copper-fastened partition, to use a cliché of the day. Trying to reform policing there was a hopeless enterprise (at a time when my duties included trying to persuade nationalists to join a reformed RUC). When the IRA ceasefire came in 1994, he accepted that this was a good thing but was not entirely persuaded by the reasoning behind it.

And, when the Good Friday Agreement came along, he was not enamoured of it. We would have long conversations about it in which I would highlight how it sought to reconcile constitutional differences and left all doors open for the future, on the basis of consent. But I could feel his scepticism: the North/South bodies were not compelling, Irish unity was still a remote prospect and he did not see how the Agreement would advance things.

We never fell out over any of this. But, when he died, I felt I had never managed to persuade him of the merits of the Agreement.

In a moving tribute at a memorial service a few months later, Hugh Logue, a prominent SDLP figure who is also an old family friend, provided a postscript. He revealed that my father had spoken very warmly of the Good Friday Agreement when he visited the Logues a couple of years before his death. From his conversations with me, my father now recognised more clearly the extent of the Agreement's protections for the identity and rights of nationalists. He was at ease with the Agreement and saw it as the right way forward. He had been impressed, furthermore, by the recent appointment of a former senior RUC officer as Garda Commissioner, something that would have been unimaginable in his youth but which the Agreement had made possible. This revelation of a changed perspective, as touching as it was unexpected, completed in a sense my own journey with him, beginning with our trip to Belfast all those years ago.

ACKNOWLEDGEMENTS

This book is mainly based on my recollections, on contemporary notes I took of key meetings and on some official records that have become available.

I have also had the benefit of conversations with a range of people, particularly members of the Irish Government's team at the Castle Buildings talks during Easter Week 1998. These conversations, and those with others who were close to the events described, have been invaluable. They have helped to refresh my memories, to fill in gaps and to elucidate factors that were in play at key moments.

I am deeply indebted to all those who gave so generously of their time and who have helped me to fashion what I hope is a reasonably coherent and comprehensive narrative. If mistakes have been made in doing so, they are entirely mine. At a 25-year remove, and given the informal way in which key parts of the Agreement were finalised in the hectic last days of the negotiations, it is not surprising if recollections vary somewhat. I have sought to present the clearest possible account of what occurred in Castle Buildings during that exceptionally challenging week.

I owe particular thanks to Bertie Ahern, David Byrne and Martin Mansergh for conversations in which they generously shared their own analysis and memories.

Among the senior civil servant participants, I am grateful to Paddy Teahon and Wally Kirwan (both of the Department of the

Taoiseach) for their assistance, as I am to Tim Dalton and Paul Hickey (both of the Department of Justice). Dermot Gallagher's early passing in 2017 robbed us of a key participant in these negotiations and an outstanding public servant. I benefited greatly from my conversations with members of the Department of Foreign Affairs team, which Dermot established and led. My special thanks go to David Cooney, Tim O'Connor, Rory Montgomery and Eamonn McKee. I am also grateful for the assistance provided by Frank Sheridan.

Sean O hUiginn, a figure of pivotal importance on the road to Good Friday, shared rich insights with me. Other companions on that road at different times, whose wisdom I have always valued, have included Seán Donlon, Michael Lillis, Noel Dorr, Richard Ryan, Declan O'Donovan and Fergus Finlay.

My account also reflects exchanges I have had over the years with David Andrews and Liz O'Donnell, two ministers who played a central role in the negotiations.

Beyond the Irish Government delegation, I had the privilege of conversations at different times with a variety of people from other delegations. I mention with particular appreciation the late Seamus Mallon; his SDLP colleagues Mark Durkan, Seán Farren and Hugh Logue; and Monica McWilliams and Kate Fearon of the Northern Ireland Women's Coalition.

A heartfelt word of thanks to those who encouraged me to start on, and to persevere with, this book. A special mention also for the advice provided by Deaglán de Bréadún, Belfast correspondent for the Irish Times in the late nineties and himself the author of an excellent book on the Northern Ireland peace process.

I am grateful to Michael Gill for encouraging this project from the outset. At Gill Books, I was fortunate in the skill and attention with which it was managed by Seán Hayes, Rachel Thompson and others.

Finally, I thank my wife, Jill, and my son, Adam, for their love, patience and support on my long journey to Good Friday 1998. As Molly and Oscar, Adam's children, grow up, I hope that they will live in an Ireland which realises the full promise and potential of that Agreement.

David Donoghue
Dublin
June 2022